BRITISH LEYLAND

Also by the Author (non-fiction)
Motor Museums
Bugatti Blue: Prescott and the Spirit of Bugatti
The Classic Car Adventure
Bugatti Type 35 & Variants
Jeep: Second World War
Porsche 911
Secrets of the Spitfire
Secret Wings of World War Two
Supermarine Spitfire Mk V and variants
VC10 Icon of the Skies
Porsche Model by Model
Saab Cars: The Complete Story
Saab 99 & 900: The Complete Story
Citroën: The Complete Story
Allard: The Complete Story
Vickers VC10
Heavies
Giant Airliners
Long Haul
Jetliners
The Revised New Illustrated Encyclopaedia of the Automobile

BRITISH LEYLAND

FROM TRIUMPH TO TRAGEDY
PETROL, POLITICS AND POWER

LANCE COLE

PEN & SWORD
TRANSPORT
AN IMPRINT OF PEN & SWORD BOOKS LTD.
YORKSHIRE - PHILADELPHIA

First published in Great Britain in 2020 by
Pen & Sword Transport
An imprint of
Pen & Sword Books Ltd
Yorkshire - Philadelphia

Copyright © Lance Cole, 2020

ISBN 978 1 52674 823 2

The right of Lance Cole to be identified as Author of this work has been asserted by him in accordance with the Copyright, Designs and Patents Act 1988.

A CIP catalogue record for this book is available from the British Library.

All rights reserved. No part of this book may be reproduced or transmitted in any form or by any means, electronic or mechanical including photocopying, recording or by any information storage and retrieval system, without permission from the Publisher in writing.

Typeset in 12/14.5 pt Times New Roman
Typeset by SJmagic DESIGN SERVICES, India.
Printed and bound in India by Replika Press Pvt. Ltd.

Pen & Sword Books Ltd incorporates the Imprints of Pen & Sword Books Archaeology, Atlas, Aviation, Battleground, Discovery, Family History, History, Maritime, Military, Naval, Politics, Railways, Select, Transport, True Crime, Fiction, Frontline Books, Leo Cooper, Praetorian Press, Seaforth Publishing, Wharncliffe and White Owl.

For a complete list of Pen & Sword titles please contact

PEN & SWORD BOOKS LIMITED
47 Church Street, Barnsley, South Yorkshire, S70 2AS, England
E-mail: enquiries@pen-and-sword.co.uk
Website: www.pen-and-sword.co.uk

Or
PEN AND SWORD BOOKS
1950 Lawrence Rd, Havertown, PA 19083, USA
E-mail: Uspen-and-sword@casematepublishers.com
Website: www.penandswordbooks.com

Contents

Acknowledgements		7
Introduction		8
1	Questions	29
2	An Empire Ends & Another Begins	58
3	Fifties Style	72
4	Car Craft: P6 to MGB	101
5	1960s: Strike-bound Before Stokes	111
6	The 'Fordisation' of BLMC	128
7	'In Place of Strife'	139
8	1970s Numbers Games	145
9	1980s The Edwardes Effect	170
10	'Reds' Under the BL Bed?	191
11	BL Brilliance	202
12	Austin to Roverisation	227
13	The Way to a Rusty Death	249
Notes		267
Bibliography		270
Index		274

If you sit on the river bank long enough, you will see the bodies of your enemies float past. What a shame it takes so long!

Dedicated to the brilliance of the designers, engineers and builders of BLMC or 'BL' and its marques – unsung heroes of an unfortunate story that had many fathers.

Acknowledgements

Thanks to: Roy Axe, David Boole, Harris Mann, Alex Rankin, Richard Gunn, James Walshe, Alan Ward, Dawson Sellar, David Atkins, Sir Kenneth Warren. Special and long overdue thanks to Ray Hutton and (the late) Michael Scarlett for taking the time when I was at *Autocar* in 1984 to try and show this then young hopeful how to assess and to write. My thanks to British Motor Museum at Gaydon and to the British Motor Industry Heritage Trust. My gratitude to the various BMC and BL related car marques clubs and their members for help and kindness. Individual thanks to Chris Powell at the Rover SD1 owners' club in Swindon. Also to the Land Crab owners' club. Thanks also to editors at the *Daily Telegraph*, the *Independent*, the *South China Morning Post*, *Autocar*, *Car*, *Classic Car*, *Practical Classics*, *Classic Car Weekly*, for publishing my motoring words. Sources include my own archive and publications and my contemporaneous BL, ARG, Jaguar, *Autocar* notes 1981 to date, and my unpublished thesis, 'Beyond the Brand: British Leyland and the effects of external forces upon corporate behaviours and constructs amid a dysfunctional hierarchy'. I would like to state my personal appreciation to John Scott-Morgan and Pen and Sword Books Ltd for being brave enough to commission this book. Admiration to my Aussie wife Anna for putting up with me, my old cars, my nostalgia for a passed age and helping make my books possible. She knows what a Maestro is too! Her reward will be a trip on Qantas to Longreach via Perth, Bendigo, Hobart, Rose Bay, and Toowomba.

Oh, and last but not least, Emily and Jack, are you there?

Introduction

Somewhere, hidden in the BL story there lies a remembrance that is beyond the gates of Longbridge. Here can be found the tears of men amid the frustrations of engineering and design talent squandered or contaminated by committees, communists, and 'group think' where confirmation bias, corporate-speak, torpor and the expectation of agreement, guided those who knew what they knew.

'Oh no, not another book about BL!' Yes, but read on, because this one is different from most that have gone before in that it views many causes and effects amid the greater BL story across a differing perspective. Cars *are* vital to the plot, but there is more than cars to the BL tragedy, so this book tries to blend the various strands together in a new approach of how but also why, and who.

As car enthusiasts who buy books about cars do not expect to read about politics, it follows that there are many people who have little idea how politics played a pivotal role in the BL story. The motoring enthusiast reader is also unlikely to want, or expect to read about social politics, yet British politics and the sociology of the 'class struggle' play very significant roles in the BL story. So in this book you will find some discussion of such vital evidence, but I have, I promise, remained in touch with the key ingredient – the cars. This book is a conversation about BL cars – across their entire landscape.

In any re-telling upon BL's tale it is important to avoid 'rants' and to try and take a wider view than solely blaming the workers, 'Commies', Thatcher, Europe, or the Allegro, for the BL story is a complex drama of many acts. Other car makers, even 'great' ones went through crises – notably at Volkswagen and at Citroën, Fiat and even at General Motors, but they all bounced back, they recovered and restored their reputations, brands, products and consequently their finances.

Yet BL did not quite make it. The reasons why are very interesting indeed.

My own fascination for all things Rover, BLMC, and Austin-Morris had a start in my early childhood days, but the defining moment remains clear to me.

One of the most exciting memories I have about cars is the day when aged 18, I walked into the Austin Rover design centre to start an experience that had been arranged for me after we had had a lecture on car design from one of the Austin

Rover designers at my school. I had grabbed him and whinged for a visit and some work experience at the altar of advanced British car design.

On arrival, in the car park I saw not just a Rover SD1 V8S, but one in Triton Green – a bright, 'electric' green of intense metallic hue. This SD1 was specially trimmed and had non-standard wheels. It had been de-chromed and it seemed to sit and seethe on the car park's tarmac. I simply stood and took in the shape and the stance of the thing. Every line, every panel, every piece of the car's sculpture seemed to work, to gel into a form that looked as though it was moving even when static. The shape of the windscreen seemed as 'emotional' as that of a Porsche 911; the line of the windows, the nose or 'face' of the car simple reeked of style – all defined a new age. From the rear, SD1 was brilliant too. SD1 reminded me of the style of a Vickers VC10 airliner – a piece of totally integrated sculpture in metal. British engineering brilliance.

This then may have been my first appreciation of SD1's superb scaling. Beside it, there was another SD1 and this was mustard yellow. It looked good, but it was not as exciting as that metallic-hued green shark of an SD1 that lay basking beside it. At no stage did I think SD1 was a Ferrari 'copy' either. It turned out that the oft-cited Ferrari 'Daytona' styling cues were more likely to have come from another Ferrari and more importantly, its designer's previous work on the Rover P8 projects and a saloon whose windscreen and window shapes were very obvious SD1 precursors.

I went inside and asked about that Triton SD1. Apparently, it was the chief designer's car. David Bache's own SD1. Bache had close Birmingham roots, had started at 'the Austin' and was the son of Aston Villa and England footballer Joe Bache. What a story – footballer's son becomes famous car designer.

There was also a smart looking Harris Mann-designed Princess in the car park that bore special paint and trims. It too, looked modern and a car of great scaling and stance – more like a 'Solihull Citroën' than a Rover P6 ever did; Princess was a truly advanced Austin and could have taken on the world.

Inside the design centre, which truly 'buzzed', there were some amazing sketches and clay models. I was addicted; the sketches I saw were fantastic. There was also the SD1 estate car – the one they did not mass produce. I saw the amazing Triumph Lynx, too, in all its cancelled glory (what a tragic waste), and the excellent SD2. It was like being at a feast hall, surrounded by inspiration and men who believed in great British design. Yet the reality was also that outside in the car park there lay examples of Allegro '3', Marina MK15, Maxi Mk3.5, and ancient but new examples of Mini (why were their cabins smeared with glue?). The contrast between these cars and the SD1, Princess, Rover P6, and to the abandoned 'nearly' cars of Lynx, SD2, AR6 and more, was massive.

The very rare sight of the 1966-1967 Innocenti Sprite two-door based upon the chassis and mechanicals of the Austin Healey Sprite. Unlike the Tom Tjaardi-designed Innocenti 950 Spider, only 487 of these Sergio Sartotelli-designed coupés were ever made and this is the rarest of all the BL overseas interpretations. It used the A-series engine and the body was built by O.S.I., with Ghia input.

Was it there, back at the home of BL, that I was infected with the car design bug? Or had it happened in a childhood surrounded by BMC, BL and many other marques of amazing cars of the era before 'Euro design' and its rules were applied across black slatted radiators, oblong chrome brand badges, vestigial under-bumper-spoilers, rubber-ended bumpers, black paint around windows and slush-moulded interiors – as seen on every Euro-clone wheeled box of the 1970s-1980s, then to be applied to the 1969-era Morris Marina as the utterly stunning Ital for the 1980s?

Our family owned a series of BMC and BL cars which included A40, Mini, 1100, 1300, Morris Minor 1000, its van derivative, Spitfire, Dolomite, Rover P6 and an early Land Rover Series One which dominated my teenage driving years, for I learned to drive in BL cars; they imbued in me an admiration for British industrial design in its great post-war decades. Think Vickers VC10 airliner, think Concorde, think Rover P5B 3500, think QE2; works like the English Electric Deltic, the Western Class 52, or the Blackburn Buccaneer, all these were the greats of British 1950s-1960s design. Genius created these metal beasts, as had genius built the de Havilland Comet, the Avro Vulcan, the King Class locomotive, the A4 Pacific and notably, the Shorts C Class 'Empire' flying boats, to name just a few of our world-beating heroes of British industrial design. All that before we even mention an Anglo-Grecian-Germanic genius named Issigonis.

As a boy, I used to take a bus to school and one day, a Michelotti-styled bus that had style and a sculpted roof-mounted pod, came howling into view. This bus also had brilliant suspension, an advanced drivetrain, safety structure and was to sell all over the world, despite some initial problems with the engine. The bus was built by Leyland, and it was called the Leyland National – although such a name would be deemed racist now (unless it was Scottish). Inherent within it could be found part of the British Leyland story and Britain's long history of building brilliant commercial vehicles. Leyland Bus Ltd is long gone, but bizarrely, an old, ex-Leyland, Indian company named Ashok Leyland has recently stepped in to purchase the remains of a bus company that itself rose from the 1980s sell-off of Leyland Bus.

Travelling to school on a brilliant Leyland bus and having had a Leyland tractor on our farm, and a rusty old wreck of a Scammell truck in a field, all meant that I was immersed in Leyland. I also learned the craft of driving on our Land-Rover Series 1, a rare early-1950 model.

Leyland built superb and class-leading buses, trucks and tractors – a fact all too often forgotten in the 'cars' narrative. So there were design greats inside *all* of BL, but BL's tale of wonder and of woe truly is worth re-examining, but it can leave us with the same questions that have hung in the air for decades. How and why?

Academics have studied the fall of BL and Rover Group and produced many papers upon the story, yet few have gone deeper into the actual thinking of the men that contributed to the outcome – notably in the political beliefs, causes and effects that lay deep inside the mechanicals of BL.

Let's not forget that not only was BL subsidised by the British taxpayers, so too were the likes of Honda, Nissan, Toyota, Ford, Peugeot/Talbot – all as direct, British-based car building competitors with some invited by Margaret Thatcher to compete with the very BL that she and other people complained received too much state aid – just before she gave BL's competitors hundreds of millions of pounds, in cash and in kind. This did of course signal just where Thatcherism was going – the international market place and the abandonment of domestic loyalties.

Critically, in the 1970s, a BL 'narrative' was set down by the media, politicians, the motoring public, and even by BL's workers themselves. Just as in today's politics and corporate 'spin', the narrative is just that, not always actually factual but a woven construct of opinions and placed agendas which 'the people' come to assume are 'fact', or paradoxical 'fake fact'. Once such a narrative is set, it becomes difficult to escape from it, or for anyone to challenge it, and if they do, they are attacked. This is what happened to BL and at BL. It also infected our politics and BL's remains via New Labour and now infects everything.

The mass-media and tabloid headlines created an anti-BL mindset (the narrative) and brainwashed the public amid the BL crisis years. Of this there is little doubt, and I write that view as an ex-national press journalist. But such media mind games *did* reflect the culture of strikes and stricken cars. But once the die was cast, there was little hope.

Mel Nichols, the revered editor of *Car* magazine in the crucial late 1970s-early 1980s period of BL's affairs, pointed out in September 1981 that the media gave Michael Edwardes' efforts a negative treatment over factory closures and lost jobs, but that in fact, Edwardes' actions, notably those ignored by the media, were, in their totality, positive moves designed to secure a vital future for BL.

Unravelling that BL narrative has taken decades and is still not settled. I hope this book kicks that can further up the road to clarity.

As an example, the Allegro and its designer have been defamed by the narrative. BL at large has also been cited and blamed for cars with problems, yet the likes of Renault, Fiat, Citroën have been forgiven for their 1970s produce that was dire. Ford turned out some truly dreadful build quality and re-warmed old cars in the 1970s, yet are rarely cited for it. Poor old BL still gets it in the neck however. Oh, and BL did not design and produce the wretched Ford Pinto and its serious design problem either. Neither did BL stick a modern car's fuel tank up under a rear wing and near the rear bumper – no, not the 1970s Pinto but the 1980s Sierra.

Renault 14, AlfaSud, VW Polo MK1 and Passat Mk1, Citroën GSA, Datsun Cherry, Ford Escort Mk III, AMC Pacer – they all rusted and failed to proceed at some stage. Lack of build quality was *not* unique to BL! Automotive 'lemons' were also built beyond Birmingham and Oxford.

The mighty Volkswagen (VW), so often hailed as BL's successful rival, saw its sales in America plummet from half a million cars a year in the 1970s to under 80,000 a year in the 1990s. Why? Because of quality issues and inappropriate model ranges pitched higher into the market than traditional VW fare. In the early 1990s, the company that gave America the Beetle had no base model, volume car proposition on sale to America. But who knows about – let alone remembers, this great VW failure?

At the same time, BL as Austin Rover made a fantastic mainstream 'bread and butter car' – one of the best cars in its class of its era that competed head-on with all its main competitors. Yet it sold in low numbers and was obscured by the narrative that had been constructed around its manufacturer. That car was the Montego estate, notably in its top-of-the-range 2.0-litre fuel injection variant. I drove one at length and knew its greatness. Like many owners, I loved that car. Only a Volvo 740 GLT estate tempted me away. Yet Montego, like other BL cars, and the BL 'nearly cars' – the ones that were nearly made, all suffered at the hand of the narrative and the hidden agendas of the politics of the Left and the Right that framed the BL story.

1990s 'Roverisation' of the old BL and Austin Rover product line, amid Rover-badged Hondas, both diluted and confused the marketing message and brand foundations of BL.

Yet Rover's 800 series, specifically as the post-1988 2.7-Litre V6 Vitesse Fastback (or even as an 827si fitted with the optional sport's suspension tuning pack seen on the Vitesse), was a fantastic car. Roy Axe, Gordon, Sked and the design team, with Roland Bertodo (engineering) and Kevin Morley (marketing), turned out a real winner in the Vitesse – stylish, fast, and efficient, with improved handling. Here was proof that BL – or Rover Group – could create a winner, something with real appeal, a car people really wanted and it had build quality. I drove one for a while and loved it. Where the engine's extra power came from compared to the standard unit, who knew, but 827 Vitesse was a superb tool, a real flyer. However, things did start to fall off... And underneath lay the 1980s Honda Legend structure, which did not make reassuring watching at the *Auto Motor und Sport*/ADAC crash test of that car; the cabin intrusion, footwell collapse and A-pillar movement was horrific and inexcusable, notably in comparison to the performances of contemporary Mercedes Benz, BMW and Volvo cars in the same tests.

Sadly, the new 800 Mk2 model never came for the 800 range – just another facelift of Mk1 for the 1990s and a stick-on chrome grille where branding took preference over its product – which was an old car based on an old Honda. Above all, not even Sir Graham Day's hopes for 'Roverisation' could throw off the old BL narrative, however good the 800 Fastback and its Vitesse were.

Another rarity, Ian Creese's LeyKor South Africa Apache. Looking like a baby Triumph that never was, it is of course a Michellotti-styled reinterpretation of the ADO16 1100-1300. BL stupidly failed to market the car in the UK.

Below, are the words of a very senior ex-BL personage who wishes to remain anonymous. They are calm, carefully considered words, thought about for decades. They are not in error.

'Something else was going on. For all sorts of reasons that include money, politics, power and maybe even the stability of the government and the nation, the lid was kept on the underlying cause. Many political deals were done between Longbridge and Downing Street. A lot has not been told.'

Something else *was* going on inside BL's factories. And it affected the cars, even the outcome of their design and production viability. That something else was of a 1970s socio-political nature, maybe even of revolutionary intrigue.

Did the Morris Marina's 'TC' trim badge stand for 'Trotskyists Cowley'? Or maybe 'Try Communism'?

Editorialised hyperbole? Not at all; read on to find out how both would have been factually accurate.

Ray Hutton, the greatly respected editor of *Autocar* in the 1980s, referred to 'revolutionary union leaders' in that revered publication on 11 October 1980 when he reviewed the story of the then new Metro and its political context and birth. Ray may have been referring to Derek Robinson – 'Red Robbo' – and like the rest of us, probably had little idea that some members of the BL workforce were so far-Left that they considered some of their own union leaders (even Robinson) not to be revolutionary but to be 'Right-wing', 'Tories', and being in 'collusion' with management.

Who knew that the 'revolutionaries' were real, ultra-far-Left and actually believed in social and political revolution for Britain (and not just for BL) by various means. Bringing down the government and altering society by industrial and other means was their ethos. Was BL their mechanism?

So, deep inside BL there lay a struggle, and it went beyond cars and their badges. There is a largely untold story about politics inside BL's factories – politics that affected the cars. The truth is that the extreme perspectives inside BL, Communism and Trotskyism, the left and the far-left, all were at war with each other, as well as with the unions, the members, and not just the management.

Today, in a bizarre outcome of history and a once strike-bound society, you can buy a Chinese MG in England and make your payment to the coffers of the thing that America and Britain have spent several wars and more than seventy years trying to destroy – a Communist State. This one is called the People's Republic of China, with its own People's Revolutionary Army and its own auto industry.

Oh, what a tragic irony.

Over thirty years on from BL's darkest days, the late 'Red Robbo' the Communist Party of Great Britain member, *Morning Star* stalwart and strike-leader at Longbridge, would have smiled wryly at the one.

Only a marble hearted soul would fail to react.

Ex-Talbot and Peugeot workers from Coventry may also smile at the reality of Peugeot now being part-owned by China's communist state. Because I do not wish to give money to China, I no longer buy Peugeots nor new Volvos. It's a free world – but not in Beijing, in case you have forgotten.

Others, who occupied a different political position, said that under Thatcher it was all a 1980s plot to kill off British car making and remove Europe's and Germany's biggest car competitor – to the benefit of German car industry and

German economy amid the European Union adventure. And Britain would get something in return – a quid pro quo.

This sounds like a conspiracy theory, but there were many of those inside BL, Austin Rover and the EEC/EU.

Still with MG – the last sad remnant of a great British brand, even the Chinese State-owned Shanghai Automotive Industry Corporation (SAIC) that owns MG, has just had to give up its British, Longbridge-based final local assembly of MGs from imported kits and resort to Chinese-built fully finished cars arriving on a ship. MG's plan to restart full-scale MG manufacture in Britain is dead in 2019. For the second time, Longbridge is turning off the lights and selling off scrap. The MG dream has died – again, probably because it was a dream that was beyond a manufactured and planned reality.

The EU is a vital part of this story, as is China – which now owns part of our history. The EU currently has a trade deficit with China to the tune of €185 billion! But that is 'ok' says the EU in its strange logic, because 'other investments' make up for it. So that's all right then . . .

Britain joined the European Economic Community (EEC) in 1973 and Europe and the resultant European Union (EU) are writ large inside the BL story then and now. Britain was full member of the EEC/EU when BL, Talbot and Peugeot ceased car making in the Midlands. Europe did not ride to the rescue, and Brexit had not been thought of.

So I make no excuses for citing past and current European matters and their legacies.

All these years on, we also have a tranche of younger people who have little idea of what really went on at BL, because they were not around to watch it, let alone sleep in a Maxi or try to drive a wobbly Marina or bouncy Allegro. So maybe they need telling? They certainly need to know about the genius inside the likes of Rover, Triumph, Jaguar, Austin, BL Technology, and the cars that were and 'nearly' were. Today's youngsters need to drive an XJ-S, a proper Range Rover, a TR8, or an XJ6, but many have not – instead they have been brainwashed into cars of digital authoritarianism amid the worst ride qualities and steering responses in the history of motoring.

Modern cars are wonderfully safe and very efficient, but they are also chemically extruded from a mould of blandness. Many are numbing to drive and utterly anaemic in character. True, there are cars of excellence and design, yet many cars separate the driver from reality. As for low-profile wheels and tyres and stiff springs and dampers, today's young do not know what 'ride quality' is, do they? BMC and BL did, for sure.

There were some very fine cars, and a great engineering and design history inside BL. So perhaps with the benefit of hindsight, we should try to be fairer upon BL, its cars, its men, and its marketing. Some of today's critical motoring media mouths are given to the automatic slag-off of BL, and so are their readers, but there is more to the story than they know from their current context or memories of Leyland bashing.

My attempt at even handedness cannot ignore the Marina's front suspension, the SD1's lack of build quality, or the hobbling of Metro, or XJ40's wheel bearing woes to name just a few moments in the ebbing tide of BL. And did not strikes become an *endemic,* daily condition for BL's workforce? 1975-78 were horrendous years for industrial relations at BL – under a Labour government and contrary to perceived wisdom, *not* inspired by Mrs Margaret Hilda Thatcher who did not launch her psychological experiment upon Britain until 1979. But read on to discover more about strikes and their relevance.

Seen from the today of the here and the now, it is easy to knock the great past of the empire of badge-engineering and re-engineering that was variously known as British Motor Corporation (BMC), British Motor Holdings (BMH), Leyland-Standard-Triumph, and British Leyland Motor Corporation (BLMC), British Leyland Ltd, (BL) and more – resulting in Leyland Cars, then Austin Rover Group and various Jaguar Rover Triumph branding iterations. A story perhaps best or worst known after the post-1968 amalgamation to be eventually known in 1975 as British Leyland or just BL as it became framed amid its era of infamy. A shout of 'BL' became a colloquial exclamation to describe much.

Indeed, the very issue of the Corporation's name was the stuff of internal debate, with Donald Stokes and his team insisting in a 1970s branding document[1] that it should always be styled as 'British Leyland Motor Corporation'. Yet as late as 1974, the company's head office was advising that it should only be abbreviated to 'British Leyland' or 'BL'. The company categorically stated in 1974 that 'BLMC' should not be used as it was cumbersome, ugly and reminded people of BMC which had died in 1968.

Inside the BL monolith could be found the components of historic marques which were eventually to be cited as Jaguar, Rover Triumph, Leyland Cars, Austin Morris, Austin Rover Group, Rover Group. Further final iterations of these once great names did, of course, transpire and then succumb in a more recent history. The flames of a MG Rover's phoenix have left many a scar.

Meanwhile, the names of Riley, Triumph, and Wolseley, lie dormant in a lawyer's file, while the once essential marque that was Rover hovers in invisible limbo awaiting its fate, which we can only hope is not that of MG of Abingdon-upon-China.

Perceived wisdom can be a contradiction in terms and in this book my aim is to usurp the constraints of the conditioned mind and re-frame so-called perceived wisdom about 'BL' and its cars. Indeed, numerous writers and observers have stated that BLMC came into being in 1968 and that the problems started soon after, or that the fault lay solely with its cars. Both statements are incorrect.

For the cars were not the only problem. Some writers about BL have looked at the story from a Right-wing perspective, others have taken a more Left-leaning view. There are people who *entirely* fault the workforce for destroying BL. Or you might solely blame management and the Tories. There is also a differently educated new generation of people who, principally, blame the cars.

It is all too easy to solely the blame the workers. And in case you do not know, the BL production lines moved at a speed that made careful fitting and utmost quality, hard to achieve. Stopwatches were used and men were timed in their tasks – that is a truth, not a piece of hyperbole or hearsay. Today, toilet breaks are timed in at least one car factory that I have worked in. Transgressors of allotted toilet time *will* be interviewed and placed on review!

Lots of BL snippets and bits referred to here came from inside BL and ARG, from the various marque histories and from motor industry men, as well as my own notes across the years. I have recalled what I have seen and heard during time within or at BL and the industry across my early, youthful days as a styling apprentice and then as an annoyingly confident young reporter.

I think the 'maddest' car I have ever driven has to be the MG Metro Turbo. How close to death it took me.

BL was not alone in its poor build quality and badge engineering. Renault's 14 was a corrosion castle of the direst build quality, Fiat's Tipo a nightmare of poor parts and flimsy structure, and Citroën's GS a spaceship that rusted. Even Ford had its issues of build, rust, ride and old technology under the cover of its expensive marketing budget. Saab had a rusty period, as did Mercedes. And BL was *not* responsible for that most expensive of follies of the 1980s era that was the Talbot Tagora.

So BL were not alone in taking some dumb decisions, but the media would have you believe that it was; BMC and BL were not unique in their badge madness and beige banality. But there were so many BL 'nearly' cars. Hidden in the depths of the British Motor Museum, there lie some of the stunning ideas that nearly made it such as Lynx, and AR6 – and also including the Harris Mann-styled, Charles Spencer King-engineered ECV 3, a car that was futurism personified and a world-beater in all but production reality. ECV 3 was a glittering future, yet one cast to the winds of a fate that was so damn British in its tragedy.

Introduction • 19

Princess 2 – stylish, modern, beautifully scaled, Harris Mann's design has aged well. Princess should have put BL back on top of the international stage, but BL's issues affected its fate.

Rover SD1 3500V8 S. Bache's masterpiece design in all its scale and stance. Another brilliant BL car that was ruined by build quality issues.

This book is an affectionate but sometimes scathing look back at all the good and the bad of BL, its era, the cars that were heroes and villains, the saints, the knaves, the waste of genius. Many of the BL cars were authentic and superb, but many had only those ingredients as potential and relied upon the customer to prove the prototyping phase of their development at private cost.

We do not design or build home-grown, mass market cars in the Midlands any more. Nor anywhere in the UK. Instead, the likes of Honda, Hyundai, Kia, Suzuki, and European others, meet the needs of British motorists.

In case you have forgotten, we no longer make much in the critical field of mechanical, industrial design and engineering, ships, trains 'planes and automobiles. All, once of our original invention, have gone – Formula One cars excepted.

It's incredible when you think about it.

For years, I have wondered how it happened. This is a book I have spent over three decades researching and have always wanted to write. The first chapter (only) is written in the first person of BL recollection – you will have to forgive me for that – but it *is* about cars. In the now, this tale is a drive through the ups and downs of the good and the bad of the BMC-to-BL years. I am a middle-aged old grumpy now; looking back at BL has been fun and I know that many car enthusiasts do, like me, share a need to remember BL and its cars.

I suppose the trick in properly telling the BL story is *not* to try and smear opprobrium evenly by calling it objectivity. Instead, can we offer praise where it was due and yet be correctly scathing of the imbecilic when it drives up in front of you and expires?

Sadly, there were indeed not just heroic failures within the BL story, there were also acts of absurd and bizarre engineering, design, manufacture and management which defied belief, took the mickey out of the paying customer and drove the franchised dealers to breakdowns on a par with those of the cars they were tasked with selling and repairing.

My old school friend's dad was a BL dealer named Peter Stirland. Peter was an ex-Royal Enfield 'works' rider and latterly owned and ran his own BMC-BLMC dealership. Driven to despair by BL's cars, notably recalcitrant Maxis, the loyal and trustworthy Peter switched to a Ford franchise and never looked back. People like Stirland were BL's loss, however hard the brilliant BL director Tony Ball worked to keep them on board.

Quite how clever men steeped in a century of British industrial heritage and industrial design created the BL disaster has long been debated. There are many tales to be told, many false trails, and many sad case studies.

Perhaps the only way of looking at what happened is to try and reach an even handed view – but that itself risks a plot of political correctness or at the other extreme, the blame game.

Although laced with my personal experience, the narrative which follows is based in design, engineering, politics and the events of cars, amid what I hope is a fair record and a fair stab at framing a unique moment in our motoring and its occasional madness. It is currently fashionable to look back in anger, but a more rational review of BL is called for.

I was lucky enough to have worked in the motoring media and car design world from the 1980s onwards and met and talked with several of the key characters in the BL story. Men like Jeff Daniels, Michael Scarlett, Ray Hutton, and BL's own Edwardes, Musgrove, Horrocks, Egan, Ball, and others, told me things when I was a young motoring writer and I have tried to remember their integrity of view in my own telling of the wider BL story. Recent chats with BL luminaries have confirmed past tutors' words.

I have used several reference resources beyond my own to create this book and they are credited here. Jeff Daniels' *British Leyland and the Truth About the Cars* has been of great clarity, although it is a shame that the author's belief of a sound BL future was beyond the reality of politics and power. Daniels was also perhaps, unlikely in light of his job, to examine the politics of the affair too closely or expose certain underlying concerns. The British Motor Industry Heritage Trust works offered much guidance. Graham Turner's *The Leyland Papers* were of note. Graham Robson's *The Cars of BMC* has also been useful. Keith Adams' views are worth reading and his AROn-line archive helps many and takes a very interesting view; Adams also owns a Citroën GS, sensible man. The Rover SD1 owners' club has also been of assistance. The British Motor Museum at Gaydon is also an invaluable resource and so too has been the British Motor Industry Heritage Trust that lies within the museum – a 'must see' museum and one of the best in the world.

Car magazine also printed some great and very rational BL stories – perhaps even too hopeful about BL on occasion – so let's tip our caps to editors of those days such as Mr Nichols, Mr Fraser, and to Mr Cropley, for their innate sense and fair play towards BL despite its transgressions. *Car* always believed in BL's engineers and designers.

Conversations with retired BL 'insiders' have informed my commentary, and they reveal much. Some of it known but unsaid and unpublished, some of them have had to remain anonymous. I worked inside Austin Rover at the end of the 1980s. Now that *was* an education.

In a rolling narrative, I have tried to avoid lifeless and numbing numbers, statistics and boring figures, but on occasion they *have* to be cited, and read, for they are the proof, the *evidence* of what happened.

I have had a lifelong love of Swedish and French cars and owned over twenty-five of them. To my taste, the Citroën GS/A was and remains, one of the greatest cars of all time. The CX is on a par of design excellence. Likewise the Saab 99 and 900 – which added build quality to the mix. I also like old BMWs and Porsches, and old Bugattis strike me as rather wonderful too. What of obscure yet amazing devices like the Lancia Gamma, and the NSU RO 80? All are wonders to be adored in my mind. So I may be abnormal.

But I also have a love of Jaguars, Rovers, Triumphs and other British cars, notably Allards (one of which I have co-restored). Quite how I ended up buying not one Maestro but two, is deeply worrying even today. The first was a Maestro diesel. The second was a green MG Maestro (red seatbelts!). And there was brief affair with the 'Turbo' variation – which was indeed a variation likely to lead you up excreta creek without a forward implementation device in a 0-60mph time of 6.7seconds. Putting a turbo in amid unequal length driveshafts and low profile wheels led to certain . . . *tendencies* . . .

I had read the positive reviews for Maestro in *Car* magazine years before and was still infected with belief in BL's cars – or Austin Rover Group (ARG) as it was known when I was Maestro bound.

I loved my diesel Maestro. It was comfortable, adaptable, reliable and made long-hauls easy. It really was a good car. It was very well designed. That Perkins-derived engine was superb – so tractable and smooth. But in the first weeks that I owned it, the Maestro's sudden attack of rust advanced faster than flies on a turd. My Austin Maestro D was good – seats, drive, cabin, handling, ride – except for its rust and temporary trim items. Within six weeks of buying it (used) from an Austin Rover dealer, a rash of rust acne appeared across all its lower panels. It spread, daily. I took it back and the franchised dealer so stupidly said to me, 'What did you expect from a cheap car?' I pointed out that it was not a cheap car, not a 'banger'.

He offered to take it and 'sort' the rust. He did – by refusing to rub the paint back down to the metal, instead simply 'blowing' over existing rusty paint with new paint. I had the car back. Four weeks later it was covered in red acne all over again.

I simply took the Maestro back and made him swap it for a lightly used, 40,000 mile, red Rover 214SLi hatchback for the same price. This Honda Concerto-based Rover, a 'Blonda' or 'Ronda' *was* a good car, well built, good to drive.

But it was under-damped, felt so flimsy, so thin and low-fronted. It took only a few months to discover just how weak and 'wrong' it was (the dashboard and front bulkhead was seemingly at below the knee height). I sold it and went back to Saab and Volvo where I felt safer. En route, I had a brief diversion to a Ford Escort Mk3 diesel hatchback which drove like a tractor, rode like a plough and was thin, oh so thin of metal and structure; the sills and roof pillars were like twigs when they should have been branches.

I would also latterly drive a Honda-Rover – the 800 and it too shared the same feeling as the Rover 214SLi hatchback – that very low bulkhead and front end – with its not unrelated, incompetent damping amid short-travel suspension that was a Honda design trait carried over into the Honda-Rovers. We had an MG Montego EFI in the family and it *was* brilliant. We briefly had a Range Rover too, and I latterly drove a three-door Bahama Gold Range Rover, at length. It was beyond brilliant, an act of sheer design and marketing genius that was timeless beyond fashion.

I think I bought these cars because I grew up in a family that owned a number of interesting 1960s, 1970s, and 1980s cars – from a Citroën DS, a Saab 99, a Triumph Spitfire, a Herald, a Land Rover Series One, several Austin 1300s, three A40s, a Maxi, an MGBGT, and Rovers from 95, 100, P6 3500. My granny had owned one of those almost-pink lilac Morris Minor 'million' celebration editions; then she had a new Mini Clubman, an execrable Mini Clubman whose interior seemed to be smeared in glue, it truly was an unmitigated disaster of a car.

My parents had an Austin A40, a Datsun 120Y and a Renault 4 at the same time. My mother loved her Austin 1100 and her 1300. My father celebrated being divorced by driving a tuned up VW Beetle 1502. There were also a string of Toyotas in the family of which the 1970s Celicas (the coupé was a mini-Mustang) were real highlights. Meanwhile, our Ford Fiesta Mk1 was interestingly dreadful – thin skinned, pared down and rust prone. It would not start on cold mornings and possessed the build quality and ride of a shopping trolley. Tom Tjaarda's brilliant design skills were hobbled by a poverty-spec build.

My mother's Triumph Spitfire had spewed oil, and she crashed her A40 into the back of a lorry and lived; her Austin 1300 had whined its way to a dusty death but its elegance and packaging efficiency was supreme. My Aunt's Dolomite Sprint never really worked properly and all the trims came unstuck. How could the wonderful old hulk that was our Maxi be so terrible in its act of mechanical operation? What gremlins inhabited its castle?

We had a Rover P6. It was quite simply the best, the cleverest car of my youth. Ours was a 2200TC, not a 3500V8, yet it was never less than brilliant in all its ingredients and everything it did. Forget Rolls-Royce or Mercedes-Benz, P6 was for a time, truly the best car in the world, only to be usurped by the Jaguar XJ6. But even these true icons were dented by BL's drive to low quality.

Our 1950 Land Rover Series One was part of the family, latterly, I drove a Land Rover 110 Tdi over 5,000 miles through East Africa and it never missed a beat and nothing fell off. It just stormed onwards. All I did was clean the air filter every day and change the oil twice. What a vehicle.

We sold our Ford Fiasco as soon as we found out about its truly dreadful offset frontal crash test performance (in an age when such tests were not legally required), and yet we took longer to discover the Mini Metro/Rover 100's equally abysmal structural collapse in crash tests. I taught a girlfriend to drive in an orangey red Metro. Both it and she were soon despatched when the truth about their foibles emerged (both whined on long drives).

More recently, we have had a Rover 75 diesel estate and bloody marvellous it was too. Times with a superb XJ-S will never be obscured amid a car which taught me much and gave me wonderful experiences. That XJ-S V12 was a superb analogue act of mechanical driving yet one cloaked in silk, leather and caviar-trimmed waftability. I used to fly down the A303 on clear, empty days in the XJ-S, and those are memories to treasure. That silken purse was not of a sow's ear, it was a king of a car yet one despised for decades, only now to have a following.

There came my own Rover, an SD1 3500 which was also superb but went off tune and off the road into a garage too often; on a good day it was great, but why did it leak? All this was amid ownership of Saabs, Volvos, and assorted Citroëns. In the main though, I dabbled in BL and Austin Rover cars. Ultimately, I reverted to a Saab 900 classic and truly brilliant, run-for-ever Volvo V70s. I can definitely say the worst car I have owned was not a BL car but a General Motors, Vauxhall-derived Saab 9-3.

I briefly dabbled with a Mini. It was great fun, I loved its drive. its dartability and its sheer joy, as so many do. But being tall, I could not get comfortable and my back complained. I wondered about my legs in a crash, too. And why were the sills, pillars, and doors so thin and light? My fears were soon confirmed and I sold the Mini very quickly indeed. I had listened to Murray MacKay (of the University of Birmingham School of Engineering) on Mini's structural and crash-test issues. Issigonis it seems, refused such discussions when confronted by MacKay.

All I knew was that if I had been in a Mini, rather than my Volvo, when I was involved in a major car crash, I would not have survived, or worse, might have lived with what they now so euphemistically call 'life-changing injuries' – or in another word, vegetablised. Thanks Professor MacKay.

Safety? It becomes more important when you see it up-close. I attended all the early EuroNCAP tests and learned a lot. Car safety –in structural, passive-safety, terms – has indeed come a very long way.

Rover and, of course, Riley, were once the class act as the ultimate driving machines of their day. MGs were once brilliant, Austins were advanced and even Morris fare was clever. We might well suggest that the Austin Morris 1100-1300 range of the 1960s, with their clean, Farina styling and advanced Issigonis engineering and packaging, were examples of British car making and BMC at its best; in fact a world class car to take on the best of Europe's small saloon cars. The Australian version – a Nomad-badged five-door hatchback with 1500cc and a five-speed gearbox – was brilliant, so too was the booted and suited saloon version known as the Apache or the Victoria.

Yet the bestselling 1100-1300 replacement was the Allegro, which was brilliant conceptually, but somewhat diluted in its reality. Some people still (erroneously) attack the Allegro's designer Harris Mann. Yet, he is a hero and the critics miss the point. Allegro was hobbled *not* by its creator, but by the committees of men that tooled it into redesigned reality in a push to save money and reuse old, very old, paid-for components. Allegro had huge potential that was diluted at an altar of conservatism and penny-pinching. Don't blame its designer!

For those that do not know, Mann also created a potential new two-seat open-top sports car design for BL in the mid-1970s. He categorically drew it and labelled it as an MG. MG needed an MGB replacement. Mann called it 'Magna'. A senior BL figure took up Mann's idea but turned it into a Triumph. Good if you like Triumphs, a disaster for MG. Once again, Mann had the right idea but senior management, shall we say, 're-framed' it.

I was a teenager in the late 1970s, so knew little of the BL strikes as reality for the workforce or the company's politics. All I know is that we had our BL-built family cars 'Ziebarted' and not even that could save them, whereas it *did* save our Lancia Beta; how about that for mad. Ziebart smelled of high-octane parabens and molasses. It oozed out of rubber-capped injection holes for months and must also have acted as a sound-deadening, anti-resonance material within the Lancia's structure. The Beta 2000ie was by the way, a wonderful car.

Flavour of the times. Car magazine always believed in BL's engineers and designers. These covers of the essential BL era prove the point. (Author via Bauer Media)

From Ziebart and other such post-purchase rust protection treatments, a question was obvious; why on earth did all the big car manufacturers not include such treatment on their production lines? If Volvo, Saab, and Mercedes Benz could, why not Citroën, Renault and Ford? Indeed, Ford's 1970s 'rust-proofing' was a joke – with 'wax coating' falling off the inside of Cortina wheel arches in weeks.

I hope you enjoy this new approach to telling the BL story. I have tried to avoid too many statistics and facts, but some are very necessary. I have tried to present the story chronologically, but on occasion it has been necessary to provide evidence out of sequence and to repeat it where appropriate. Your understanding is sought.

Today, there is a huge nostalgia for BLMC and its BL cars. Far more love now exists than it did in 1977 for these cars. The club movement and the pages of *Practical Classics*, *Autocar*, and sometimes even *Classic & Sports Car*, are often laden with BL cars and owners' stories. BL nostalgia is great fun and a viable business too. Club members embrace with their BL friendship and fond memories.

This book is my own, different conversation about cars and more. Like BL's cars it is presented 'warts and all'. This is what I saw, heard, and what I thought and what I found out. I have commented on politics, but not set down a dogma, simply opinion based on a wide variety of factual evidence. This is *not s*peculation; it is an examination of the evidence trail amid obvious patterns of behaviour – an approach I have used in my other professional disciplines, notably within academic and aviation research. BL's internal inconsistencies are exposed for the reader to consider.

Talking to some of the men who were there was interesting and even Tony Benn was emotional about the fate of our car industry, which is more than we might say about Thatcher, Blair or Brown. Michael Edwardes was hugely interesting to talk to. Small, sharp, clever, dynamic, but he must have been hard to disagree with. *He* was convinced that something else was going on with BL.

The late Roy Axe, Harris Mann, and many others were so loyal to BL. It seems we the owners have been too. Today a Gaydon, BL gathering is one of joy.

This book is what I (and others) think happened; you may disagree and if you do, why not write your own book and 'correct' what you feel are my errors? Just don't whinge on the web and expect no comeback. Speaking as a lad from the 'outback', a place where life or death decisions are more important than celebrity status and news, more vital than soft egos of entitlement and pampered business class feelings, a place where people skills are vital, I say this is my book, drawn from a range of informed evidence and if you don't like it, try examining your own down pipe.

Before we start off, I have removed the drip tray, run my hands over brown velour, beige vinyl, 'fake wood' and pushed the chrome embellishments back into place. As long as the coolant lasts, the head gasket does not rot, and the electrics remain live, we may make forward progress. I hope you do not have trouble engaging gear herein. I have at least tried to grease the cable-operated transmission between today and our trip to the memory of an automotive yesterday, one that incredibly, failed to have a future.

I ask but one thing of you, do not 'Leyland-bash'. Please do not pre-judge the issue. Try and be nice about BL's great engineers, designers, managers, and men; for they were, in the main very talented people indeed, of world class works and deserve much respect. It's time we took a kinder retrospective on what happened, yet at the same time, investigate the crash, for it really was fascinating.

Lance Cole
Round the bend – not far from Cowley

1
Questions

A brief personal pontification upon to BL or not BL

I once worked for BL's mutation, the Austin Rover Group (ARG) or better known as Austin Rover (AR) and that only cemented my frustration at the cars of BL legacy. Arg indeed.

Checking a Montego for final acceptance, I noticed it had been built with basic L trim check-patterned rear seat trim fabric and with totally different HLS velour trim on the two front seats! The supervisor seemed unmoved. 'Oh,' came the disinterested response as if such incompetence was the norm. It was sent off to the dealer and he could sort it out there. There was also an orangey red Metro with beige stripes applied on one side and grey stripes along the other, both cars being straight off the production line.

I saw bodyshells arriving from Pressed Steel Swindon on a rain-soaked transporter. I also saw raw bodyshells sitting outside in the rain before being taken into the factory. I saw tinted glass fitted in one window and not in another in the same Jaguar. Mixed-up wheels and wheel trims, missing bits, specification anomalies, bare metal showing through a new Jaguar's paint, poor rust proofing, glue smeared in cabins, all was 'normal'. And why would electronically governed, brand new Maestros utterly refuse to fire-up properly, run cleanly, or stay in tune?

Possibly the biggest blunder I saw was a new Maestro with base model steel bumpers (in black) at the front, and the upper range car's full-width, painted thermoplastic full bumper valance panel at the rear! Such imbecility was impossible, *surely*?

Why did the plastic spoilers on Rover 827 Vitesses wilt and bend? Why did the Rover Sterling interior plastics change colour after exposure to the sun, to create a mix and match quilt of rioting hues across the dashboard?

Why did Jaguars of the 1980s eat wheel bearings and dashboards? What was wrong with the electrics – always? Why did BL's Jaguar paint seem so thin? I saw new XJ6s that seemed to only have one layer of paint applied, with such thin paint not just on the sills, but on the roof too! Often there were swathes of primer or raw metal showing through. How did these escape from the factory?

Why did bits fall off so many of our BL cars? Why did my Rover SD1 fail every month?

I nearly caused a mass walk-out when I carried a drawing from one office to the factory floor. A union rep stopped me and asked if I was a member and had the drawing been stamped and approved? I was not a union member. He exploded and shouted, 'All out!' then began to rant about rights and exploitation. Oh, and was I a management stooge, because I sounded 'posh'? His reaction was irrational and not proportional. This is how bad things had got on the factory floor. It was, it seems, a tribal war.

Back in the 1990s, I drove a Honda-based Rover 827 Vitesse for a while; I also ran the 'Sterling' version. I enjoyed these cars but they were a it seems a bit of a con-trick. How brilliant their Honda 2.7 litre engines were (the 2.5 was weaker), how brilliant their Rover-designed interiors, yet how appalling were their fittings, build quality and suspension damping – except the revised Vitesse. What didn't fade, fell off, and the electrics – *please.* The 827 drove though, and drove well; I remember a wonderful drive through the west highlands of Scotland in the 827 Vitesse, the creamy, cammy 2.7 multi-valve engine screaming and the front end turning-in with precision on wet bends. But of course, in time, it all went awry. Oh, and the rear spoiler wilted and went limp.

The Sterling was Atlantic Blue – a lovely deep cobalt hue. I loved its interior and fascia design, but after one hot summer, all the mouldings in the front cabin and fascia had changed colour – but independently. The dash top coaming was now green not grey! It broke down, just as Sterlings did all over America, thus invalidating the great British car reputation very quickly indeed.

'Export or die' ran the old Donald Stokes' mantra. Death soon came.

These so-called Rovers looked good when new, but soon faded, and what was it about their structures that worried me – huge apertures for the windscreen, and cut-way doors, a very low front, thin panels, and long A-pillars? The bulkhead or firewall seemed low, the footwells so shallow. Where did these design traits come from? A lack of depth at the front of the car really worried me – it meant that there was less metal to crush and absorb impact, and less rigidity to resist intrusion. The thoughts lay dormant until I saw the ADAC, EuroNCAP, IIHS, crash test results for the then Honda Accord/Rover 600, Honda Legend, and the Civic – the cars of Honda-Rover basis.

The Germans testers criticised the original Legend for its poor impact performance but contrary to such findings, Honda said there was no risk of serious injury. EuroNCAP noted Rover 600's serious cabin intrusion. In America, the Insurance

Institute of Highway Safety (IIHS) gave the 1995 Honda Accord only an 'acceptable' rating due to its risk of leg injuries stemming from front footwell collapse and intrusion (as also seen in the original Legend/800/600). In 1999, the IHHS tested the 1999 Honda Accord and commented that Honda had still not resolved the issue of its car's leg injury criteria from footwell intrusion.[1]

Some years later, I worked in the Honda factory at Swindon and did some new model development driving for the company. It did not go well. I asked too many questions.

Why, I asked, did some new Civics have anti-intrusion steel bars fitted in the doors, but other identical models being built on the same production line for export to Europe's mainland, did not? Were we prioritising safety by market profile, PR, customer 'expectation' and costs? Or were the 'floating' door bars when fitted, pointless anyway?

Why did Honda insist on such expensive double wishbone suspension (dictated from on high?) only to ruin the quality of ride effect with short dampers and springs in a low front that failed to offer correct damping or spring absorption rates? Why was there a brand new VW Passat being stripped apart in the new model development laboratory? Why did Honda end up paying Volvo about £400million to build it a new safety test centre?

I worked for Peugeot and for Saab too. The differences in their cars were interesting. I owned several Saabs and also two 'real' Peugeots – a 304 and a 305 – but soon Peugeot's past quality and strength seemed to have departed. My mother's 205 three-door was a nightmare and split at the B-pillar.

My uncle's Rover P6 3500V8 had 'Ambla' seat trim with a 'Huntsman' vinyl roof. At least it was not BL puce or excreta hued. It was a truly great car. Our Montego estate was superb. Our Land Rover even better. BL made such good cars, but the narrative wants you to remember the bad ones. It is however rather hard to forget the bad moments. But there is more to BL and its story than that.

My aunt owned a truly bizarre Chrysler 180 and an Australian relative owned the Aussie version of the same car – which came with an extended-aircraft carrier deck-like nose job.

Chrysler in the 1970s and 1980s was not unlike BL in that it turned out rehashed and facelifted 'series four' badge-engineered cars, left right and centre. The Chrysler Sunbeam hatchback of the 1980s was in fact the underpinnings of the lurching, rear-wheel drive, two decades old Hillman Avenger, recast and draped over with a cleverly disguised 'modern' hatchback body that even used the Avenger two-door shell's front doors. Inside, the cabin was cramped by the massive transmission tunnel and gearbox housing. Apart from the Lotus-tweaked version, the Sunbeam was a marketing con-trick. So it was not just BL who played games with the brands and the consumer.

So others got things wrong too. But they got things right as well. Think Peugeot 305 and 505, think Renault 30 and 20, think Saab 99 and 900, think VW Passat; think Mazda 626. Yet the Princess, notably the Princess 2, 2000 HLS was a superbly designed car of huge refinement – but it too was hobbled by BL built quality and also the BL narrative. Princess was brilliant – but you are not allowed to say so.

'Badge engineering' gone mad was not just a BL thing; we saw that old late-1960s Hillman Avenger of Sunbeam underpinnings ruse live on in Argentina until 1990 (initially as a Dodge 1500) and then utterly incongruously as a Volkswagen! This was the British Hillman Avenger recast as the VW1500, the original, soft, 1960s Hillman bodyshell being dressed up with black painted trim and a front end straight off a Euro-clone car or a Morris Ital and a VW badge affixed.

In the 1980s, the Mazda 323 was in fact the 'new' front-wheel drive Ford Escort in drag (with more aerodynamic drag too). The Vauxhall Astra latterly became a desperate Daewoo. Kia's first supermini was in fact an old Ford and Mazda device. Proton sold Mitsubishis on the cheap. Eventually, General Motors sold Subarus as Saabs. But Volvo's 360, based on a DAF but built like a Volvo was a brilliant, rear wheel drive, trans-axled driver's device. I owned four, including the fuel-injected GLT which ate MGBs alive.

A curious riddle in the welding lies in the twistings and turnings of politicians in the BL story. From Benn to Blair via Callaghan and Thatcher, BL cost them all a sleepless night and more. At times, it all reads like a BL-Lab-Con pact. And how odd that three *women* should be so prominent in the affairs of BMC-to-BL-to-Rover RIP; Barbara Castle in 1969, Margaret Thatcher in 1979, and Patricia Hewitt in 2005.

BL did something unique in business terms too. It stepped outside normal corporate and automotive business mechanisms, structures, strategies and model cycles. Now, that confused a lot of people.

It is fashionable to decry the cars, the management, the 'Red' workforce, the politics, the corporate-speak robots, and the whole carbuncle that became the BL affair. And the truth is that there were some very bad things that happened in the essential BL era.

But 'Leyland-bashing' became a sport that pre-judged the issue. Yes, it *was* about cars as products, but it was also about *more* than cars.

In air crashes, it is easy to blame the pilots, especially if they are dead – scapegoats that cannot answer back. In the story of the BL crash, it has been easy to blame the workers, but just as with blamed pilots, it is too easy, too simple and too obvious to blame BL's workers – or BL's cars, as so many observers have.

Blame the workers! Blame Stokes! Blame Mrs Thatcher! Blame Edwardes! Blame BAE! Blame BMW! Blame *anyone*! So goes the BL-to-MG Rover cacophony of blame. But there is more to this story than such headlines or such positions. In fact, this is one of the most complex dramas in British history. It goes beyond transmission fluid, a lack thereof, or wonky wiring.

However, even if blame might be non-constructive, the BL affair was someone's fault, *surely*?

Yet behind the lurid headlines, behind the failures and the defeats snatched from the jaws of victory, beyond the 'nearly' cars, there *were* some clever, dedicated, talented engineers and designers. History, media headlines, and the court of public opinion have been unkind to BL – not least as other car makers turned out some terrible cars. Yet the talent pool inside BL's design and engineering departments was of global status – a collection of designers of world-class quality and equal to any from Germany, France or America, and way above the 1970s 'copyist' techniques of the greater Japan Auto Inc.

You might say that the BL cars were badly built because the workers were 'Lefties', disgruntled and strike-prone, but would you ask how they were so-minded and why? And was there more than one cause beyond theories about Communists and the very different Trotskyists?

What of the original Rover cars? They were truly were advanced and upmarket. The Rover P9 mid-engined coupé could have taken on Porsche and beaten them, yet it was binned. Who the hell thought of BL's 'Freight Rover' division? And why taint Rover with sticking the Viking longboat's legend on a tarted up old Metro. Strange to recall that Rover was always 'posh', but BMW started 'common', having built basic fare (with honourable 1930s exceptions) and 1950s micro cars. Yet a reinvented BMW is now deemed to be both posh and flash, an ultimate brand; yet Rover is dead, via van manufacture, cross-dressed Honda-badged 'Ronda' Roverism and BMW ownership. And the Chinese Roewe cars were re-engineered by brilliant ex-MG Rover men into an even better car than the Rover 75.

Rover's research department was in the opinion of many, one of the finest in the global car industry. But Communist China is where Rover's last stand became Roewe, and MG became truly worthy of its red seatbelts.

Some of BL's people have said that there was not a problem for BL selling Rovers, Jaguars or Triumphs. This is an opinion stated from a viewpoint rather than a peer reviewed fact, and it flies in the face of things that customers and dealers have stated about these cars' dire quality, notably in export markets. As one British main dealer told me in 1983 of Jaguar XJ6 and Rover SD1, 'Frankly I'd be worried about giving them away, even to a relative. In fact I wouldn't.'

He told me that after I had visited him to pick up a white XJ6 4.2 S3 (with rare 'pepper pot' alloys) that had been repaired after yet another electrical malady.

To me, BL's cars were inanimate lumps of British steel, vinyl and plastic yet somehow they lived, had souls, often they were arse souls, but still, they were part of our families.

If you still think Rovers, Jaguars, Triumphs were an easy sell, try the first six months of 1978 in Europe for clarity about BL's sales figures. In Germany, BL sold just 7,950 cars in this period, ranking 18th of 23 car marques listed on the German market at that time. In July 1978, BL sold eighteen Maxis in Germany, yes, eighteen! Allegro? Try less than seventy in a month. Princess – hobbled by driveshaft failures, engine issues, trim problems and a dire reputation, it sold thirty, yes, thirty cars in Germany in July 1978.

BL's cars in Germany, Italy, France, Sweden, and the Netherlands, achieved a remarkable low in 1977-78. The BL reputation was *not*, therefore, just a British perception stemming from the British mindset or media brainwashing.

In the mid-1970s over thirty per cent of the British workforce worked in the British motor industry making cars and their components. In 2015, less than ten per cent of the British workforce worked in the motor industry and those that did, worked for foreign manufacturers based in Britain. Ford was never British (despite its marketing) and Vauxhall, which was British in 1903, is now French-Chinese owned. Jaguar Land Rover? Who knows if it will still be Indian-owned by the time this is printed. Maybe it will be part of an 'empire' again, a great American, or Chinese empire? More likely German – they have always fancied getting their hands on Jaguar.

Let's hope none of their respective 'bubbles' do what bubbles always do and burst.

Behind it all lies the sorry saga of BL in all its brilliance and all its bad times.

The businessman Michael Edwardes would surely have stared at such a 'free-trade' situation and blinked in confusion at its contradictions. Intriguingly, some commentators, even those in official obituaries and narratives about BL, categorically state that Michael Edwardes was put into BL by Margaret Thatcher and then credit her for what they say were his achievements.

The *Birmingham Post*, commenting on matters BL and Longbridge, described Margaret Thatcher as being a form of spiritual leader to Michael Edwardes. This is an example of the BL narrative in action as Edwardes was brought in by the prior, Labour, Callaghan Government. Thatcher did not employ him at BL, the Labour Party did! What is more, long before Thatcher was elected to run Britain, Edwardes was appointed a member of the Labour Party's own National Enterprise Board (NEB) and was voted on to it by union leaders – including the deputy general secretary of the Transport and General Workers Union.

If Michael Edwardes had been a 'union-basher' (he was not and had no record of such) and a blunt tool of capitalist extremism, as per the narrative, would a Labour prime minister and a bunch of union leaders *really* have appointed him? Of course not – unless, as the Trotskyists claim, they were 'Right-wing'. And Thatcher hated the NEB, so she must have held her nose when embracing one of its members – Edwardes.

Yet as part of the 'narrative', the *Guardian* categorically stated on Monday 21 July 2008, in its obituary of Lord Stokes, that in 1979, Thatcher (then the new Tory prime minister) had brought in Michael Edwardes.

Although he knew little of motor cars, Edwardes knew a great deal about management, its psychology and the application of change to teams of managers who had become stuck in their ways amid a torpor of managerial conceit. Love him or hate him, the little man could manage with command. He was an early exponent of 'change management'. This was why he was a success at Chloride and why he then achieved much at BL – rightly or wrongly, depending on your personal views. When he left BL, its market share was down and so was its output (in comparison to when he arrived) but does this 'prove' failure? Not at all.

External forces and the BL 'narrative' were to blame.

I talked to Michael Edwardes about BL. He shattered my preconceptions about him and what he did. I still did not agree with some of it, but I could see that he was trying to address something that had festered for a very long time. Amputation has often been required in such circumstances.

If you can see beyond your own dogma or his, Edwardes' choices were very limited indeed – as were those of Donald Stokes.

Edwardes was fascinating to talk to. If you were a Lefty, you might have missed the fact that he actually believed in BL and its workers. But he also knew that change was needed. In a way, Edwardes the South African was a British patriot, yet at times he too has been unfairly framed by a perverse narrative. You or I might disagree with some of the things he did, but he believed in BL and Britain, which is more than you can say for some of the players in the BL story. And did not 87 per cent of the workforce vote for his plan in 1979? Had they all *really* been 'conned'?

In fact, the man who really carried out Thatcher's edict upon BL as Austin Rover Group (ARG) to achieve its sell-off as Rover Group was not Sir Michael Edwardes, it was Sir Graham Day. Day did what he was told do with the options available. There is little point in subjecting him to blame, say some, but 'Roverising' everything was Day's decision, and an allegedly flawed one. And most people forget the man who ran BL between Edwardes and Day – Sir Austin Bide. But Bide and Day also did what they could within the limited options on offer.

Blinkered observers cast Donald Stokes as the villain of the BL piece, others absolve him completely. As we shall see, he was *not* the villain, but neither was he quite as removed from the process as some say. Ex-MG workers from Abingdon will however have their own view due to Stokes' decisions over MG and Triumph model strategies.

Stokes was a clever and swift operator – faced with Ken Costello's home-made 'men-in-sheds' MGBGT V8 engineering conversion, Stokes asked to try the car, then he agreed a factory engine and drivetrain parts supply line to Costello's low-volume production to buy time and let Costello build up awareness of the idea. Meanwhile, BLMC chief engineer Charles Griffin looked again at the MGB bodyshell, as he had previously decided it was too difficult and too expensive to fit the ex-Buick, Rover 3500V8 under the bonnet.

Then, BLMC's Special Tuning Department actually bought one of Costello's V8s direct from him. Very quickly, there came BLMC's own version of the idea and Stokes immediately cut off Costello's supply of direct, factory engines and parts. This was, to put it plainly, pretty ruthless stuff and, despite building 200 or so of his conversions (which included MGB as well as the GT), Costello's opportunity was shot. However, Costello – straight talking, combative, cap-wearing, brilliantly irreverent – had the last laugh, as his conversions were better, faster and advertised under the great strapline of 'Beware of imitations!'.

Stokes and Costello must have been interesting to watch.

There were many BMC/BL stalwarts who kept the faith – talented men like Harold Musgrove, John Egan, Tony Ball, Ray Horrocks, Spen King, Harry Webster, Gordon Bashford, Jim Randle, Harry Mundy, Charles Griffin, Roy Haynes, David Bache, Harris Mann, Roy Axe, Gordon Sked, Fred Coultas, Peter Harris, Gordon Birtwhistle, to briefly name a few corporate and engineering/design heroes. We must cite the maverick design genius that was Alexander 'Alec' A.C. Issigonis, not least because he thought laterally and knew that the application of mathematics constrained creative thinking. His mind was not crippled by dogma or prescribed learning, as so many are.

Today, dedicated BMC and BL owners clubs keep the cars alive and prove that there were some great cars inside the story and the saga. Take a look at the trimmed-up Land Crab driven by the chair of the Land Crab owners club and you will see just how clever the Issigonis 18-22 series was.

Oh, to own an Austin Ambassador now, yet so few are left. With tuned hydragas suspension and new special valves added to the suspension's gas spheres, Ambassador was one of the world's best cars in terms of ride quality and comfort. 43,000 were built and a just a handful remain.

The gates of BL remembrance are shot through with nostalgia and it seems, with shame.

There came an end time when the Rover 75 range was reincarnated and begat the MG ZT 160, ZT 190 and the amazing but pointless V8 ZT 260. But under them came the MG ZS120 – a weak, 20 year old Honda Civic re-badged beyond the millennium despite its ancient and very soft underpinnings. As for that TATA Indica badge-engineered as a City Rover, what tortured mind conceived this?

So badge-engineering, good and bad, continued beyond the ashes of BL.

What is really interesting is to learn about the schism between so-called 'Lefties' and some of their own union brethren who stand accused of being 'right-wing' or in collusion with management. There was, in case you do not know, open war between sections of the Left – with the Communist Party of Great Britain revolving around its factions and splinter groups, all amid the schisms of Trotskyism and various socialist or workers' 'revolutionaries'. Remember, in Britain (or America), a Leftie, or a Communist, is a firebrand to be scared of (unless he is a Chinese corporate or government official to do business with), but in France he is likely to be your local mayor, neighbour and garage owner. The French had their revolution and went on to free-thinking – how else do you explain the Citroën 2CV, the DS, or the Panhard Dyna, or the Citroën Ami?

'What about the Mini?' I hear you shout. Yes, but it was designed by a foreigner whose thinking was not constrained by middle class British values! Issigonis lay beyond such rules, such blinkered mindset.

I have viewed left-winger Allan Thornett's books, including *Militant Years: Car Workers' Struggles in Britain in the 60s and 70s*. Mr Thornett's politics are not my own, but his book is essential evidence of what went on at BMC and BL as seen from a far-Left viewpoint. You may disagree with its claims, but this should not limit your observance. The Far-Left may be extreme when seen from the middle of the road, but our British class divide, the system, helped create that thinking and those that believe in such extremities of opinion. Thornett's works have their own agenda – he is not unusual in that. However 'Left' they are, his words present very logical evidence of just how bad physical conditions, manufacturing processes, and human relations were inside BL's antiquated, old factories, albeit amid a mind-set. Thornett, it should be noted, latterly modified his views on Trotskyist groups (which had been active inside BL).

In his Foreword to Jeff Daniels' book *British Leyland The Truth About the Cars*, Graham Turner author of *The Leyland Papers*, quite correctly suggests that it is products that can make or break a company and not management or workers and their unions. This may be so, but what if the products in question reflected management decisions, workers' behaviours, society's attitudes and political imperatives forced upon the company that designed the products in the first place? And what if the products were an amalgamation of diverse and often opposing marques and their brand ingredients amid contradictory product planning?

Good as Turner's report was, it apparently came with its own pre-determined and prescribed viewpoint. Turner agreed with Leonard Lord – it was all about the product and how it would sell itself if it was good enough. Quite how he would, using such logic, explain the Triumph Acclaim is beyond me.

Although I tend to agree with Turner that if the great marques of BL had been sold off in about 1973, they might have gone on to success, as the weaker ones were culled – as they since have been by a reverse process anyway. However, I think a more nuanced perspective needs to be forensically appreciated in order to understand just what the hell happened at BMC and then at BL.

Britain joined the EEC in 1973. It was supposed to open the doors to trade in a single market. BL was supposed to be a big player.

Recalling that every new MG you buy sees you paying money into the Communist, People's Republic of China, it all gets funnier. Because if you purchase a new car or van from Peugeot, Citroën or Vauxhall, you are also paying money into China, in this case via the Dongfeng Motor Group of Wuhan, and the Chinese state; both now own a share of Peugeot PSA.

On the one hand we berate China, its Communism, its human rights and its society, and on the other, we throw ourselves at China begging for trade and investment, notably in the motor industry. The hypocrisy is astounding – as it is towards Russia – whom we also do massive deals with, not to mention borrowing their spaceship.

In shades of 1970s British Leyland, the French Government has just had to pump billions into Peugeot to save it. But don't worry, because Peugeot has just threatened to 'punish' Vauxhall and not build the next Astra in Britain if we dare leave Europe and its rules and invest in the outside world on World Trade Organisation (WTO) terms – with somewhere like China perhaps?

But again, don't worry that China is *outside* of the EU, its currency, safety legislation, trade deals, human rights, or anything else that is reportedly absolutely vital, because as we know, Peugeot is part-Chinese owned and has a car factory guess where – China – you know the place outside of the protection of Europe. Oh, and Volkswagen makes cars in China and South America too – on those wretched WTO terms that we have all been told are so bad.

But we British don't make cars in China – because China makes cars here instead – well, it did until recently, and even China has given up on that!

Who was the numbskull at Jaguar that thought it would be a good idea to seemingly rely on the Chinese 'bubble'? Why put all your eggs in one basket and ignore other loyal customers? Bizarre, utterly bizarre. I only met Sir William Lyons once, but I reckon he would have had something to say about the China syndrome.

The ironies of it all, post-Thatcher and post-New Labour do seem rather funny, unless you are an out of work ex-BL, ex-Rover Group employee looking at the Longbridge wasteland through a wire mesh fence.

It is an odd game this EU in-out, rules or no rules game. It is one that affected BL when Britain was a full member of the EEC and the resultant EU. In case you have forgotten, the EU latterly complained over the state aid given to British Aerospace (BAE) when it bought Aunty Austin's Rover. And £48 million had to be given back by order of the EU! Things were different when the British taxpayer initially helped save Talbot in Coventry for Peugeot, or poured money into Nissan and Toyota start-up factories inside Great Britain.

Peugeot, VW, BMW and others all have massive investments in China, despite China and the investments lying completely outside the EU's own rules and edicts. As stated, Peugeot is part-owned by China's Communists. This the very same Peugeot SA (then minus Chinese part-ownership) that needed British taxpayers' aid to keep its Coventry operations going over three decades ago and which killed off both it and Talbot's car making in the Midlands – all while Britain and France were full members of the EEC/EU.

Today, the EU trades with China in a massive deficit and after years of negotiations, is yet to sign off a finished trade agreement. Strangely, the EU and its major motor manufacturers (notably Peugeot via Vauxhall) now threaten Great

Britain with dire consequences of its possible post-Brexit position based on the same WTO terms that the EU deems perfectly acceptable in its dealings with China and the rest of the non-EU-agreement world.

Our roads are packed with German and French cars, but also with Korea's Kia and Hyundai cars which are (finally) safe and sound, and the irony is that their modern place in our motoring was originally cast by an ex-BMC/BL senior director named George Turnbull whose talents were appreciated elsewhere.

These Kia and Hyundai cars are sold into Europe amid non-EU licensing, legislation, external supply chains, employment and protection practices. It was not until 2015 that the EU and Korea fully implemented a trade agreement first signed in 2010. Prior to that, tariffs and WTO ruled! Indeed, Italian and French car makers believed the EU-Korea agreement would harm their interests and vetoed the original agreement. Finally, the agreement was ratified on the grounds that Korean car imports and sales within the EU were so small their effect would be minimal. But look at Hyundai and Kia now! BL's Turnbull who made Hyundai's first car (the Pony) reality, would surely have smiled.

So you don't need a trade deal to trade – not least as the EU takes ten to twenty years to negotiate its trade deals, while it trades on WTO terms!

Does anyone remember when Renault built 1980s 'Alliance' cars in Canada with American Motors Corporation (AMC) for the North American market – on WTO terms long before any trade deal was toyed with for a decade?

Can you recall the fuss the EEC and notably Italy made over BL's attempt to sell its British-built Honda Civic/Ballade as a Triumph Acclaim in Europe as a 'British' car? Can you recall how little fuss was made when Alfa Romeo tried to sell a Nissan Cherry in Europe as an Italian Alfa Arna? Oh, and what of the Nissan version of the same car – the Nissan Cherry Europe? Did that have a trade agreement?

What of VW's current imports into Europe from Brazil and Mexico, or BMWs built in America or Hondas built in Thailand? Of Protons built in Malaysia? Of German cars built in South Africa? Are all these 'at risk' because they are not built to EU rules amid EU safety legislation, employment, design, currency and tax rules?

Of intrigue, BMC once built cars in Dublin. Austin and Morris cars were built on CKD-basis in the 1960s to supply the Irish market. British Leyland Ireland existed until 1979. Rileys, MGs and Triumphs had also been locally fabricated and trimmed in Eire in the 1950s – as were low numbers of Citroën Traction Avants.

In 2016, BMW allegedly threatened to reconsider the viability of its Cowley, Oxford plant due to the British EU referendum and potential Brexit issues.

BMW wrote a 'warning' letter to its Oxford employees *before* they voted in the 2016 Referendum. The letter – from the boss – seemed to urge them to vote 'remain' for a host of EU-related reasons. How strange then that BMW is quite happy to build its cars in other, non-EU countries (including America) on WTO rules to non-EU legislation, in a non-Euro currency without supply-line, legislative or workforce problem or threat?

Did BMW also write to its employees in Spartanburg, South Carolina, to 'warn' them about the risks of making cars *outside* the EU? Did it write to its employees in Africa, China, India, Mexico, Russia, Egypt, amongst thirty sites in thirteen countries on four continents beyond Germany, to 'warn' them of the risk of not being in the EU and having to work under WTO (the so-called 'no-deal' terms) terms?

The answer is of course, that it did not.

So, you can build BMWs at Spartanburg USA without problem (or even in South Africa), outside the EU, but dear Oxford BMW worker, your job may be at risk if you vote Brexit and force BMW to retreat into fortress Europe. And did BMW write to all the thousands of Turkish workers it employs to build its Bavarian masterpieces *inside* Germany, and warn them that as Turkey lies *outside* the EU and all its protections and rules, that their jobs were or are at risk? Of course not.

It all is very bizarre indeed and defies logic utterly and is less about voting 'remain' or 'leave', and more about politics and power – as was BL itself in the 1970s.

The cars of Britain were writ large over Indian motoring history – beyond the Rover SD1 as an Indian-built car and into the gripping realms of the Tata Indicar badged as a British Rover for sale back in Britain. Today, there are more mass-market cars made in India than there are in Britain. We must surely wonder why?

With BL and Rover gone, big European and global car companies build cars in India too – and we hear no fuss about the lack of a single currency, supply lines, or meeting EU legislation, notably safety rules. Renault and Nissan have been selling their old, discontinued European market cars in India long after such cars have been eclipsed by modern safety standards post-EuroNCAP in Europe. A recent Indian market Renault, and a recent Nissan, have both suffered terrible Indian crash test results. So bad were the results that calls were made for sales of the cars to be suspended.

So much then for Europe and its vital safety standards and the British need to conform to them; curiously a different safety standard, as found in modified *old* European market cars, has been offered to the Indian market.

The sainted EU 'legislation' and EuroNCAP, so often cited by these two car makers (and others) here in Britain becomes seemingly invisible. But hey, India, you can have the old, 'less safe' stuff.

So is the safety of Indians less important then?

It is all very strange in terms of logic. And a raging hypocrisy.

BLMC's Lord Stokes – a man of eminently sensible pro-European business sentiment – might have been mystified. Stokes even sold Leyland buses to the communists of Cuba! Stokes looked to the world and the Commonwealth to sell cars, beyond Europe and thus was not a 'Little Englander' nor a 'Little Europeaner'. Stokes, love him or hate him, was a big beast on the world's stage – running the fifth biggest car company on the planet.

But today, it appears that car making has been politicised, again. Yesterday, in the past, amid the origins of BMC to BL, there lies a series of stories whose fates lined up to create a crash of epic proportions. We have to go back to a now politically incorrect past, to meet the men who commanded the ship of fate and set the runes of today's reality.

Way back in the 1930s MG laid down its genesis: few would predict its fate as a Chinese 'State' car of Communist and Peoples Liberation Army economics.

Above: A Riley Sprite from the 1930s when Rileys really were ultimate driving machines – to coin a phrase...

Below and overleaf above: Riley's post-war 1940s RM-series truly were the last gasp of greatness. The interior speaks volumes about 'Britishness'.

Frogeye Sprite. The quintessential and accessible British sports car of the great era.

Triumph's early TR-series carved out the beginnings of the British sportster legend all over the world.

Above and overleaf above: *MG's post-war sportsters did likewise. Such cars took America by storm.*

A Ricardo Burzi-styled A35 line-up. Looking great and having such an 'Austin of England' character.

The true face of Morris. 'OCD' seems a good numberplate!

The classic Morris Minor 1000 – the car that sold a million and more.

When Rovers were redoubtable. Solid, and 'Empire' styled. Captain Mainwaring would surely have had a P4-series.

Gerald Palmer's cleanly styled 1950's line was applied to Wolseley, Riley, and MG versions of the same bodyshell.

Above: When Jaguar bought Daimler it was the end for the SP250 Dart, but this one looks great.

Below: Michelotti created a funky face for his cars – never more so than on this top of the range Triumph Herald convertible.

Michelotti's hand touched the later TR series. This TR4 IRS has just raced up Prescott.

Austin Healey 3000. Quintessential and ready to race nearly 60 years since it was made.

Above and below: *The defining Jaguar E-Type of XKE-Series. Malcolm Sayer and Sir William Lyons created something beyond an icon. Seen here in convertible and also in fastback fixed-head forms.*

Early MGB long before BL ruined it with rubber bumpers and increased ride height that led to a certain skittishness...

The classic MG interior – naturally.

Questions • 53

Above and below: *These two photographs depict how many different 'nose-jobs' BMC could graft onto the same body. This was the beginning of badge-engineering gone bonkers.*

Above: MG Midget – the nimble post-war interpretation of the earlier, pre-war MGs. Also available with squared-off rear wheel arches!

Left: A later Mini as 'Cooper S'. Still racing.

A-Series – antique but still excellent and an engine that had driven around the world.

Land Crab heaven. Early Morris-badged 18-22 capturing the essentials of Issigonis austerity design.

Same car different nose treatments – Land Crab evolved.

Land Crab modified (right), Land Crab original (left). The more modern modified accessory-styling car looks so modern!

Land Crab became an Austin 3.0-Litre. This is its lovely cabin.

2

An Empire Ends & Another Begins

Never in the field of badge-engineering had so many panels been owed so much by so few.

The British gave the world the Dreadnought battleship, the great ocean liners, and superb cars. We, yes us, we made the Supermarine Spitfire, the de Havilland Mosquito, and the Hawker Hurricane, and the Hunter; the Avro Lancaster, the TSR2 – these were all world class. TSR2 was like one of BL's cancelled 'nearly' cars – a world-beater strangled at birth at huge cost to the nation not just the humble tax payer.

We created the Great Western Railway (GWR) under Brunel, the London Midland Scottish Railway (LMS) and the famous, high-speed London North Eastern Railway (LNER). We Brits exported brilliant cars, motorcycles, trains, planes and ships to the world.

We created the Riley Sprite and the RM, the MGA, MGB, the Allard J2, the Healey 3000, the Triumph TRs, Spitfire, GT6, the Land Rover, and the Lotus Elan. We gave the world the XJ13, the truly innovative Rover P6 and Range Rover, Mini, Jaguar E-Type and XJ6-series, the Ford Escort 1600RS and Lotus Cortina, the Humber Snipe, the Rolls-Royce Silver Shadow and the Bentley Continental as well as the Rover P5 and the P6 series. We also gave the world the Laycock de Normanville overdrive unit.

There are many other great cars that we created.

There was no reason at all in 1960-something to assume anything other than a golden age of British automotive excellence lay ahead. Soon would come TVR and Lotus. What of the gas-turbine Rover? Soon would come Jim Clark, Ken Tyrell's cars, Stirling Moss, Graham Hill, Jackie Stewart, Roger Clark, and more racers and rally drivers and magic cars. Years later, even as it entered its death throes, the great genius of British engineering at BL gave us the ECV3 – one of the most intelligent and advanced design concept cars of several decades, and surely the basis of many themes that we are about to see in electrically-powered cars. BL gave us the AR6 too – another act of genius killed off just before it was born.

We Brits knew our stuff and we could beat the biggest budgets in the world. We might secretly have pinched missile and rocket technology, supersonics research, the delta wing, and the diesel hydraulic locomotive off the Germans at the end of the war, but at least our *cars* were ours (yes, we know Bristols had BMW bits in them, but that was different). The Americans got to the moon, and to the swept-wing jet age, through doing the same thing – 'acquiring' Nazi science.

Yet in the 1950s, national hero and Londoner Sydney Allard had won the Monte Carlo Rally in a car of his own design and manufacture, then he led at Le Mans in front of Ferraris, and was placed in subsequent Le Mans in his own Allard! Oh, and he had taken the 1949 British Hill Climb Championship in an Allard (Steyr-engined) too. Then he designed the first British dragster and invented the British end of the global dragster movement. One Englishman did all this – and got himself in the *Eagle* magazine too. What a hero.

Donald Healey achieved global fame with his cars too.

Standard Triumph made great cars, Sir John Black saw to that. So too did Standard's top man of 1960, Alick Dick, who rose from apprentice in 1934 to managing director by the age of 37 and to chairman in 1960. Dick 'drove' the new age of the Herald into existence. Curiously, having co-engineered Triumph's move into the Leyland fold, he left the company and moved on.

Morris cars powered a nation of shopkeepers and Leyland lorries and buses ruled the highways. Austins were a British family institution. Buying a 'foreign' car was bound to make the neighbours mistrust you!

Herbert Austin, William Morris, Leonard Lord, George Harriman, these were the men of the indigenous, true British 'motor industry' as it was then called. Sir William Lyons was Jaguar's hero and hallmark, as were his designs (Malcolm Sayer was his key post-war designer). Alec Issigonis, the Wilks brothers, Spencer King, Harry Webster, Walter Hassan, Harry Mundy, Frank England, Don Hayter, Gordon Bashford, Harris Mann. They are legends all.

These were just some of the names of the greats of British car design amid its Midlands crucible that was not a Ford or Chrysler outpost, as the new age of the swinging Sixties dawned.

Others? Norman Dewis, Innes Ireland, Pat Moss, Paul Easter, Paddy Hopkirk, Andrew Hedges, all these brilliant Brits drove equally brilliant British cars.

'Flat cap' Ken Costello would soon make the 'best' MGB GT V8 – in a shed. The list of genius, greasy palms, hand drawn designs, and exploits of integrity, frames a truly great era when we Brits were aces of the air and aces on the road (we sailed and built ocean liners too). Our cars were of the best and the world bought them. Birmingham, Coventry, and Oxford were the true centres of industrial design and engineering.

From here came the great cars of the 1960s. This was a golden age that truly existed and clever men made it happen.

One of the cleverest was a Rhodesian, Gerald Palmer. He designed some of the best, most elegant and timeless 1950s cars, yet his name remained obscured in the suburbia whose driveways contained the Jowett, MGs, Rileys, Wolseleys and more that he shaped.

An oft-quoted wind of change swept through late 1950s and early 1960s Britain – principally to its empire and the British Commonwealth. Old ways, old attitudes, old practices, all had been shaken up and stirred by the Second World War and the new society that followed it. But Britain itself was still enmeshed in the class system and symbols of status. Motifs of hierarchy and of servitude still cast their shadow upon many aspects of British life – including the motor industry, its cars, their badging, and the towns and cities that supplied muscle and metal to build our cars.

The Jaguar E-Type may have shocked the world, as did the original Mini, but the Triumph Mayflower and then the Herald were more accurate symbols of how mass market Britain, its drivers and their cars chose to be seen at that time. Yet BMC and BLMC were lucky with Jaguar, for they inherited not just the E-Type, but also the newly launched Jaguar XJ6 – very probably the best car in the world at the time and for some years afterwards. It took an almighty effort to stuff that up!

Wolseley Pathfinder, Jowett Javelin, Ford Anglia, Standard Vanguard, Humber Super Snipe, Vauxhall Wyvern, Austin Cambridge, Morris Oxford, *et al*, these redoubtable beasts and their badges of British motoring defined what we and our cars were. As for 'Johnny foreigner' or the flashy Americans, well that was for them; we Brits knew what was what and that we could export to our colonies, Dominions and the Commonwealth, and the inhabitants thereof would buy such cars and dare not grumble and be bloody grateful.

Meanwhile, the rest of the world would think fresh thoughts. Companies like BMW and VW would abandon their conventional and boring cars to create new technology and new hallmarks that would build defining brands and engineering traditions – and earn large amounts of much needed money. Fiat, Saab, Renault, Citroën, and others would embrace new design language and new engineering. General Motors would sell cars by design! How dare they?

The Turkish-born Greek-German but Edgbaston, Birmingham resident Alexander 'Alec' A.C. Issigonis (Knight, CBE, FRS, RDI) must have been a frustrated man in 1949. He had worked for Humber pre-1936, raced an Austin Seven (with his own design of rubber suspension), then worked for Morris before 1939, soon to create a new post-war car for the masses – the Morris Minor, evocatively and bizarrely code named 'Mosquito'; this monocoque car had been designed with front-wheel drive, a curved, highly aerodynamic front-end with faired in headlights, a super-stiff hull, and a flat-four engine. But it was deemed to be far too radical for the minds of the British motor industry and the men who would prescribe what the public wanted in their cars and what they should be told to purchase. A twin-cam engine in a Morris! Never – so dictated, not Nuffield but Leonard Lord, who knew what he knew...

Issigonis' original Minor had shades of the Saab 92, or something French. But the powers that be ordered it to be squared up, the front to be made more conventional (with high-mounted headlamps and a proper wing line); rear-wheel drive from an in-line four cylinder engine was prescribed, the car was widened by four inches and made to be look and feel like a pre-war dinosaur that had re-warmed 1930s themes for a 1950s market. And of course, this more conventional Morris Minor sold in its millions as utterly reliable, predictable transport for the masses. And very good it was too, but it was not of the engineering revolution that lay within Issigonis' mind.

Issigonis liked to use the torsion bar/spring suspension set-up, but most people forget that neither he nor Citroën invented it; the torsion bar system patent lay with Ferdinand Porsche until its expiry in the 1950s.

Stunning though the Morris prototype with the original, front-driven, aero-styled design as per Issigonis thoughts would have been, it was simply too revolutionary for Leonard Lord. But just imagine how too far advanced, too ahead of its time and the car buyer's tastes that original Minor was. Yet its theories came back to light in the 1959 Issigonis Mini (as an Austin Seven, Austin Morris MiniMinor, mouthful until 1961 as 'Mini'), but the aerodynamic body and the stiffer hull, were missing.

Inside Morris, and then inside BMC under an Austin banner, Issigonis was his own man who stamped his own mark of genius very firmly upon the cars that were produced. In fact, many people who were there at the time thought he operated far beyond his remit and was beyond the control of a management that was either weak, fractured, or both, the Austin 1100/1300 and 1800/2200 Land Crab and the Maxi both being examples beyond the Mini that evidence such views. The ADO16 – the 1100-1300 – really ought to be perceived as one of the greatest small car engineering and design packages ever created, yet the 'narrative' has apparently decided otherwise.

For Issigonis, there were no 'customer clinics' marketing research, or even a debate amongst a 'diverse' design team. Issigonis thought up the brilliant idea, and he told his employers what to do with it. Issigonis was a 'God' and few dared argue. He also resisted suggested updates to his original 'pure' designs and this created cars such as Mini and Maxi that stepped outside the normal model refresh or replacement cycles. This was to prove a vital commercial and operating issue for BLMC and BL.

As long as Issigonis kept the successes coming, he remained powerful, But he was slow to adapt and commercial reality overtook 'pure' engineering. But he and Austin had advocated front-wheel drive early on, when Saab, Citroën and only a few others had truly embraced it. The Austins of Issigonis were truly amazing; Austin was a 'technology' brand.

If you want to know how clever he was, take a look at his 1950s sketches for a car of the future. There we see a vehicle shaped like a modern 'people-carrier'. We also see Issigonis' suggestion of an alloy frame with plastic panels, electric hybrid drive with wheel-mounted motors and interconnected hydraulic suspension. This was true futurism. Imagine if Renault was to produce a composite, hybrid-drive, Espace-type car for 2020 and it might begin to approach Issigonis' 1950s design.

In 1956, Issigonis worked on a design code named XC9000. Here was proof that his thinking was different because it had shades of the advanced Citroën Traction Avant yet reimagined into a smoother and more 'British' iteration. Shades of DS and of a four-door Mini (Mini not being extant in 1956) were all obvious in the rear-driven XC9000. It was a big car and could have been a new star for the 1960s but was killed off by the Suez crisis which led to the immediate need for a small car – the Mini. So here was proof that geo-politics did influence British post-war car design early on. The ADO 17, the Land Crab, was of course a later reincarnation of XC9000 and its XC9001 front-wheel-drive variant – but with less style! And a smaller version of the 1950s XC9000 was XC9002 – which became the ADO16 – the 1100 and 1300 success story.[1]

Market research was, said Issigonis, 'bunk'. The Mini, said the great man, would never have been born if market research men had had the chance to influence it. Issigonis thought that customers had been brainwashed by marketing and advertising into thinking what car manufacturers *wanted* them to think – into buying into a prescribed set of car design and sales parameters. He was correct, but he might just have taken it a little too far in his prescribing his own, 'know it all' choices inside BMC, but of course his was the path of advanced design, not regurgitated contraptions. So he was right! At least he avoided 'Fordisation' and the claptrap of 1970s marketing and bling.

But what of a small car with a hatchback? Certainly not, said Issigonis. So was development and update delayed at the hands of the master. He was probably right – what on earth was the point of adding a hatchback to tiny car with limited cabin space for people let alone cargo? However, Innocenti's own hatchback take on the Mini sold rather well, but not in Great Britain...

One of Issigonis' key acts was the move on from the constrained Morris Minor 1000 to the Mini in terms of concept and function – was the Mini the first car to be designed around people and not an engine and pile of parts-bin bits? It probably was, but it is a shame that the consideration of its occupants' use of the car did not extend to protecting them in impact safety terms.

Yet Issigonis came up with a Mini replacement – the 9X was based on ADO19 and indeed ADO 20. 9X was a prototype project for a 'new' Mini – and ADO20 was used as a base for a 1970s prototype for a 'gearless' car, based on a modified Mini using the more compact 9X-coded engine. This engine had an alloy cylinder head, crankcase and gearbox. Issigonis' revised Mini was to lose its gas and air suspension and the subframes, and receive conventional vertical strut suspension in the name of cost saving. The body used alloy panels over a reinforced structure with 'crush cans' inside the front wings to aid impact safety and a clever 'gearless' (modified torque converter) transmission; he experimented with hydrostatic and hydrokinetic converters. Issigonis refused to call the car 'automatic' as there was no variable gear ratio, nor conventional 'transmission'. Engine speed was tuned to torque delivery via a forward and reverse 'drive' setting; this resulted in somewhat critical engine speed-to-torque ratio problems at low revs. He abandoned the idea – which was unusual for the man.

Issigonis categorically stated that, 'It is inconceivable that people would put up with so much work gear shifting when this could be completely eliminated while also achieving better fuel economy.'

There were four such ADO19/20 prototypes, registered as: NOB 5289F; SOL 258H; LOK 576P; and GNP 677S. Issigonis drove what was listed internally in BL as the 'green car' SOL 258H, as his personal car for some years. Today it is part of the British Motor Museum and has been on loan to the Atwell Wilson Museum.

Issigonis lost his post as BMC Technical Director in 1968 in the BMC-BLMC merger and was appointed Director of Research – a role with less power and influence. He retired to act as a consultant in 1972, yet he built and constantly modified the 9X prototypes in the 1970s – having to use existing Mini production cars as a cost-saving basis.

The true 'X' replacement Mini project was axed as the 1980s arrived and instead we got the Metro. Although you could have bought an 'ERA' tweaked Mini in the 1990s or a 90bhp Mini with an airbag fitted!

Like Frederick Lanchester, André Citroën, Ferdinand Porsche, and Vincenzo Lancia, Alec Issigonis was a philosopher, and not all followed his thinking, as would become apparent in 1968. The 'Fordisation' of BLMC and its cars was very far from Issigonis thinking. He was the man who, (not unlike André Citroën) had believed in cars that were different by design. Issigonis stated (to camera) that, 'The easiest way to win . . . is to make a car so unusual that it automatically becomes a status symbol.'

That might have been true of the Mini or the 1100-1300, but it was not proven to be true by the 1800 was it? 1800 was good, it was clever, but its looks constrained its acceptance and status.

Front wheel drive, 'cab-forward' cabins with a short nose, a long wheelbase, long-travel suspension, stiff hulls, transverse engines, massive room inside, great handling, Austin under Issigonis was the pathfinder, yet, later Mini variants would lose the original car's interconnected hydrolastic 'displacer' suspension set-up. The clever rubber rings inserted into the camshaft sprocket to benefit tensioning and operating noise were deleted to save money in the 1970s.

The brilliant Issigonis, beyond his genius, and beyond the comprehension of his admirers, was allowed to create a paradox, a contradiction of design research culture; an advanced design language that was not designed for those who did not speak it. This then was another rune in the route to BL's eventual problems. It seems incredible given his genius and his cars, but it is now obvious that after 'Fordisation' and BLMC's on-off affair with front-wheel drive, all the potential of the Issigonis work was to be wasted.

L.J.K. Setright was an Issigonis admirer and reckoned the man was an engineer and an artist who considered people, not style, in his designs.[2] Yet Setright never asked the obvious question. If Issigonis and his designs were about people and their needs, why did the great man fail to incorporate adequate structural and crash safety features into the Mini? Indeed, we might ask why he allegedly created features that many, including experts,[3] thought were positively 'unsafe'. Curiously, Issigonis' Land Crab was strong, safe, torsionally rigid and resisted frontal intrusion well.

Yet Issigonis's front-wheel drive cars were brilliant, but few people are prepared to state, as is done so here, that his engineering ethos and dominating effect were actually to become an unintended part of the BL problem as BL gave way to 'Fordised' marketing, chromed-up glitz, vinyl-roofed glamour, superficial design, built-in obsolescence, and cheap-as-chips engineering – *none* of which was within Issigonis' thinking or his effect upon BL and its cars. The contradiction was a painful one.

Ironically, Issigonis was maternally related to a certain Bernd Pischetsrieder – the man who would latterly run BMW (with a hand in the 1990s Rover story) and then Volkswagen!

At this time, and often forgotten, there was also the advanced thinking of the Rover company amid the Wilks brothers' effect and that of the likes of Bashford, Randle and others. They came up with gas turbine types, aerodynamic bodies, advanced structures, 'active' suspension, and engine developments, and two early 1950s version of a 'Road-Rover' (but with real off-road ability) precursor to the Range Rover that could have defined a 1960s market niche. Rover was packed with brainpower. So too was Triumph. And both teams would end up inside the BLMC tent.

Rover gave us the P5, the P5B favoured by royalty and prime ministers, the world-class P6 series, and almost gave us a P9 as the mid-engined two-seat sports car that could have won over the world and beaten Porsche and others at their own game. There were P8/P9/10 saloon prototype projects too.

Triumph was similarly of high-IQ design engineering, but BLMC's answer was to make Triumph's ever confident Harry Webster deliver the Marina and claim success.

Somehow, British car design got stuck in a rut of prejudged outcome and entrenched opinion and fashion. There were six, yes, six, independent British car companies based in the Midlands of Britain and over fifty factories employed half a million men.

Each marque had a wonderful heritage of skills, tradition and success. That they would merge into a giant single conglomerate was seen as good idea – twice over, first in 1953 as BMC, then adding the Leyland-owned marques into the mix in 1968. Amongst this affair, the once great Alvis died, and Alvis had been huge – a real player.

Of all the car branded companies such as Ford, or Vauxhall, it was the amalgamation of brands that was BMC-to-BL that seemed to get its wires crossed. How did this occur? The answer may lie in the fact that the companies, principally Austin and Morris, previously of differing design culture, different design language, opposing engineering thoughts and output, all of which rather unwisely, became joined at the hip as unintended twins. Throw in the personalities of the leaders and chaos was perhaps inevitable.

Austin had known qualities to its designs – its chief designer, Albert 'Joey' Hancock, was superintendent of the designs department across thirty years up to

1941. Austin hired an Italian-trained designer long before others thought of it. His name by the way was *not* Battista Farina (Pinin Farina) but the Argentinian Riccardo Burzi who had worked for Vincenzo Lancia's company in its 1920s heyday. Burzi brought a distinct style to Austin, the Atlantic being a clever example yet one that was a sales failure. Yet we must credit Burzi as being the first to sculpt Midlands steel into an 'Austin of England' design language. Eric Neale joined Austin as a designer from Singer and Lanchester in 1938 and latterly worked for Wolseley and Jensen.

But then came Issigonis, and the contradictory ingredients of front-wheel drive, efficient structures and packaging, but now wrapped up in austerity styling, spartan cabins and trims, and yet often having to use old engines – much to Issigonis' annoyance.

Known as 'the Austin' by those local to its location, the company, from 1946 to the 1960s, churned out set values and known designs under the lead of Leonard Lord. He was not really interested in the new 1950s art of styling, let alone industrial design.

Products sell themselves, said Lord, but that attitude might be framed as somewhat complacent. And who would prescribe those products ingredients and qualities? Lord of course!

At this time, there was a massive gap between engineering and the art of design or styling. Engineering departments ruled and rarely talked to body designers, unless a minor aerodynamic consideration was in the offing and even that was an unlikely joining of departmental minds. As for 'styling' – that was a separate world.

Things were different in Paris, Stuttgart or Detroit, but who cared; the British Empire still lived and car buyers would do what they were told, buy what they were prescribed! So was set the great weight of industrial torpor that afflicted the British, and especially the Austin!

But Lord knew that his cars had to have *something* to make them sell and Burzi's characterful shapes as body stamping was cheaper than advanced engines and suspensions. So we got the A series – A35, A40, A50 – and then the Austin Drawing Office or 'ADO' cars that eventually benefited from another Italian designer's talent, that of Battista 'Pinin' Farina and then his Pininfarina SPA Company of Grugliasco, Turin.

Amazingly, at one stage Lord even paid Raymond Loewy Associates, the American designer, to come up with some ideas to freshen up the BMC brands. Loewy's men descended on Longbridge from their transatlantic castle in a rage of couture and perhaps, seen by British beige and brown standards, a somewhat theatrical attitude. Needless to say, it was an exercise in British torpor; the Loewy design ideas stayed in Austin's drawer. Still, two-tone colouring soon made it inside BMC cars as well as outside, long after Renault had embraced such transatlantic fashion.

'Good God man, we don't do things like that, we are British!' So must have gone the refrain around the Midlands. Over in France, the plastic-roofed, hydro-pneumatic, biomorphic, Citroën DS was compounding such narrow-minded certainty. And Rover copied bits off it too; hence the sobriquet of 'Solihull Citroëns'.

At Rover, under the conservative yet forensic Maurice Wilks, a young designer began a career. His name was David Bache.

But at that stage of the 1950s, Rover was still 'redoubtable' and not really interested in style. Rover and Bache would work on the staid P4, but would however soon produce the great P5/P5B and then the defining P6 series – truly one of the best British cars ever designed, styled, and built.

As an aside at this point in the story, we might wonder how on earth Jaguar's 1960s design language and Malcolm Sayer's exquisite ideas ever saw the light of day, given such British attitudes? The answer is that, until 1966, Jaguar was independent and Lyons had vision as well as the ability to cut costs and piled up money (and a few problems). But Lyons also made the 1968 Jaguar XJ6 which was one of the world's landmark cars, a truly serious moment in the history of car engineering, design, and driving.

Also consider Donald Healey, master of suave sportsters.

Such men were made of greatness.

Back with the 1950s Austin merger, the big rival to Austin for the hearts, minds and wallets of the Midlands middle classes and other British car buyers, was the Morris Company of Oxford under the Nuffield brand. Morris made cars of a different nature, appealing to a different customer. Mooted as far back as the 1930s, a merger between Austin and Morris was deemed to be a financially sensible idea. Also to be considered in the great amalgamation to come after Austin and Morris, was the name of Leyland. Yet if Morris and Austin had merged in the 1920s or 1930s, would the terms have been more favourable than the later merger? Would Leonard Lord have had the chance to turn 'difficult'?

Long before the grand 1968 BLMC alliance, Sir Herbert Austin begat much, not least an American company initially called the American Austin Bantam Company, which, through various incarnations and twists of corporate fate, ended up being responsible for no less a defining vehicle that the original Jeep, whose origins are now obscured by the names of Willys and Ford.

Herbert Austin was British-born (1866) but an Australian resident in his youth after leaving his Yorkshire home with an uncle returning to Melbourne. Herbert was a man whose Austin Motor Company was founded in 1905, yet he died before the British Motor Corporation became what it did as BMC, then BMH and then BLMC. An artist and prolific sketcher and inventor since his childhood, as early as the 1890s Herbert was running a machine tooling outfit in England, as the British end of a colonial Australian entity. Following various episodes that included the creation of one-off cars that, shall we say, borrowed ideas from pre-existing rival vehicles, and a Vickers company involvement (Vickers then owned the rights to Wolseley), Austin set up his machine and tool making shop in Longbridge, Birmingham and quickly designed his first true Austin-type car for late 1905. After the First World War, Austin's fortunes faded on a disastrous car model policy and huge overheads and operating costs from its massive 200 acre site in Birmingham.

Having nearly gone under and lost control of his company, Herbert Austin, the trained and time-served engineer, provided the motor industry's first turnaround and comeback through *design* – creating cars for the 1920s that people purchased in their many thousands (notably the Austin Seven Type). By 1932, Austin was making nearly 50,000 cars a year; so was born the great automotive entity of Austin.

Of 1930s note, General Motors (GM) nearly bought Austin – but were turned down by Herbert Austin, so they purchased Vauxhall (and Adam Opel) instead! Such were the origins of automotive history. Herbert became Baron Austin yet had no obvious corporate heir – enter Leonard Lord in 1938, just before war would interrupt the motor industry. Lord had previously worked for William Morris but also for Wolseley earlier in his career. Morris denied Lord his just rewards for reinventing Morris cars and branding in the 1930s, so Lord was off. An internecine 'war', a need for revenge, seemed to have manifested, which would have consequences undreamed of at the time. Lord is reputed to have stated that he would return to take Morris apart – brick by brick.

So Austin's rival (and eventual merger partner) was William Morris (born 1877) who was not an engineer yet was to head a company that began as W.M. Morris in 1912, thence to become Morris Motors. William Morris lived to become Lord Nuffield of the Nuffield Organisation, manufactured over 20,000 cars a year in the 1930s and played a vital role in war time production. By 1951, Nuffield, with Morris Motors within it, was selling over 100,000 cars a year. So too was its rival, Austin. Leonard Lord would play each off against the other, it seems.

Morris, of course, began in the mechanical world of bicycles and from a small beginning in Oxford in the Edwardian era. After 1910, the Morris workshops had given birth to work on early cars and the Morris Garages and its first car of 1913. Morris did not go to the expense of designing cars from scratch; instead he utilised other people's components – even engines and drivetrains – and created a production line process that aped Henry Ford's ideas, albeit on a smaller scale. In fact, Morris visited America in 1913 and returned to Oxford to import well-priced US car parts into Great Britain in order to set up his business. His first 'Cowley' used such parts but production was interrupted by the First World War. Post-war, his Morris Cowley was an all-British affair in terms of components and build – except that the Coventry manufacture engines were of Parisian, Hotchkiss derivation, built by a British subsidiary.

Morris, it seems, had no dream of pursuing a personal engineering ethos. Morris also turned one of his own bull-nosed cars into a 1920s tractor and that would set a course that resulted in the greater Nuffield brand. By 1939, Morris – as the newly titled Nuffield – owned Riley, Wolseley, MG, Morris Commercial, Morris Marine, and SU Ltd. Fast-forward to the post-1952 merger with Austin to form BMC, the Nuffield tractor brand would be allowed continue under its own brand name – only to then put 'Leyland' badges on Nuffield tractors soon after the BMC-Leyland merger of 1968.

A suggested merger between the two major British companies of Morris and Austin – both domestic and global suppliers to the British Empire – was made in the mid-1920s by several interested industrialists, and again in the 1930s, but nothing came of such moves. Yet Wolseley would end up under Morris' ownership, as would other marques, and of course Cecil Kimber's MG branding stood for Morris Garages – part of the original Morris portfolio. The Riley brothers' marque would also fall into Morris's hands as Riley imploded financially – so this is how Riley became part of Morris and latterly part of BMC. Vanden Plas of London (originally van den Plas of Belgium) would also become a suitable upmarket branding mechanism to be acquired for Austin. Triumph (founded by a German!) enjoyed its heyday and post-1935, having separated off from the motorcycle brand, produced wonderful British sports cars, yet would soon be dumbed down by BL.

But did General Motors also try to buy Morris as it had Austin? Some say so.

Leonard Lord was clearly a man on a mission, with brain bubbling with ideas for cars, trucks, machinery and all things mechanical to be sold. Lord would become managing director and then chairman and chief executive of Austin by 1945 and it is to Lord at Austin that we look to see the basics foundations of the huge post-war success that was Austin of England. It was Austin's sheer range of across-the-market cars and engines that were the foundations of its model range success and security. The A-series 30-90 made Austin its money – over 120,000 cars a year and an £38 million pound profit by 1951. Soon Austin, under Lord, would be powerful enough to devour Nuffield's Morris.

Revenge was to be taken cold.

Morris made post-war money by building as many cars as it could, but these were not greatly innovative cars. With its previous management leader long gone (Sir Miles Thomas went to run the national airline – British Overseas Airways Corporation) and with Lord Nuffield tweaking the corporate tiller by remote control from afar, Morris entered the mid-1950s with production up, but little innovative being planned for a design-led future. Morris was not a designer. Yet he had Issigonis!

The Morris Minor may have been reliable, sturdy and a best seller, but despite Issigonis' efforts, it represented the past made new. Its 1930s engine did not help either. How ironic that its original prototype's form was a sleek, curved, aero-weapon of a car with front-wheel drive and advanced configuration, only to be reverse engineered into more conventional dinosaur, yet then to see the innovative Mini manifest within the same company.

Riley made technically advanced post-war cars, but retained ancient, wooden-frame coach-built bodies of vast expense and poor safety. Wolseley cars lost their way en route to being Oxford based. Both these illustrious marques became part of Morris under the Nuffield umbrella. In an early act of badge-engineering, Morris stuck the Wolseley name and trims onto a tarted-up Morris Minor! So began mix and match car design of declining integrity.

Austin started to 'design' a new range of cars. Morris and Austin were clearly going to clash. Yet merger was back on the cards and talks between the titled egos saw the 1948-1952 on-off talks to merge the two great marques and their leaders into a brand that was supposed, or envisaged to be devoid of personality clashes or behavioural traits.

Nuffield and the Morris board stood firm against a merger with Austin, but the reality dawned that Austin's innovative new cars like the A40, Devon, Dorset, A60, Atlantic and A90 ranges might kill off Morris car sales over the next five years or so. For Morris, unless major investment and new corporate 'design' vision could be secured, the writing could well be on the wall. And this was before the advent of the Austin Healey tie-up and the export-earning and domestic 'halo' branding cars that it produced.

On 31 March 1952, the two giants of motoring, Austin and Morris were finally merged, two decades after such a merger was mooted in the 1930s and four years after post-war talks began. So was born the Austin-Morris entity that was named the British Motor Corporation or BMC. Competition from Ford, Rootes, Chrysler and the Europeans would soon hot up.

This BMC merger would turn out to be hugely prophetic in its underlying issues.

The polymath workaholic that was Leonard Lord, a man who had worked for both Austin *and* Morris, had by 1953 created something truly important on the national stage, a vital crucible of design, manufacturing, employment and British global branding. He had also had his revenge.

Lord (later ennobled as Baron Lambury) truly was remarkable, although apparently not all found him easy to get on with. He seems to have been utterly driven, ruthless say some. Yet his cars were remarkable too, cars that poured from 'his' BMC in the 1950s and 1960s. But there were errors apparent.

One significant internal inconsistency was that Austin and Morris dealers, as well as MG, Wolseley, and Riley outlets, were actually encouraged to compete with each other inside the BMC circus, with sales and earnings targets, yet were asked to do so by selling cars that were soon to be identical to each other except for their badges, trims and 'shared' engines. This was how BMC's early badge engineering undermined the its own brands and brand – here lay the seeds of trouble.

Ford knew it, and was with its model range 'family' which could take the loyal Ford owner from youth to retirement, soon snapping at BMC's 35 per cent domestic market share as early as 1957.

Lord had also decided that Austin should purchase the company that made its cars' bodies – Pressed Fisher, then Pressed Steel. Firstly, in 1963, Lord swallowed up body-constructor Fisher and Ludlow Ltd of Castle Bromwich, then by 1965, the Pressed Steel (Cowley) concern that had American roots via Morris and a link with the Budd Corporation in the 1920s. There followed Pressed Steel Fisher, who would also make the bodies for many other car manufacturers, including Rolls-Royce at Swindon. The integration of Fisher and then Pressed Steel into Austin was the first big act of amalgamation inside the British motor industry and might be framed as setting the scene for further such ventures.

3
Fifties Style: Seeds of Trouble
Rule Britannia? Or a Wind of Change?

No one seems to have realised that offering a rationalised, single car type sharing an identical body and components, but just wearing differing badges, to two (or more) differing buyer bases of differing tastes, was a potentially risky idea. Strangely, no marketing experts pointed this out to the bosses of Austin or Morris, or if they did, they were ignored. But before this scenario transpired, BMC *would* produce some very clever 1950s cars.

Surely the product should define the brand not the brand define the product? BMW, Citroën, Saab, VW, Ford, Renault, Volvo, even Fiat, etcetera, *all* latterly demonstrated this. So too did Triumph, MG, Jaguar, and the main British brands. But BMC abandoned the logic and then reversed it.

So occurred the great merger of Austin and Morris. With them went the smaller, independent Midlands car brands that they absorbed. So was born the seeds of the internal and tribal conflict of the Austin Morris-based, British Motor Corporation as BMC – as would become British Motor Holdings and then British Leyland Motor Corporation (BLMC).

Inherent within BMC was an internecine corporate behemoth; here lay the seeds of destruction, of compromise, of an Austin being an MG, a Morris being an Austin and vice versa. Also of a Riley being a Wolseley, and a Mini becoming an Austin, Morris, Riley, derivative – one with a posh grille and a boot box tacked on.

Initially, the two groups' design studios and engineering functions would remain in separate locations, but it would not be long before they would be thrown together and forced to function jointly. Inside BMC (and then BLMC), engine design and engine development were run as two separate, independent departments which could give rise to conflict. Sadly, there were deep divides between management, engineers, designers, and the workforce.

Competing management tribes soon produced competing cars under the same roof! MG Midget or Austin Healey Sprite? Big Austin or the Wolseley 6/80 as a Morris Minor 1000 in drag? Austin A40 – or would you prefer the bizarre

1954 Metropolitan of Nash, Hudson, Austin, Fisher, provenance and on sale in America and then in Great Britain 1956-1961 as a Longbridge-built product?

Riley Pathfinder or the almost identical Wolseley 4/90? MG Magnette or Wolseley 4/40? Or a 1959-onwards Farina-styled Austin Cambridge versus the identical Morris Oxford, or its sub-brands of MG, Wolseley etc?

BMC had to have five, yes five different front and rear ends on the factory shelf in order to build these modified variants of the same car thus: Austin A55/A60 Cambridge; Morris Oxford MkV; MG Magnette MK111/IV; Riley 4/68; Wolseley 6/99; and 6/110 Mk1, MkII, Then came the A99 and the A110 Westminster all based on the same car! Six iterations of the same body shell but most with differing engines, fascia and cabin trims, rear lamps and front grilles. This was mass badge-engineering that destroyed 'brand equity' – the value of the brand – by diluting its cars authenticity.

In these, the origins of badge-engineering and class conscious brand snobbery amid the costs of individualising these cars, there lay the seeds of the later troubles. Very little was coherent. It was a bit like a big airline (BOAC for example) buying three different types of airliner to do the same job. Branding, training, maintenance and operating costs went through the roof. BOAC did just this with its Comets, 707s, VC10s, BOAC being another corporation with too many masters including Government.

Meanwhile, over at Ford and Rootes, entirely rational model lines and trim options were being created. Triumph, however, created the Mayflower as perhaps the world's first retro-pastiche car design as an utterly pointless car. Standard would purchase struggling Triumph in 1944 and eventually that once revered marque would come under the BMC banner, but not before the TR2, TR-ranges, Herald, Spitfire, and large sporting saloon series (2000/2500) had achieved their respective sales successes.

Surely it was back in 1949-1959 that the disordered personality of Austin-Morris merger that was laid down in the DNA of a genetically modified car maker staffed by engineers and designers with differing ideas and talents. Here, in the archaeology of BL, lie the beginnings of all the trouble latterly blamed on workers, managers, designers, and politicians.

Unlike BMC, Saab would not abandon its brand hallmark of front-wheel drive amid advanced design, and suddenly produce a rear-wheel drive dinosaur in direct contradiction to its previous ethos of products. Citroën would not do that either. But BMC did this with a rear-driven Land Crab conversion – the Austin 3.0-Litre – and BLMC did just this with the post-Maxi family car that was the rear-driven Marina; it turned turtle in its technology and product offering and expected its loyal buyers to follow it, only then to re-offer them its previous front-drive Issigonis-era philosophy. Mad, truly mad.

Back at the 1960s Birmingham-Coventry axis, Standard Triumph, Riley, Wolseley, then Rover, and Jaguar, were all merged into a corporate entity of Leyland and BMC that led to the BLMC or BL.

Strangely, the great independent British aircraft manufacturers were also forced at this time into a giant merger by government edict (via the Sandys Report). So died the great names of Vickers Armstrong, Handley Page, Bristol, de Havilland, Shorts, Airspeed, Miles and everyone else. It signalled the end of a British ability to supply the world with class leading aircraft, Concorde and the VC10 being the last gasps along with the cancelled TSR2, Rolls-Royce Medway engine and other projects that had world beating potential that was to be deliberately crushed by men in in suits.

By 1966, Britain had won the football World Cup, but it had also seemingly gelded its major car making and aircraft making companies under a big umbrella of corporate power and corporate 'group think'. So died engineering and design opportunity, so died a golden age. And politicians of Left and Right had had a major role in creating the rolling disasters that resulted.

Even Joe Edwards, as the time-served Austin and BMC senior man, resigned. Yet via Pressed Steel he ended up back in the BMC tent as managing director and had the unenviable task of navigating these vital years as 1968's birth of BL took its first steps into the 1970s and a looming global recession and fuel crisis. But faced with Board and management confusion, Joe Edwards resigned and who could blame him.

Also walking away from the BMC/BMH behemoth was Jim Woodcock; he was a long term Morris man and, like Edwards, knew about strategy and planning. He too would be on the BMC Board and was led by George Harriman. Woodcock ran Morris into the 1960s but walked away before it became part of BLMC.

It was the BMC leviathan, via the Austin-Morris merger, that unleashed the cancer of design compromise that would help kill off British car making in its vital crucible, within just three decades. And no amount of patriotic flag waving, from Left or Right, was ever going to save it.

Inherent within the thinking and the behaviours were all the societal and behavioural factors cited above. Austin and Morris, as the great merger and subsequent amalgamations, told themselves not just what to think, but what others such as the car buying public, should think and desire. This was how our 1960s cars and the forthcoming 1970s cars were created and their ingredients prescribed. Fashion had not been followed at BMC in the manner it was at Ford with the

Cortina. Instead, BMC set the fashion via the Issigonis cars, and then abandoned them and then contradicted itself. Mini, 1100-1300, Land Crab, Maxi, but then Marina, but then back to front-drive and the Allegro!

BMC's Issigonis design policy and front-wheel drive ethos years were halted and then 'Fordised' in a mixed and matched policy of its engines, bodyshells and trims to make several versions of the same car. Thus it extended 'badge engineering' on a scale seen neither before nor since. Thus it also created the Morris Marina.

Indeed, if the rationale of chief designer Roy Haynes had been followed, BL would have done a GM (or Ford) and clothed a range of individually styled, different cars over the chassis and components of *shared* platforms and engines – at vast cost savings and efficiencies yet still able to appeal to the 'tribes' of the marques and their buyers. But this was not correctly enacted and a vast panoply of engines, tweaks, panels, toolings and trims gave rise to bizarre legions of variants and specifications amid a confused range of cars that cost a fortune to design, manufacture, sell and repair. This was not Haynes' fault!

Paradoxically, in this act of supposed highly profitable, lower unit cost, badge engineering, lay the second of the causes of BL's eventual failure behind that first step of an unwise and unworkable merger. But none of this was seemingly obvious then.

How on earth did it go wrong? Specifically, how did we commit industrial suicide and end the genius of British volume car production by the British, as British designed and built? Before this occurred, there lay a new thinking, one that was so different from BMC's ethos and experience and the cars it had designed for its customers, that it was a change that needed total revolution in order to work.

In the 1950s, Leonard Lord immediately saved money by rationalising the costs-base by sharing Austin engines in Morris cars and mixing and matching engines, bodies, parts, and trims across the marques.

As the 'perfect' example of BMC engineering genius gone wrong, witness the Austin 3.0-Litre, a car created from another that was fundamentally opposite in its thinking yet which would form the basis not of a hybridised derivative, but a completely opposite philosophy.

The Austin 3.0-Litre, or ADO 61 as its Austin design code tagged it, was a clever, technical, yet bastardized paradox of a rear-wheel drive car based on the front-wheel drive design and bodyshell of the Issigonis-designed ADO 17 or 'Land Crab', thus utterly invalidating its engineering concept and abilities in the ADO 61's attempt to try and create an upmarket silk purse out of enlarged Mini; an idea that was never going to lead its class.

Yet this *was* an interesting car, loaded with engineering and today they have a respected following of niche and cult status and rightly so, for the car is 'technical' and rather special. But at launch it was, seen up against the obvious competition that was the Rover P6, Triumph 2000 and more, surely rather pointless.

ADO17, the 18-22 or 'Land Crab', was diluted in brand and marque terms by it being on sale in identical form as a Morris. But Austin used it to go upmarket. Yet above ADO 61 as the 3.0-Litre in the Austin line-up, lay the ancient Austin Westminster which was still on sale. Also on sale had been the Austin A99/A110/Princess/4.0-Litre R Type (VDP) 3.0-Litre and then came the Westminster, to top off the range just as ADO 61 was being created and readied for sale– talk about internal conflict. Is this why the 3.0-Litre was held back from launch until 1967?

Initially conceived as early 1963, 3.0-Litre ADO61 did not achieve series production until 1967, taking three years to convert an existing car that was the 18-22 ADO17 and itself not launched until 1964. But how interesting (and at what cost) that the ADO61 variant was considered *before* ADO17 as the 18-22 was finished or announced. Few outside BMC/BL were aware of this until Jeff Daniels revealed it.[1]

Heavy, ugly, cramped inside by its intrusive (and expensive to engineer) new rear-wheel drive floorpan, the 3.0-Litre cost a lot of money to develop (not least major revisions to the old C-Series engine lump) and was a badge-engineered mutant that flopped. It totally contradicted the Issigonis ethos upon which it relied for its base 'chassis'!

The bus-like driving position and cabin layout were as if lifted from a Mini on steroids, and hardly stylish or luxurious. Why on earth didn't Austin spend the time and the money building a 'proper' new class car! Yet bizarrely, the 3.0-Litre boasted high-tech, 'active' interlinked hydrolastic self-levelling suspension powered from an engine-driven pump a la Citroën.

The Austin 3.0-Litre managed a meagre 10bhp gain over the 1800 as ADO 17, yet was hobbled by its significant weight increase. Set alongside the tuned-up Morris S version of ADO 17 – the 100bhp 1800S, or the Wolseley-badged variant – the 3.0-Litre's performance became pointless and it drank fuel like the aircraft carrier it resembled.

Even at launch it was not right, and a 'De Luxe' version with improved interior trim and seats was rushed out to meet criticism. The 3.0-Litre lasted three years on sale and sold just 9,092 examples.

Most sensible people would have bought a Rover 2200/3500 or a Triumph 2000/2500 instead – surely? Both of these other types of course being produced by the same over-arching brand as the Austin – BMC and thence BL.

The 3.0-Litre was a folly and a massive waste of money. As such, it was typical of what went wrong at BMC (note, pre-BL) when accountants and managers tried to reduce and amortise spending at the cost of actually making a car people would want to pay for in the first place! This was not a 'designed' car, it was bean-counters' camel created out of a horse. Was no manager brave enough to stand up and say so? Probably not, not in the 1960s hierarchical authority gradient of the BMC boardroom. Did 'group think' and subservience allow this mad car to be born?

As with the Austin Maxi, these men in charge took some existing parts, an old engine, four doors off another model (and the windows and windscreen), some borrowed instruments, lights, and seats and literally cobbled together a so-called new car that was a pretence, but one badged up as new. And patriotic British buyers were briefly fooled, again, but only 10,000 of them!

If the 18/22 series ADO17 was thought a sound basis for the Austin 3.0-litre, how come it was also thought sound for the basis of the Maxi – the bigger Mini that wasn't? What mind created this internal inconsistency? Indeed, why not just shorten the nose of a Land Crab, chop off its boot and give it a nice swoopy hatchback rear end. Simple! In fact, BMC actually created a one-off prototype of this very idea and it had huge potential.

But, oh, no, BMC had to do it the hard way and dump the existing Land Crab fastback hatchback prototype and then reinvent it as another car – the Maxi itself. If you ever wondered where the money went, Austin 3.0-Litre and Maxi provide the answers...

There was more to tell and to cost too. The BMC and BLMC 'empire' reached across the world and produced a series of incarnations of cars that defied rationale or accounting sanity. Much like the thinking behind the Austin 3.0-Litre based on the 18-22 Land Crab, it was a 'designer' madness or an engineering expedition into the bizarre. Had not even Rootes abandoned the idea of 'strange' cars, such as their large, rear-engined saloon that made it all the way to pre-production prototyping before sense was seen?

Export or die remained a mantra for BLMC. So at vast cost, was supported local production from CKD kits and fully-locally manufactured pressings and trim items as manufactured cars in a range of countries that included Argentina, Belgium, Ceylon, Colombia, Cuba, Denmark, Egypt, Ghana, Ireland, India, Indonesia, Italy, Kenya, Malaya, Mexico, Nigeria, Portugal, Rhodesia, Sweden and, it is reputed, in the Philippines. In fact, it operated sixty factories across more than twelve nations – even small scale in Malta. At its height, over 330,000 vehicles were CKD built or fully manufactured overseas circa 1968.

Full-scale tooling and pressing production of local market cars took place in Australia, Canada, New Zealand, and East Africa, and South Africa. Little known were the fibreglass Minis and ADO 16 1100/1300 cars that were locally built by a rural BL outpost in Arica, Chile with local content and fibreglass bodies. It is also known that a few ADO 16s were built in Colombia and an outpost in Ecuador has also been cited.

Triumph 1300s were also locally built in Israel, as were Leyland buses.

Donald Stokes' export mantra was truly delivered. Millions of pounds were poured into supporting such concerns.

In Italy, the 1960s tie-up with Innocenti in Milan resulted in licence-built BMC cars (notably Farina-styled ones) being locally produced and uniquely trimmed. The CKD-built Austin A40 fabricated in Milan also used local trim materials and was constructed to a build quality some think was higher than the British-manufactured cars achieved. The Italian A40 sold over 50,000 units in Italy alone as an Innocenti-badged car. It was known as the 'Innocenti A40s Combinata' and even saw the MKII version utilise the full-height rear hatchback, which rural Italians apparently found very useful. 'Trattatela pure duramnente' was the very non-politically correct advertising strapline.

In 1960, a special-bodied Innocenti Spider (Spyder) was styled over the base of an Austin-Healey Sprite. Also available with a steel hardtop as a C-Coupé from 1964, it is today one of the rarest of all Italian specialist sports cars.

Innocenti and BMC also created an improved ADO 16 1100/1300 with local trim tweaks, a tuned MG twin-carb engine and of real note, a reduced steering wheel angle rake. Known as the IM3/ 3S and 4, Innocenti followed this range up with their less successful Allegro-based Regent.

Quite why BL did not buy the British and global rights to the pretty and pert-handling Bertone-styled Innocenti Mini-based 90/120 hatchback of 1973, is beyond comprehension – it would have wiped the Renault 5 and VW Polo off the sales charts. And BL's later Mini replacement echoed its themes – right down to being cancelled! Yet Innocenti re-engineered the little car and gave it a fuel efficient Japanese engine to replace the old A-series unit; a five-speed gearbox and trim updates saw the brilliant Innocenti Mini continue into the 1980s.

Despite producing over 50,000 BMC cars a year, BMC and BL never took the Innocenti relationship and its many dealership outlets further – which, given the entry of the UK into the EEC in the 1970s, would surely have been a prescient move.

Intriguingly, Innocenti was purchased by the Argentine, Alejandro de Tomaso after BL abandoned Italy. And it had been in Argentina that a saloon (and a pick-up or ute) version of the Farina-bodied A55/60 series known as the Di Tella 1500 had been built in the early 1960s as a remote and little-known BMC offering.

In 1960s Africa and India, a five door Triumph Herald (1959-71), and Austin Morris 1100/1300 range, including the hatchback (including a 1500cc version), all sold well in local markets.

Triumph's Herald, notably in four-door guise, was found in India. The car was given revised and very European rear end styling and four doors as the Herald MkIII. Even the normal British-spec Herald was restyled – the basic car featuring the quad-headlamp set-up, yet often with the outer lamps blanked off or used for indicators. From 1964 onwards, a range of Herald and local-market Herald derivations were created for the Indian market.

A Herald-based 'true' hatchback was designed by Michelotti and one prototype completed. This car found its way into private British ownership, yet in India, a modified Herald five door estate was actually produced. Soon Triumph would be within the Leyland BMC tent and competing with Rover and MG.

The decision not to manufacture the Herald hatchback is the perfect example of the 'nearly' car that could have been a sales success – rather like the TR7-based Lynx coupé of the 1980s which was so close to mass production and global sales success.

Down under in Australia in the 1930s, the Nuffield organisation had created a car factory near Sydney under the Nuffield (Australia) Pty (Ltd) brand. It was an easy step for a post-war interlude that created the BMC Australia concern, where modified British market cars were tweaked to appeal to the Australian buyer.

A second plant near Melbourne meant that BMC Australia was casting engines, forging parts, pressing bodies and creating unique model variations out of existing British domestic market cars. For example, the 1957 model the Austin A95 had become the Australian-built Morris Marshal. Australian-built Austin and Morris cars also included Riley and Wolseley derivatives. Key model names in the lexicon of BMC's and BL's Australian automania included:

Kimberly;
Lancer;
Marshal;

Major;
Nomad;
Tasman;
Marina;
P76; and Coupé.

But by 1959, a car of higher local content, a car more tuned to Aussie needs was to be built by BMC as an Austin Lancer or a Morris Major. This was a restyled variation of the Riley 1.5/Wolseley 1500 range from Britain. At some expense, mix-and-match front grilles, dashboards, trims, and latterly, re-tooled rear wings with add-on rear fins, were grafted into and onto pre-existing shapes. Even a longer wheelbase was incorporated. Yet the UK-standard specification Wolseley version of the car was also on sale in Australia!

Mixing Austin items with Morris items created the Austin Lancer. Again, blending panels, badges, grilles, hubcaps, bumpers, and trims such as instruments and seats created a plethora of special, Australian-specification design iterations with all the attendant costs associated with parts, stock and marketing. The Lancer died in early 1962, yet was soon to be re-born as the Morris Major Elite – which replaced the Morris Major, itself related to the Austin Lancer. By 1963, this market saw the Austin Freeway and a luxury-trimmed variant known as the Wolseley 24/80! The Wolseley 24/80 emerged as a six-cylinder variation of the British market Farina-bodied Austin and Morris A60 ranges. Just like the six-cylinder Marina that would follow it over a decade later, these cars were front-heavy and of ponderous dynamics.

So was created BMC's first range of 'dedicated' Australian cars. But the truth was that even patriotic 'Anglo' minded Australians wanted bigger engines, huge cabins, great torque, long range and tougher suspension. Holden and Ford would soon create cars to better meet that need – even if they had US market origins – that were better hidden than the BMC cars' DNA.

The Fisherman's Bend BMC plant at Melbourne soon faded and local assembly of CKD cars from Britain (with added local content) was solely located near Sydney.

Austin Lancer, Morris Marshal, Morris Major Elite, all died. Yet in their place came the brilliant Nomad and the Austin X6 range of 'Land Crab' derivatives. These led to the P76 range (which may have had Rover P9 origins), and in the opposite direction, the Australian Mini-Moke production line. Think of the costs!

Then came a brainwave for Australia. BMC – by now BL – spent millions putting a novel hatchback and extra windows into its superb 1100/1300 series ADO 16-series cars for 1970 launch in Australia. This included a new rear structural support hoop-pressing to support the hatchback and the hole that had been cut in the previously stiff rear end. Small, Maxi-style windows in the D-pillars added a fresh look too. Even better came a 1500cc ohc engine for the Australian market (yet so stupidly never offered in the UK) and the Maxi's five-speed gearbox.

Named the Morris 1500 in the saloon version and the Morris Nomad as the five-door hatchback, this was a superb (gas suspended) car range that reinvented the 1100/1300 series and also made it a hatchback as the craze for that type dawned. But this car, based on a pre-existing best-seller, was never offered in the BL home market of Britain, which was another opportunity inexplicably side-stepped; another 'nearly' car.

Triumph had built Heralds at Port Melbourne long before the 1968 BLMC merger and had two plants in Victoria State. BMC also had a plant in Australia and would soon spend money converting the Austin Morris 1800-2200 series 'Land Crab' into the Australian market-only Tasman, and Kimberley series of badge-engineered devices. New bonnets, wings, lights and new rear aprons and different engines distinguished these cars.

The transformation of the original, British market Land Crab's 'anti-styling' was quite something. A new long front with four square headlamps lurking under a proboscis-like shovel-nose gave the car an ant-eater like appearance. At the rear, the roof and D-pillar and 'six-light' rear three-quarter windows were draped over with a steel duvet that 'boxed' off the rear end of the car. These were significant styling alterations designed to make the car look tougher, perhaps even 'butch'.

An upmarket version – the Kimberly (2.2-litre) – boasted twin SUs and 115bhp through the front wheels! But these cobbled together cars were the ultimate acts of badge-engineering and failed to survive the tough conditions of Australia's long-distance, 'hot and high' operating conditions, let alone outback corrugated roads and 42 degree ambient air temperatures.

You could even buy a rather wonderful 1800-based pick-up or 'ute' especially tooled to the Australian trader and farmer. This had a bench seat and provision for three front seat belts to meet local legislation. Even rarer was the pick-up based upon the Riley/MG tooled version of the Farina A55/A60 range, the ute being seen in tiny numbers in Australia and Argentina and known as the Di Tella 1500.

Unknown to many, was the 1.5-litre diesel-engined version of the A60 Cambridge and Oxford series that was sold in export markets such as Australia and Africa. Slow, but torquey and economical, it was the ultimate outback engine.

Quite why the ultimate development of the A60-series, the A99 and A110 Westminster series with six-cylinder power, were not promoted in the Australian market, is a moot point. Surely this, the proven development of a tough, rear-drive car, should have appealed to sheep farmers and Sydney lawyers alike. Even the rear-driven version of the front-driven 1800/2200 series, the Austin C-series 3-Litre of 1967 to 1971, was denied to the Australian market.

These were the myriad toolings, pressings and trimmings that cost BMC so dear to maintain its presence in the 'colonial' export market.

Of some profile, there came about the 1970s 'Leyland Australia' branding, and a Leyland Marina with a choice of E-series engines (not the A-series or B-series of the UK market) and even a six-cylinder E6-series engine. Also at this time, BL spent millions on the ill-fated 'proper' BL car for the Australians – the Michelotti-styled P76 saloon, coupé and estate ranges – which died after a few thousand of the saloon (and less than 100 coupés and fewer than ten estates) had been built. A few were shipped back to Britain for domestic development and testing as potential new British model. MG at Abingdon were rumoured to have done the assessment and modification works on one example that was sent to the MIRA test track. Many BL insiders think that Rover P9/P10 project origins lay within P76.

P76 was big, strong and had wide, steel anti-intrusion panels inside the doors (the first BL car to possess such technology). Its handling needed some work for wet UK roads, but it had potential. Yet BL's management decided not to proceed with a car that might have undermined sales of the larger Rover 3500 or its intended P9 replacement, and the big Triumph 2000, and the smaller-engined Jaguar XJ.

The result of the P76 tangent, was of course near-bankruptcy, set amid the wider 1975 BL crisis in Birmingham, Ryder, and the need to nationalise, rationalise and slash operating costs. Decades of Australian BMC and BL production was dumped, millions of pounds were misaligned in losses that hurt.

BMC also built cars in South Africa, East Africa, and Rhodesia (from CKD kits and local pressings) and set up a plant at Pamplona in Spain. Bizarrely, the 1100/1300 was transformed at vast cost in design and tooling terms, into Triumph 1500/Dolomite lookalike by BL at the contracted pen of Giovanni Michelotti. This car was marketed in Spain as the Authi Victoria, and also sold in South Africa as the Apache.

Leyland South Africa was known as LeyKor (Suid Afrika) or as the colloquial British 'LeyCor' and had built standard ADO16s since 1964. The 1970s Austin Apache was the engine, cabin, central section and structural underpinnings of ADO16 with Michelotti's new front and rear portions. Changes to the subframes were tooled up by the local Datsun factory! Was this the first BL-Japan tie-up?

Indeed, Apache was in the Triumph Acclaim niche years before Acclaim happened and was more authentic than that badge-engineered Honda. It also used an improved and locally cast A-series engine that added to the A-plus efficiency improvements seen in Ital and Metro.

Apache was a classy, four-door, three-box saloon with good looks and just the sort of appeal to middle class buyers that you might find in Surrey, Hampshire, Devon or Yorkshire. Why on earth was it not marketed 'at home'? After all, the Spanish got it as the more appropriately tagged Victoria! What about an Apache Vanden Plas!

Yet instead, BL spent millions on creating the Allegro and then bastardising it into a failure. Surely Apache, or Victoria, could and should have propped up the BL home-front empire at a much lower cost and let an Allegro type car be developed along more rational, less hobbled lines?

Today, two (imported) Apaches are on the road in Great Britain, several Victorias are known in Spain, and more than a handful of Apaches quietly rot under an African sun.

Naturally, BL sold off its Spanish plant as its 1975 crisis loomed.

In East Africa, from Kenya to Rhodesia (Zimbabwe), the ADO 16 as 1100/1300, was locally built under the Authi project title and represented by wonderfully named subsidiaries such as Leyland Albion Uganda and Leyland Albion East Africa/Kenya. ADO16 performed sterling service with colonial families and would soon pass into the hands of indigenous peoples, but even dry conditions could not stop the dreaded subframe rust that did for these African incarnations of a BMC classic. BMC had produced Austin, Morris, Standard-Triumph, Rover, cars and Leyland trucks in Rhodesia until political issues and the nation's declaration of independence (UDI) in 1965 forced BMC to close its Umtali plant. This would not reopen until 1979 in Southern Rhodesian under BL International Ltd and would continue up to the creation of Zimbabwe itself.

We might also wish to recall that BMC exported a special edition, automatic, two door ADO 16 Austin 1300 to America with special trim and badging. 59,000 such 'Austin America' badged, 1275cc, 4-speed autobox equipped cars were sold in America from 1969 to 1971. It was discontinued to allow an American-spec or 'Federalised' Marina to be marketed under the new U.S. federal regulations – which included changes to the bumpers and carburation settings.

So it was that BMC and BL had a foreign empire and, just like the British Empire, it failed upon the winds of change and not inconsiderable amount of blinkered conservatism. Oh, and the BL empire cost a fortune too. Yet it lived on via locally-badged cast-off BL and Rover cars built under new names and new flags and new badges. How apt.

Leyland (prior to the 1969 merger) had long run a factory in India at Madras and could produce over 9,000 vehicles per year for the Indian market. Hindustan Motors had also been building Morris cars for years in what was then Calcutta.

So the fact that, decades later, Rover's SD1 was reincarnated in the old colonial marketplace of India, reeks of karma. 12,000 SD1s were supposed to be locally welded up in India from as early as 1985, through to 1989, and some were fitted with the ancient engine of 83bhp, 1,991cc or '2.0-litre' Standard-Triumph 1940s provenance. A four-speed gearbox replaced the correct five-speed Rover unit. Curiously, the Rover was marketed under the old British brand name of 'Standard' – having been locally built by the Standard Motor Products Company of Madras.

'Standard 2000 – Nothing else comes close to it'. So ran the Indian advertising for the car, and at the hefty price they were new, no wonder less than 4,000 were sold.

Many Indian SD1s were also latterly rebuilt with a heavy, Nissan diesel engine and five-speed gearbox that truly was asthmatic and noisier than a tractor engine. Curiously, the Indian-manufactured SD1 body-panels were to be sold as new spares in Britain by Unipart!

The revised rear window and tailgate styling of the latter SD1 was also incorporated with the frontal revisions. Badge anomalies were common, as were locally sourced trim items. Some Indians also fitted the cheaper to source, US-spec round headlamp kit from the original British-built US export SD1.

Raised ride height, twin SU carburettors and a Triumph-type cylinder head were all part of the car's intriguing mix of re-warmed SD1 engineering and old BMC parts. The fuel consumption of the 2.0-litre 'four' was worse than that of a well-serviced ex-Buick V8 as found in the original SD1.

Today, a few hundred Indian-built SD1's with Standard brand badging survive in unloved retirement across India. Above all, this car saw the last use of the Standard-Triumph badge and did so four decades on from that company's demise. Who said badge-engineering was dead?

Well, it wasn't because the TATA Indicar would make it back to Britain over a decade later badged as the new CityRover, and the rest is rather sad history.

As the great 1960s badge-engineering experiment faded, we might suggest that, never in the field of badge-engineering had so many panels been owed so much by so few buyers. Yet there was to be a curious final twist in the tale of the BL and Austin-Rover branding.

Fifties Style: Seeds of Trouble • 85

Above, below and overleaf: *Owned by Ian Creese who restored it and loves it, this Austin Apache is beyond rare in BL circles. Michelotti added a boot, restyled the front and created a Triumph-like design that was an overseas market-only Austin. Also sold as the Authi Victoria in Spain. This was badge-engineering got right – as more than just the badges were changed. Why on earth did BL not built them at home? We might ask the same of Australian -market ADO16 'Nomad' hatchback?*

86 • *British Leyland: From Triumph to Tragedy. Petrol, Politics and Power*

Fifties Style: Seeds of Trouble • 87

ADO16 as a Vanden Plas Princess – slinking away like Dowager Duchess on the sherry.

More ADO16 badge-engineering – MG and Riley variants.

Rover's imperious P5B V8 Coupé: simply magisterial. The Queen had several P5s and Labour and Conservative Prime Ministers rode in P5s. Surely one of Rover's best cars.

Rover's P6 was advanced, innovative, safe and oh so stylish. Only the steering wheel design dated the interior. BL inherited this car and sold it to the world. Probably the best Rover and the the bravest and most successful post-war British sporting saloon car ever created – alongside the Jaguar XJ6 of course...

Mineral blue MGC-series six-cylinder looking wonderful.

Fifties Style: Seeds of Trouble • 91

Above: *Range Rover three-door as designed by Spen King, David Bache and the team. Timeless beyond fashion or foible.*

Right: *This is the very rare Carawagon Range Rover camper – ideal for safaris when sleeping on the roof is safer!*

Above: *Spitfire was wonderful, but like several Triumphs, used a clam-shell bonnet that revealed a lack of inner-wing crash cans or impact structure.*

Below: *GT6 came in several version with several attempts at the rear suspension! A brilliant straight-six of car in a fast-backed body: only the British could have created this 1960s icon.*

Fifties Style: Seeds of Trouble • 93

It's a Mini, but not as Issigonis would have approved of... Badge-engineering again.

Maxi. An early-build car seen alongside later iterations of 'Maxiness'. A fundamentally good car yet one tainted by BMC-into-BL.

Left: *The later Maxi interior replaced a 'Ford' type plastic moulded cowled fascia design with a wood or vinyl 'plank'. Austerity ruled.*

Below: *Maxi in its element – a later car in a lovely 1970s hue. Maxi and a caravan – how British!*

Fifties Style: Seeds of Trouble • 95

Right: *Maxi's 50th at Gaydon. Despite its issues, Maxi was loved and sold well across 1969 to 1981 without body tooling changes. No badge-engineering for Maxi!*

Below: *Marina Coupé out of Cortina and the 'Fordisation' of BLMC. For the want of better front suspension and a bit more money on the body, it could have been great. But it wasn't.*

Above and left: *Allegro. Much better than its press. The 1750 really flew and the estate was a superb car – BL's forgotten hatchback. Mr Mann's original Allegro design was diluted by BL but today we can see that it was about more than a 'square' steering wheel (a marketing department idea apparently). And when did you last see an 'Allegro 3 HL' – with four round headlamps?*

Fifties Style: Seeds of Trouble • 97

Above: *The Mini Clubman – more 'Fordisation' much to Issigonis' horror. The Clubman came with glue smeared all over the cabin as standard – and an aerodynamic drag coefficient so bad it was positively Edwardian (CD.53)! Still 1275 GT went like the clappers.*

Below: *1980s Triumph's Dolomite Sprint was fast and good-value, but eclipsed by more modern cars whose origins did not lie in the early 1960s.*

98 • *British Leyland: From Triumph to Tragedy. Petrol, Politics and Power*

Above: *The revised Triumph 2000 saloon gained more length and more power (2500S/ PI). Elegant and fast, yet costly to build and to own.*

Fifties Style: Seeds of Trouble • **99**

TR7 was new, innovative, safe and sold to the world, especially as a convertible and as a TR8 V8. It also made a good rally car.

TR7 had a very modern interior that has often been overlooked. The plaid seat trims were of their era. Comfort and safety as well as handling were key TR7 qualities.

Nose-engineering. The 18-22 /Princess came with three differing nose treatments even before it morphed into the Ambassador.

4
Car Craft: P6 to MGB

'The resulting car, the Rover P6, is one that is so beautifully free of inherent design compromise that it ranks as one of the greatest achievements of the British motor industry'

Statement by Rover P6 Owners Club

Inside BMC there was one of the best cars ever designed in Great Britain. This was not just a good car, but probably the most significant post-war mass market British car in terms of design, driving, and of note, global sales and brand reputation. Here was true brand equity. But the fact was that this car was *not* of BMC creation, for this car was inherited by BMC as part of the 1960s mergers and acquisitions and it entered the post-1968 BLMC merger as a star that had very little to do with BMC or BLMC in pure engineering terms. That this car went on to be perceived as a BL product with all that meant, was just another part of the story of the collapse of the British car industry.

You might think I am referring to the world class, 1966 Jaguar XJ6, for Lyons and his Jaguar was the shining jewel inside BMC and its post-Jaguar merger BMH. Jaguar and its cars, not just XKE as E-Type but also the earlier XK-series, its MK10, its XJ13, deserve all the praise that their incredible designs and careers garner. We cannot ignore the 'Lyons line', the men of Jaguar and their achievements. Yet the car being referred to here is *not* the Jaguar XJ6 of 1966 onwards, it is the Rover P6 of 1963 and beyond.

Here was a car famous the world over, desired the word over and delivered to the world. The car was the Rover P6 – better known as the 2000, 2200, and 3500 V8. Punters, policeman, and government ministers loved them. Rover was inside Leyland and Leyland soon became part of BMC. Triumph was inside Leyland too.

Rover's P6 stemmed from the Rover Car Company of Solihull, Warwickshire, and Rover was a global star of design engineering – the engineering headed up by Charles Spencer 'Spen' King, and the design/styling function under David Bache.

C. 'Spen' King – 'CSK' – was an ex-Rolls-Royce apprentice who happened to have two uncles who ran Rover – the Wilks brothers. After defining the P6 (and then the Range Rover), King worked on Triumph developments after the two marques had been forced into a parallel existence inside BL in 1971 and his engineering genius touched the later TR7 and TR8. King latterly headed BL Technology.

Key to P6's development was engineer, Gordon Bashford, who had joined Rover aged just 14 before the Second World War. Bashford was instrumental in the development of the Wilks brothers' Land Rover concept (and the later Range Rover) and notably, in the design engineering of the P6. A touch younger than Bashford was an engineer named Jim Randle who joined Rover post-war and achieved later fame at Jaguar, firstly under Bob Knight's engineering tutorship (both men working under the legendary William 'Bill' Heynes as Jaguar's Technical Director, and then, not least with the XJ-S development and with the Keith Helfet styled XJ220 project. Randle was famous at Jaguar (as was Walter 'Wally' Hassan) – ultimately for XJ40, but it was at Rover where he started and the P6 was his favourite. His son is also an auto engineer.

The late Michael Scarlett, ex-Technical Editor of *Autocar*, had the highest of praise for the forensic and calm Randle (who was also a private pilot) yet also cited his humour and ability to break rules and get things done. Randle was described by many as a visionary engineer who also knew how vital build quality was.

Although Triumph's men might argue over it, Rover in the 1960s probably had the most capable design development team of any British car company in the post-war automotive era. Jaguar would say that the E-Type, XJ13 and XJ6 proved that *they* were the leaders. But P6 has a secure claim to be the most innovative British post-war car design – doesn't it?

Although latterly famous as a 3500V8 – even better as a V8S – the often ignored truth is that the launch version of this car with the smaller-capacity four-cylinder engine, actually created the market niche for the accomplished, sporting 2.0-Litre saloon and did so long before BMW got its act together and went on to dominate the market.

P6 offered the style, size, safety and performance of a much larger car but using a smaller engine (until the V8 arrived!) and at a lower price. 1978cc of alloyed and iron, free-breathing engine delivered 115mph and 0-60mph in just over 13 seconds – enough to keep up with much larger -engined cars, yet using far less fuel. The 2200TC made P6 even better.

Of note, despite its heavy and strong base unit under- frame, P6's bonnet and boot lid were lightweight alloy.

Car designers and engineers (two separate breeds, yet people who thankfully collaborated in the P6 story), often talk about a design research culture, even a design research psychology. Get that right and get the engineering-design-styling collaboration correct, and a great car will result. In P6 it did.

First conceived in late 1956, Rover's research and design team took over six years to deliver the P6 but the wait was worth it. The originator of the car's concept is cited as Robert Boyle. Every part of this car was totally new – a massive technical and financial undertaking for Rover. The sadness today is that that the car marque that created this type of sporting saloon is no more and its German rivals now provide what it did.

It is perceived that Rover was a 'conservative' company, yet Rover's pre-war cars, notably its 'airline' range were far from conservative or boring. The P4 series might have looked staid, but they were in fact technologically clever. Post-war Rover's research unit, packed with genius – truly a post-war apogee of automotive intellect – gave us the Rover T4 Jet Engine, twin-rotor turbines, advanced structures, suspension and styling. It also created the P9 as a still-born sports car and a potential new big saloon project.

The P5/P5B might have looked a bit upper crust, but it too was an example of advanced and refined design principles. Here was a safe, stylish, robust British car with that rare thing, a sense of occasion.

Then came P6 – a 'Concorde' moment before that machine was built; P6 was of the future. Not quite a gas turbine future, but nonetheless, a car to shake up Citroën, BMW, Mercedes, Volvo, the American marques, and many more. P6 was not just a new car to lead its class, it invented a new class, a new definition of what was possible and what the car-buying public could expect if they were minded to investigate.

P6 really was a new world order. Today, we forget just how defining this car was. That BMC and BL inherited it and eventually cast a wicked spell on it and its SD1 successor, somehow sums up just how bad things got in the BL years.

£10.6 million of Land-Rover generated profits went into the P6 design project. This was huge amount by 1957 terms and over £6 million more than Jaguar would spend on its new saloon – but then Lyons was known for his parsimony of perfection on a shoestring budget.

In BLMC terms, Triumph was where Donald Stokes cut his motor industry teeth and therefore likely to be deserving of his attention inside the BLMC circus tent that P6 joined. But Rover's P6 was its saloon car star – Triumph 2500 PI notwithstanding.

P6 won the first 'Car of the Year' award in 1964. The 2000 model alone – via SC, Auto, sold over 325,000 cars from 1963 to 1972 – add in the 2200, TC, and 3500 V8 sales thereafter, and the Rover claims that P6 was 'More than a car' and

'Takes motoring years ahead' was proven correct. P6 production did not cease until 1977 in Mk2 guise. By which time, the 3500 V8 had become a sporting saloon legend with its high top speed and sub-10 seconds 0-60mph time.

Like a big Saab or a big Citroën, so advanced, so authentic, so technically ethical was the P6, that its stood the test of time and did not fall behind the competition for many years.

The Citroën analogy is not without accuracy in the P6 story. Examine the Rover's A-pillars, windscreen shape and surround, and the design of the exterior panels around the front wings to windscreen intersection, allied to the curvature of the windscreen, and you will find a very close resemblance to those features on the Citroën DS. In particular note the 'chrome' trim on the windscreen pillars and windscreen-to-roof header rail. It is all very DS and the answer lies in Rover learning from Citroën's aerodynamic expertise and deploying it in the P6. The sides of the car also used curved sections to control localised airflow and the high, boxed tail helped provide a clean rear airflow cut-off.

Similarly, the P6 was not a monocoque car body (nor was the DS). Instead, P6 hung unstressed exterior body panels from a 'base unit' inner frame or skeleton built up from a floor unit or 'punt' – not a twin-railed or boxed chassis. However, the DS's under frame was notoriously weak in the A-pillar, B-pillar, and C-pillar design. The main side B-pillars were not integrated into the sills and the result was very poor frontal and side impact protection in the DS. The DS's floor was deep, thick and strong, but this was low down in the car, the upper body was weak, the non-structural roof was plastic (latterly metal). Although it had a big front firewall/bulkhead, the DS lacked inner structures in its front wings and crash impact was forced back into the A-pillars which then intruded into the cabin as they collapsed.

Citroën's wonderful car, its defining sculpture, its technology beloved by so many (including my family), had a secret – an elephant in the room – its crash performance did not reach high standards.

Rover knew about this alleged flaw and ensured that their use of the 'base unit' structural underframe technique incorporated significant improvements to increase its crash safety. Rover fitted steel fillets to the A-pillars, armour-plated the bulkhead and front floor pan, securely welded the stiff B-pillars to the sills and strengthened the C-pillars. Rover made the sills very deep and also sited the fuel tank ahead of the rear axle. Extra-thick steel was used in the doors, too. Rover's designers also created the first-ever use of leg protecting 'shin pads' as absorbers in the 'glove lockers' that were the lower half of the heavily padded fascia – remember this was before people wore safety belts by default or law. Only the rather thin steering wheel arms were at variance with the 'padded' thinking of the cabin.

The steering box was mounted high up to avoid it being pushed back into the cabin in heavy impact.

As a result of all this extra engineering, in the standard 100 per cent full-frontal crash test, the P6 performed very well indeed (the later P9/10 did not and was cancelled). Even in the non-standard offset or partial overlap (50 per cent or less) crash test, not then part of any regulatory testing, the Rover did well, the only issue being that forces were transmitted by the front suspension's cranked arm via its scuttle/bulkhead mounting into the A-pillar which could suffer some intrusion.

'Sold on Safety' was the headline for the P6 which was awarded the first AA Gold Rosette for Safety (1967). Volvo's extra-strong 140 would soon receive AA plaudits too.

Rover's advertising told a safety story:

> 'Safety by design: The strength and safety of the 2000 is founded on a steel base unit which carries all the mechanical components and forms the passenger compartment. Occupants therefore sit in what is virtually a steel cage with a very strong bulkhead forward of the fascia to afford good protection in the event of an accident. In respect of a head-on collision this bulkhead prevents the engine being pushed back into the passenger compartment.'

When we remember that this was all designed prior to launch in 1963 and was several years ahead of Volvo or Saab's own armour-plated, reinforced cabin 'safety cell' designs in the Volvo 140 and Saab 99 respectively, the true engineering achievement of the Rover team should become more obvious. P6 was structurally 'safer' than most cars at launch and stayed that way for years.

An advanced rear suspension deploying the expensive de Dion mechanism was modified and fitted to reduce rear-wheel drive oversteer effects and roll rates. P6's front and rear suspension mechanisms had the wonderful thing – plenty of depth and 'travel'; long travel suspension in dampers, springs, and loadings allows bad road surfaces to be absorbed and noise, vibration and harshness to be minimised – something today's car drivers have little experience of.

The front suspension used expensive double wishbones (racing car practice) and saw a bell-cranked type spring mechanism mounted on the armour-plated bulkhead. One added benefit of this was that the car's structure absorbed 'bump thump' and road vibration far better than normal. The idea had been to leave the inner wings free of encumbrances so that a turbine engine could be fitted in width-wise.

All-round disc brakes (in-board at the rear) added to the technical tour-de force in 1963.

Lightweight aluminium alloy was used extensively in the engine and gearbox. A two-stage duplex roller chain drove an overhead camshaft which acted directly onto the vertically inclined valve-gear through bucket tappets, eliminating the need for inefficient and noisy rocker arms. The cylinder head was flat and on the Rover 2000 models, the pistons have a deep dished 'heron' crown creating an inverted hemispherical chamber for effective combustion long before the Jaguar high efficiency heads.

P6 four-cylinder TC models were also given racing standard breathing; a four-branch tubular header exhaust system was fitted as standard to complement a water-heated ported inlet manifold with twin 2-inch SU carburettors – the largest carburettors ever fitted to a British production car.

All Rover P6 cars came with a pioneering ventilation system, safety-design headrests and despite some roll-angles, superb long-distance, mile-eating handing. The V8 arrived in 1968 – a true performance saloon with true grunt and revised handling and a big cooling vent under the front bumper. The automatic-only V8 was a huge character but drank fuel like a Super VC10 on a hot day – so in 1971, Rover finally offered manual transmission via a tweaked 3500 'S'. 0-60mph in under 9 seconds – yes, 9 seconds – and running on to 120 mph marked this car out as something truly special. Germans loved them, Americans, rated them, Aussies adored them. Latterly, the 2200 TC debuted in 1973 and was a refined cruiser and performer easily capable of 30 mpg if you were careful.

The P6 cars were true to their badges – Viking flagships yet utterly British and frankly, one of the very best things to come out of Great Britain in its post-war history.

As the P6 owners' club currently so rightly states:

'Probably the most technologically accomplished saloon car the British motor industry has ever produced, the Rover P6 is the defining sports saloon of a generation. With performance, style and safety in equal measure, it is one the most innovative and attainable performance classic cars you can buy today.'

Rover absorbed into Leyland prior to the great merger, had a glittering future but inside the BMC, BMH and then BLMC affair, it found itself not only internally competing with Jaguar and Triumph, it also found its fantastic projects killed off by Stokes.

Ironically, Triumph was founded by a German émigré and his German business partner. Splitting from the motorcycle business in 1936, Triumph cars lay inside the

Standard Motor Company and then the Standard-Triumph Ltd outcome. Triumph produced significant sportsters and defining sporting saloons. It also created the Triumph Herald which was a glitzed-up (blinged!) small runabout touched by the hand of Italy's styling maestro, Giovanni Michelotti. He went on to style all Triumph's subsequent output. He also styled very many Japanese cars of the 1960s and 1970s but never had his name upon them nor was he cited by their manufacturers; Michelotti touched more mass production 'world' cars than any of his contemporaries.

Possibly one of the greatest British sports cars was the Triumph TR4/A (with or without IRS). Introduced in 1961, was it a poor man's E-Type? Whatever your view, TR4 was defining, brilliant and of course, Michelotti-styled, its sporting successes mirrored by its owners' enthusiasms. It was proudly build at Liverpool Speke.

The TR6 – a 150 bhp Triumph 'Straight-Six' – was a serious sports car but had the unenviable task of being the first BLMC sports car to emanate from the BMC merger in 1969. You would not have found Stokes intending to restyle or even cancel that! Contrary to stated views, TR6 was not 'completely' styled by Karman of Osnabruck, but 'restyled' by them from Michelotti's TR4/TR5 origins. Just under 100,000 TR6s were manufactured.

Yet when Triumph ended up inside the BLMC tent (via Leyland), there was no need for a new small Triumph like the Herald, yet we ended up with a bodyshell that gave us an in-line engine that was *front-driven* for the 1300 and later 1500, a rear-driven Toledo model, and then a Dolomite badged version of the same thing but which cost more! But wait, it gained a very early mass market sixteen-valve high performance (slant-four) engine of Spen King engineering, a chain cam, and went on to race and rally success.

In fact this Dolomite Sprint was a BMW 3-Series competitor despite the Triumph's antediluvian underpinnings which so detracted from its ride and handling offering. Confusingly, BL then spread the Dolomite name downwards to rename the 1500/Toledo types. This was badge engineering gone mad again – as applied to an antique car amid a market packed with 'real' new cars. Here lay more marketing madness.

Incredibly, the boxy little 1300 was selling over 30,000 a year when Triumph was absorbed into BLMC.

Triumph gave us the TR sports car ranges – which opened up the 1950s British car sales market in the USA alongside MG and Allard. Triumph gave us the defining TR3, TR5, TR5, and later TR6. Spitfire, GT6, these were true icons. Super styling, advanced suspension, great engines, cars with real class all came together to deliver the likes of the brilliant 2000, 2500, Stag.

The 2000 was elegant and a true sporting gentleman's saloon. It was re-styled by Michelotti into a modern facelift with a 2500 engine that was injected. These were troublesome so the 2500S reverted to carburettors. It lasted well into the 1970s and had a loyal following amid Triumph fans.

In fact, the 2500 was manufactured up to 1978 when it sold just 468 economically unviable examples – down from over 6,000 in 1977. Enter the rival Rover's new SD1 and the death of the big, sporting Triumph saloon.

As with MG, BL starved Triumph of new model opportunities, binned the SD2 and Puma prototypes designed to take Triumph into the 1980s to save money, only then for the legends of its cars and Harry Webster's work to be consumed and subsumed into the Rover-Triumph tribal battle inside BL. Then came Michael Edwardes, forced as he was by prior circumstance into the despicable act that was the Triumph-badged iteration of the decidedly un-civic, Honda Ballade/Civic badge-engineered project and its outcome as a Triumph of little 'Acclaim'.

So would die one of the oldest and greatest names in British motoring.

As at Triumph, in MG lay greatness and the foundations of British sports car legend in America and far beyond. Like Triumph, MG was to become a true victim of the BMC merger. BL and all that happened to it, led to the demise of MG. Yet MG is not dead, say some.

What on earth would Mr Kimber have made of this? Perhaps it is best not to ask. Kimber, like Sydney Allard started out as a garagiste who built his own 'Specials' prior to founding an empire and becoming world famous on a massive scale.

From the late-1920s, MG became a huge brand in Britain and amid its Dominions. Post-war mobility saw the MG marque and its revised old cars and its new cars, spread to global fame. From TF to TC Midget, to MGA, MG carved an incredible niche. MG's boss John Thornely and his Chief Engineer Sydney Enever faced the serious questions of the Nuffield organisation and then of the merged 1950s BMC, about MG's very future and even its manufacturing location. The only bright spot was the availability of BMC's Austin engines.

The MG men came up with the MGA – itself a stepping stone of innovation in design. After MGA's derivations came 'EX205' as the project that led to the MGB – a car that boasted a twenty year production run – became an icon across the decades, and a reincarnation as an excellent but pointless RV8. Yet MGB, MGC, GT, and V8 had it all. Here was a true icon, not an over-hyped icon. MG's proud men of Abingdon-upon-Thames created an advanced aircraft technology derived 'hull' for the car, applied magic to proprietary parts and created a legend.

MG advertised the MGB as 'Superlative' and it was. Men like Don Hayter, Jim O'Neill, Terence Mitchell and a small team made all this happen.

With the Healeys creating their own monocoque sports cars, MG's new offering had to be special. It also had to beat Triumph's sportsters as the main competitor and out-perform the brief but notable 1950s highlights of Allard – notably in America via Watkins Glen and Sebring.

O'Neill and Hayter 'styled' the new MGB as an evolving process and took many cues into their organic, fuselage-esque shape – all reinforced by a Mr Brocklehurst's (who would later assess the Leyland Australia P76 for British use, at MIRA) body engineering skills and some development from Pressed Steel Ltd and its ex-aviation industry engineers. MGB had a very high torsional rigidity rating for an 'open' car. So MG had made a 'safe' car long before it became either fashionable or a requirement. MGB was very safe and the only improvements later found to be structurally beneficial was an experiment of adding foam padding to the side doors and revised locks and plates. This reduced side-impact intrusion very significantly. The Pininfarina-influenced GT coupé did not however, fit a roll-over bar into its fixed roof, which was regrettable. Yet the Leyland safety project created the MGBGT SSV1 as a safety study that did include body reinforcement and a rollover hoop in the cabin. Curiously, due to new U.S. legislation, 1968 MGB for sale in America featured a new, heavily padded dashboard and further minor safety improvements to cabin and external fittings. The hardy British buyer was not offered such!

Amid the great BMC marquee, MG was soon forced to be part of badge engineering, but the tweaks, of engine, suspension, performance, handling, trim and identity that MG worked into humble BMC saloon bodyshells, can only be described as a more successful part of BMC's badge engineering and the internal wars that followed.

With BLMC in evolving cash and model crises by 1972, rationalisation began to creep in to the competing marques. Donald Stokes and then George Turnbull decided that it would be Triumph who would be the brand to lead on a new sports car for the 1970s global market. MG were not even invited to tender. Many think that this was the moment that MG began its death. Within five years, as 1978 closed, MG was at serious risk. The idea of an Aston Martin (Lagonda) consortium bid to step in to purchase MG became enmeshed amid rights, badge/trademark, finance and political issues but it did not stop an intriguing modified MGB design proposal (William Towns). Aston's Alan Curtis tried but failed to secure a new independent future for MG in 1979. By early 1980, the problems had stopped the Curtis consortium. Soon MG of Abingdon, late of Morris, its garages, and a global fame, would be gone. Utterly bizarrely, today, the MG badge is the only one from the BMC/BL story that survives as a trading entity – but in another, Chinese-owned form.

Yet Jaguar XJ6, Rover P6, Triumph TR3/4/5/6 and the 2000, MGB GT/V8, and many of the cars of these great marques represent the true car craft, the artisan, the skills of engineering and design genius that built Great Britain. The fact that they are gone, is a tragedy beyond belief. Helping them along their way, was the hidden politics of strike-bound Britain.

5
1960s: Strike-bound Before Stokes
The Paradox of Hindsight

The BL of the 1970s is said to have suffered at the hands of the strikers. It certainly did. But contrary to perceived and oft-published 'wisdom', this endemic British strike-bound condition was *not* born of Thatcher, or even of Heath in the 1970s. The 'truth' is that as early as 1959, Britain's workers and unions were unhappy, militant, and given to regular walk-outs and strikes that had a very serious effect on car production and resulted in significant damage not just to BMC, but to Triumph, Rover, Jaguar and others. But not all these walk-outs or strikes were unjustified. Working conditions were often appalling and piece-rate pay unreliable. Pay at BMC and then at BLMC was an issue – low piece-work rates and long hours lay within the causes and the effects. However, other factors, notably political ones, were at play too.

Post-war Britain was all mixed up in terms of class, hierarchies and the actual structure of our society. The Second World War had ripped up the social order, challenged set conventions and freed people from a frankly feudal society where if you were not rich and upper crust, your chances of self-improvement were minimal.

The changes to British society of the early 1960s reflected these problems and were also a reaction to them. There was also the 1950s effect upon people of the 'Cold War', rising Left-wing activism, the wretched wars of Malaya, Korea (and soon Vietnam), Suez and more. Oh, and the Jaguar E-Type and the Mini just about summed up the differing nature of British society as the 1950s became the 1960s. Patrician old-Tory 'toff' rule from Macmillan, Anthony Eden and Alec Douglas-Home would be swept away. Labour would come to power and Viscount Stansgate, Anthony Wedgewood-Benn, would become the untitled, Left-leaning 'Tony' Benn in a Harold Wilson government – an interventionist regime of policy imposition. An 'Industrial Reorganisation Committee' was the vehicle to implement such intervention and no arguments to the contrary would be accepted. And the National Enterprise Board (NEB), was set up by Labour – to become so hated by Tories of the 1970s.

It was Wilson who, prior to his premiership, when president of the Board of Trade, had relaxed controls on sterling and the US dollar in and out of the British economy. He did not realise it, but this single move would within two decades, leverage the great financial boom in the city of London just as Margaret Thatcher arrived to take credit for it amid her 'privatisation economy'. Wilson's moves, including setting up BL via the great 1968 merger, would have profound effects. Thatcher would receive blame and credit for her policies and effects yet many of them were laid down by prior governments. Similarly, New Labour would benefit from and continue these policies and their cycles – until the bubble burst.

The BMC merger would create new shares and new shareholders amid a massive company with a global reach and market share – this was the kind of prospectus that Thatcher's 1980s was built upon, yet one of the biggest such moves was BMC to BLMC under Wilson in 1968.

Behind the scenes in the mid-1960s, Prime Minister Harold Wilson had been adamant that the merger of Britain's big motoring marques *would* take place but contrary to some narratives, it did not begin with BMC. Tony Benn was the likely first mover of the motor industry merger idea in political terms as Minister of Technology – it was Benn who called the two giant companies in for exploratory discussions – but note, *not* in relation solely to BMC and Leyland, as so many have since stated.

Given the government's other troubles, notably the devaluation crisis and issues in the aerospace industry, and the looming on-off nature of Britain's EEC involvement, a motor industry merger was a possible success with good political potential at the ballot box. But did that strategy ignore the structural weaknesses that lay within the pre-planned policies of the main players? Was forensic due diligence applied? Or did Harold Wilson and Tony Benn get carried away on the wings of political and ideological expediency? Here the 'greatness' of Wilson as perceived, might be accurately challenged.

The merger idea was hardly a Communist 'five-year' plan, but *was* it ideology which curiously, and utterly paradoxically, happened to have fitted into the ideas of motor industry capitalists who dreamed of a massive global 'motors' empire?

It seems this might be so, yet the merger appeared a rational idea; was it less ideology and more strategic pragmatism? The merger might create a British big beast that could fight off the ever-encroaching American manufacturers. Ford in Dagenham was one thing, but Chrysler making waves and owning car plants across England and Scotland was something else entirely.

Despite a long-running series of 1960s motor industry union disputes and strikes (amid other national strikes), the government and the corporate men urged on the idea of merging Britain's biggest and most strike-prone car makers, and without addressing that very issue.

What could possibly go wrong?

The answer was, a very great deal. Something was wrong with society, not just on the factory floor.

BL is synonymous with 1970s strikes, but the reality is that the strike condition first manifested as early as 1959 at BMC. In 1959, BMC sacked its senior union convenor at Cowley, whom you are unlikely to have heard of. His name was Frank Horsman and he became a 'name' long before Derek Robinson – who you have heard of. There followed many walk-outs and disputes. Cowley had communists within its workforce, and so what, you might ask.

From 1959 onwards, while it was producing just under one million cars per year, the British motor industry was convulsed by a series of strikes and daily walk-outs that cost it dear. These disputes would go on for nearly four years. Jaguar was seriously affected by strikes in 1960 and beyond, Sir William's renowned 'economies' extending beyond the cars to the workforce it is claimed.

The ironical thing is that BMC and the British brands were at this time world famous, with huge marketing and customer profile and the competition was minimal. They also had a massive global export market in the remains of the empire and amid the Commonwealth and the Dominions. The likes of VW and BMW were still producing dire cars; they had yet to reinvent themselves and their cars. Japanese competition was invisible, and BMC had begun to build cars all over the world, notably in Africa and Australia, with very profitable outcomes. BMC started building cars in Rhodesia in 1960 and was soon selling 3,000 to 7,000 cars a year in this corner of East Africa alone.

Why did BMC's market share decline at this time? Bad cars? No, *great* cars including ADO16 as the 1100-1300, and the Mini, but they both existed amid an inability to build such cars due to strikes and poor productivity and BMC lost money on each car built. Customers would not wait six to twelve months for a car. Production costs were high on these cars, and profits low. And they were built by poorly paid workers using ancient pre-war technology on a factory floor that was less than ideal due to lack of investment; in fact the factories were prehistoric in terms of conditions and equipment – some of the BMC factories were said to be health and safety violations on a grand scale, reflecting the failure by BMC's 1950s-1960s management to update factories and facilities via investment, leading to genuine grievances of the workers and inefficient car production.

Over at Leyland, managing director Donald G. Stokes (to become variously entitled, Sir, Lord, and Baron) was to become the new boy on the block as he replaced Sir William Black.

Other things happened in the industry too. Standard-Triumph faltered and Rover's advanced new P6-series cars were to be badly affected at launch by strikes and long delivery waits (long before the SD1 would suffer the same fate at BL nearly twenty years later).

Leyland made trucks, heavy vehicles, buses and tractors and was born from the works of two men – Henry Spurrier and James Sumner who formed a Lancashire Steam Motor Company near Preston.

Leyland's first export sale was of a steam-powered light van to Ceylon in 1901. Leyland embraced such oddities as steam-powered grass cutters and then a steam-powered lorry or wagon. By 1905, the company had focused on petrol combustion-engined vehicles including buses. The business prospered and by 1907 had changed its name to Leyland Motors. The First World War provided accelerated development in vehicle and aircraft design. Leyland was to manufacture over 1,200 petrol-engined vehicles by 1915 and many more by the war's end in 1918. The famous engineer, J.G. Parry Thomas was Leyland's, chief engineer and he turned out lorry designs – notably the RAF-type lorry for military use. Ably assisted by no less a figure than Reid Railton, Thomas had his ideas set upon producing a Leyland car for the 1920s.

With a 6.9 litre straight-eight engine of overhead valve type, and other thoughtful features, such car was hardly antediluvian.

Leyland of Lancashire went on to build a legacy of commercial vehicles and more. They were world-class machines yet became obscured by the BL 'cars' headlines. By 1966, Leyland made heavy commercial vehicles all over the world and had absorbed the truly iconic Triumph (Standard-Triumph) marque. Leyland was profitable and Stokes was a superstar in his own world.

Leyland would sell a range of trucks, buses and excellent tractors into the 1980s.

Britain, British society, was deeply marked by a strike and dispute culture a decade *before* the better known 1970s BL union disputes and burning braziers, as part-built cars sat on static production lines awaited unhappy men to return and throw them together amid a collective mass-depressive syndrome of the disgruntled; men who may well have been 'agitated' by external factors and parties.

Could the likes of BMC and even the profitable Leyland continue? They had vast cost-bases and with BMC's badge-engineering, the operating costs, which included dozens of small factories and suppliers spread all over the country, were huge.

Leyland of course had a truly global truck and bus, commercial business that made money.

In straight business terms, there was little sense in merging the British car giants, unless you were going to cut costs, share engines, drivetrains, chassis, bodies and trims amid something other than the cynical badge-engineering that had already been tried by BMC.

Doing a General Motors by allowing separate marques to design separately shaped cars of distinctly individual characters, yet which *hid* their economies of shared engines, chassis and hidden details, could have been the answer. After all, this is how GM made its billions – by design – yet it was design which convinced the buyers that their choice of car, their brand loyalty was being met and valued, even if underneath their bodies' skins, the cars shared as many, mass-volume, money-saving engineering components as possible.

This is not what had happened at BMC nor what would happen at BL, and would not be prescribed for the big British brands such as Austin, Morris, Riley, and Wolseley and eventually beyond them.

So if clever British motor industry men were reluctant to amalgamate, if they were only going to produce the kind of badge-engineered clones that BMC had already toyed with, more powerful forces of reasoning must have been at work to achieve what happened as the great merger of 1968.

Those forces were corporate power and politics, yes politics and, specifically, Harold Wilson's Labour government and its ideology. That an officer-class sales supremo like Lt Col. Donald G. Stokes, ex-Territorials/REME, should go along with it seems rather intriguing, surely?

But did Harold Wilson threaten Stokes – with nationalising Stokes' own Leyland? Some say this was the lever with which Stokes was clouted over the head.

It has been suggested that Donald Stokes was reluctant to consider or embrace a merger, and that Benn and Wilson were the forces behind it. Indeed, this is now an oft-repeated claim. But there is evidence to a different story that few have touched upon.

Firstly, those who worked for Stokes, men in senior positions, have suggested that a man of Stokes' drive, determination and sales orientated energy, could see the massive profile and power he would personally gain from being the commander-in-chief of a merged BMC-Leyland. Stokes was popular and very far from being a hard-Right capitalist, yet he was not without ego and power. He also knew he had to make money and pay shareholders their dividends. Indeed, in 1968, Stokes told the media that he had been minded to make a takeover bid for BMC, *prior* to the suggested merger.

Stokes should not be 'blamed' for BMC to BL, but to absolve him completely from any responsibility seems odd. By his own admission, he had thought similar thoughts to Wilson and Benn about a merger, but as a takeover, amid a different commercial and political context.

But, hidden in the records, is a little-cited story that pre-dates the 1968 BMC and Leyland merger.

On 13 September 1966, the rarely-cited National Advisory Committee for the Motor Manufacturing Industry (NACMMI) held a Whitehall meeting to discuss the problems of the motor industry and the national economy. Those present included Leyland's Sir Donald Stokes, BMC's Sir George Harriman, and numerous officials, civil servants, and trades unions representatives. Chaired by Tony Benn, it was apparently (as he described to the author[1] and in his diaries[2]) a difficult discussion because the problems of the British economy, the need for exports sales, and the need to earn money from export sales allied to the needs in the domestic motor industry, were presenting a paradoxical situation – because expanding the domestic or home market was also key to the export drive and vice versa. Stokes remember was a superb salesman and global exporter. Production, sales, profit and exports needed to go up whichever way you looked at the problem.

Benn aired numerous options, but none it seemed sat well with the main players – Stokes and Harriman. Stokes opined that the motor industry should not be used as a mechanism to control or manipulate the British economy. Benn tried to suggest potential options to deal with the motor industries' issues but made little progress. An impasse was apparently reached. The meeting closed without plan or agreement.

Soon afterwards, Benn would discuss his anxieties about the car industry with Richard Bullock, a senior figure in the civil service. The issue of the machine tooling industry and its dependence on the ailing motor industry was of concern. But this was September 1966, and no known official record of a suggested merger between any of the British car manufacturers is suggested.

The ancient Rootes car company, family controlled, had run into problems in the early 1960s. Intriguingly, its problems were a precursor scenario to those that would afflict BMC at the end of the same decade. Rootes had a limited and dated model range, and it was struggling to adapt to the new era and produce its own new cars – the Hillman Imp notwithstanding. Rootes had also faced the costs of having factories, infrastructure and suppliers scattered across the map of Britain. Alternating government policies of both main parties had not helped either.

The previous, Conservative, government stepped in when it became clear that Chrysler of America were looking at investing in Rootes. That government then decided that such investment would only be allowed under the terms of a categoric, contracted agreement that Chrysler would be a smaller partner and not under any circumstances 'take-over' Rootes, nor own in excess of 51 per cent of its shares. Under such agreement, Chrysler was allowed to buy into Britain's Rootes by a Conservative prime minister.

Fast forward less than five years and a Labour government was in power and a certain ex-Viscount Anthony Wedgwood-Benn MP, (Tony Benn), was overseeing the mid-1960s issues of the British motor industry for Prime Minister Harold Wilson.

By the summer of 1966, British football notwithstanding, Rootes was still in trouble.

By 15 December 1966, Stokes and Harriman had once again be called in, to discuss the motor industry situation.

Benn and his boss Harold Wilson had been trying to come up with ideas to improve the financial situation of the nation and of the motor industry – the two being related and linked factors to national economic well-being. And Rootes was now in very serious trouble indeed. Stokes and Harriman met Wilson and Benn on 15 December in London and Benn posed three questions to the two leaders of Britain's motor empire. The questions asked if (a) Chrysler should be allowed a total take-over of Rootes which would create a third American player inside Britain alongside Ford and General Motors/Vauxhall; (b) was a 'British' solution possible or desired; and (c) if so, would the two great men consider saving Rootes from bankruptcy and or foreign (i.e. Chrysler) take-over, by *merging* their companies with Rootes as a greater national conglomerate that would receive Government backing and financial support?

Here, then, was the first suggestion of a merger, but it was *not*, a merger between just BMC and Leyland, but a tripartite merger to 'save' Rootes and merge Rootes into a BMC-Leyland-Rootes company. The sole purpose of the suggested merger was to save Rootes for the nation. The plan also fitted into Labour's own political psychology.

According to Benn, neither Stokes nor Harriman (two very different characters) would agree to such a thing and that there was conflict between them. As a result, the previous government's agreement with Chrysler that protected Rootes from a total Chrysler take-over was torn up and Harold Wilson was forced to let Chrysler purchase Rootes in its entirety. There were no other choices left other than the bankruptcy and closure of Rootes amid all the sociological and political problems that would cause all over the country, including in electorally vital Scotland.

Here, then, in 1966, is evidenced the idea of *earlier* merger – one involving three car manufacturers, not two. Stokes resisted, but did it make him realise or further realise, that he would get an ideal opportunity to consider what he later admitted and stated was his own thought – of his Leyland taking over not Rootes, but BMC?

There was more to come.

Just over ten months after that December 1966 meeting, on 11 October 1967, Benn stated in his diary[3] (and to the author) that he had heard a rumour that Donald Stokes was going to make a bid for BMC. As we know, Stokes later admitted to such a possibility. So Benn's claim of such has an external and confirmatory reference.

Acting upon such rumour, Benn called Stokes to Chequers on 15 October 1967 to discuss with him and Harold Wilson a suggested merger in the national interest. But Benn had also invited Sir George Harriman of BMC! And Stokes and Harriman were like water and oil, they did not mix. But out of such meeting came the actual merger of BMC and Leyland within just three months. Benn and Wilson had moved fast, Harriman was perhaps not able to keep up with the decisive buccaneer that was Stokes.

Sir George Harriman of BMC was a diplomat of the 'old school' and probably unused to dealing with a mind like that of Donald Stokes, for Sir Donald Stokes of Leyland and famed as 'Mr Export' in the media, was powerful, decisive, perhaps thrusting and ruthless. He would soon become well-regarded by Harold Wilson. He has often been cited as being both a capitalist and as being politically Centrist, yet no such allegiances are definitive. But Stokes openly admitted he was out to make money. And the truth was that without money, somebody's money, BLMC was dead.

Whatever the reality, surely Stokes should not be blamed (as so many have done) for what happened after the great merger. Could *anyone* have known nor foreseen what would occur inside BL and to BL? But was Stokes an innocent lamb led to the fire by the machinations of politicians? That too, is unlikely. But he would be forced into some unpopular decisions, yet they were *his* decisions.

Wilson and Benn pushed things along and Leyland's finance director John Barber (ex-Ford) was to prove key to the moving on of the idea amid talks and arbitration from the Industrial Reorganisation Corporation under Sir Frank Kearton.

BLMC emerged as 1967 became 1968 and stemmed from the forced marriage of BMC (actually now listed as British Motor Holdings, BMH) and Leyland Motors Ltd. The two companies had diverse histories going back to the dawn of our motoring. Between them they had scooped up the great marques of England.

But the non-Leyland part of the DNA of BMC-to-BL stems from Austin and Morris and the amalgamations that had swallowed the major brand names into the camps that mutated into what became BMC. The Leyland name was chosen because it was Leyland that actually led the merging of the brands in 1968 under government decree. Oh, and Leyland was in profit and BMC/BMH was not.

Late at night, around 1.00 am on Monday 15 January 1968 at Donald Stokes' flat in London, the fate of the British car and commercial industry was set and sealed in an agreement to merge British Motor Holdings (the old 'BMC') and Leyland Motors.

Ironically, just a few hours later, 6,630 Midlands car workers at the Austin plant at Longbridge, would be temporarily laid off because of a strike of just 130, externally-employed delivery drivers at the vital Pressed Steel-Fisher body plant at Castle Bromwich. Restructuring and a change of employment from one department to a new agency, likely to reduce hours and weekly wages, lay behind the walk-out.

It was an almost invisible cloud upon the great fanfares of the BMH-Leyland merger agreed on the previous day and quickly announced on Thursday 18 January to avoid share speculation.

So the truth is that the 'BL' story began with a strike! In fact it started with two, because production of the Rover 2000 at Solihull had also been disrupted due to a strike in early January. Very few observers or commentators have pointed out that these were the ironic and sadly prescient circumstances of BL's birth. As British Leyland Motor Corporation was born, a strike was happening.

Was BMC *already* in trouble?

So was founded the amalgamation of BMC/BMH and Leyland Motors with (at 1968 prices) £410 million of share value assets as a defined BLMC brand. This created in January 1968 the biggest automotive concern outside of the United States of America and the second-biggest multi-marque car company in the world – a million cars a year was within its grasp. It was Britain's fifth biggest company in terms of units of products sold. There had been a share value imbalance between Leyland and BMH and some degree of modification and financial adjustments had to be made. Leyland had to alter its share capital in order to allow negotiations to proceed.

In 1963-64, BMC sold 730,862 cars.[4] BMC sales stayed near that figure for several years up to 1968. In 1967, BMC had sold over £465 million worth of cars yet *lost* £3.2m, but *had* made £20m profit in 1966. So there was a problem with fiscal yield and costs – underlying, operating and manufacturing.

Leyland had falling profits at £16m for 1967 but *was* in surplus. The vital profit on product margins were 5 per cent for BMH and 6 per cent for Leyland, respectively.

Leyland's Donald Stokes said to the media he nearly made a total takeover bid instead of the merger that had been created at political instigation. He said he would have won such a battle, but instead, he side-stepped it in order to avoid losing the 'goodwill' of the BMC management. How considerate of him.

But remember, it was as far back as 1966 that a merger (albeit involving Rootes) had been suggested by Benn and Wilson, and Stokes had had two years to make his plans. In the end, all the cards fell his way.

Stokes acted the role of a straight-talking northerner, but the truth was he had been brought up in the south and attended a minor, 'posh' public school. He had been an officer in the war. Perhaps army service had roughed up a few soft-southern edges. In truth, Stokes and Leyland did 'take-over' BMC in many contexts. Jaguar's Sir William Lyons must have pondered his fate at the news of the merger, for Jaguar had only just joined the BMC camp.

Buried within the new BLMC name with Stoke's character stamped all over it, lay the likes of AEC, Standard-Triumph, Scammell, Thornycroft, Park Royal Vehicles, Maudslay Motor Company, C.H. Roe Ltd, Rover, Alvis, Aveling-Barford and a host of suppliers and smaller engineering companies.

Alvis had been significant in the history of Britain. It had made cars, tanks, aircraft engines, and much more. In the 1920s and 1930s, Alvis made fantastic sports cars, notably the 12/50 and the Silver Eagle series; in 1928 Alvis was at Le Mans. Alvis even made a front-wheel drive car in the 1930s and a range of 'Speed' models. No less a figure than George Lanchester designed the 1930s Alvis 12/70. During the Second World War, Alvis aero-engines made an important contribution. The 'Leonides' engine also had civil applications. Few recall that Issigonis worked for Alvis inside the early 1950s BMC tent and created a new engine and new suspension designs, which Alvis was not resourced to advance.

Post-war Alvis turned out elegant up-market sports cars and gentleman's coupés, notably the Graber-bodied cars. Under its 'red triangle' was a significant British brand of technical importance. The company was absorbed into Rover in 1965 and ceased car production two years later, although military vehicle manufacture did continue. If only Alvis' multi-bearing six cylinder engine of smoothness and efficiency had been alive inside BLMC! Intriguingly, the Alvis badge was suggested as a suitable vehicle for the proposed Rover 2000 coupé – but it was not to be.

Was Alvis the 'lost' marque of post-war England? Should, could, BMC and BL have made more of Alvis instead of sticking Riley and Wolseley badges on everything from a Land Crab, a Mini, to an 18-22, and making a Vanden Plas Allegro?

Alvis truly was engineering excellence and truly upper crust. Douglas Bader owned more than one Alvis and would shout, 'Make way for quality!' when he pulled out to perform a probably risky overtake.

Alvis was adored, but it was wasted.

We should also recall that Jaguar had only come under the BMH wing in 1966 – just as its world class XJ-series was launched. Stokes signed the merger deal as 1968 had dawned and stated that the new company would 'storm' the world's markets. With 200,000 employees and £500m per year in sales, BLMC was a huge and powerful beast. A further £25 million was made available through the Industrial Reorganisation Corporation as loan capital for future expansion.

Immediate rationalisation and cost cutting would follow, when 'badge engineering' would really take off after BMC's earlier go at it. But it would be cynical badge-engineering, where cars that were very obviously identical would be sold as being of differing brand and badge. Here lay another reason why British car buyers turned to the ever increasing competition. And MG was to be key victim of the cost-savings and rationalisation Stokes was forced to implement.

As a vignette of the problems Stokes' new BLMC brand faced, let's remember that from 1968's BMC-Leyland merger it was not until 1976 that the last of the old BMC dealerships removed their Austin or Morris signage and became BL-branded. Ironically, by 1980 more new signs were going up at the (remaining) dealerships. They stated 'Austin-Morris'. A few years later they would be replaced with more new signs that stated 'Austin-Rover'.

The final signs would say 'For Sale, business/residential development opportunity'. Alternatively, new signs would finally go up and they might say 'Ford' or 'Kia'.

But back with the merger, the production of one million vehicles – cars and commercials – per year, was the vital target. BLMC now had a monopoly on home-grown British car design and production and no one realised that this might allow the monolith to dictate to its customers what *it* thought that *they* should want!

There were however warning signs that stemmed from the merger. Integrating models, rationalising the ranges and the internally conflicting brands, and ameliorating rising operating costs while financing new model development and waiting up to five years for their arrival, could all be suggested as potential problems for the big new BLMC beast on the block. Normal motor industry cycles were to be disrupted.

Even in the 1960s, hundreds of millions of pounds in real, actual operating cash were required to run car factories and design the cars that they would be build. Assets in buildings and shares, meant very little in the car industry – as they still do because cash is, and was, king.

But it seems quite a few people looked the other way at the behest of corporate and political imperatives that leveraged the great BMC-Leyland merger. And anyway, wouldn't the share price shoot up?

Donald Stokes also said something to the British media in January 1968 that was very revealing indeed.

He said that he wanted to match the Ford Transit van, and Ford's and Vauxhall's new saloon cars; he said that he could not stop any pre-existing new BMC models that were in development but not yet in production (only the austerity-styled Maxi springs to mind), and he also said, 'I want to get our group to do the same things as Ford and Vauxhall, to be able to come out with new cars at proper intervals.'

Stokes also warned that too many factories spread too far producing too many cars was a risk, and that he hoped BLMC had enough time to sort out the issues. He referred to a battle.[5]

Clearly the writing was on the wall early on, but was anybody listening?

We might also ask, if Stokes knew the full implications of these issues beforehand, why undertake the 'merger' (reputedly, according to those who wish to defend him, against his informed judgement) in the first place? And why was he not questioned about such contradictions? After all, he wanted (and admitted to wanting) a BMC takeover and to stamp his ideas on the new giant car maker. The obituaries to Stokes upon his death many years later stated that he was 'given' the 'unenviable' task of amalgamating BMC and Leyland and turning around the British car industry. It is unlikely that Stokes would have meekly agreed to such order for the good of the nation and the Labour Party; there must have been something in it for him. It is unlikely that he buckled under the 'charm' of Benn and Wilson at Chequers to take on a task he did not wish to take on. And how many people cite the earlier meetings of these men in 1966 regarding the abortive BMC-Leyland-Rootes merger as suggested by Wilson and Benn?

Yet what Stokes' comments prove upon merger, is that all was not well underneath the great panoply of the big new BLMC tent that he and others had just erected. And he and they knew. Latter commentators like Turner seem to have lionised Stokes as a hero, but we might now ask if in fact he and his character and super salesman's charm and abilities, ignored known knowns in order to achieve his own goals? It is surely fair to say however, that he had the nation's best interests at heart.

In 1968, the engineering unions had all welcomed the BMC into BLMC merger – maybe as a way of protecting jobs by fighting off the American invasion of British car making – via Ford, and notably via Chrysler and by Vauxhall, all American owned. So the three largest unions, the Amalgamated Engineering Union, the National Union of Vehicle Builders, and the Transport and General Workers Union, all gave the merger their approval. Donald Stokes it seems, was highly regarded by them. Yet Hugh Scanlon of the AEU suggested the potential contraction of the workforce amid the contraction of cars and brands. But his views were put to one side it seems amid the headlong rush, aided by personal prime ministerial support and intervention, into 'saving' the British car and commercial industry through creating something big enough to fight off the Americans on a global as well as a national stage.

The first meeting of the Board of the new merged company took place on 19 February 1968 at Berkeley Square House. Those present included of course Donald Stokes, John Barber, Joe Edwards, Sir William Lyons, and George Turnbull. One name present was a Dr Albert Fogg – now a little-cited figure, he was running the commercial and truck side of the business to great effect. Critically, Sir George Harriman was missing (due to ill health), so Stokes ruled as stand-in Chairman, above his cited Deputy Chairman and Managing Director role, but Harriman was still a Chairman in his absence until he stepped down within months. Rover's Sir George Farmer was missing from the listed 'top jobs' of the new BLMC Board.

Little-known names of the BLMC Board also present were: T.A.E. Layborn; R.J. Lucas; J.H. Plane; R.A. Stormonth-Darling; and L.G. Whyte. The BLMC Company Secretary was T.N. Addison and his deputy was E. Pedlow. These men are the forgotten names of BLMC at its inception.

Of note, the actual share-holders' agreement to the merger and the related stock market document and shareholders' agreement, did not become official until 6 March 1968. So was born a £400 million company – one of the biggest in the world. It was not until Tuesday 14 May 1968 that everything was settled and the announcement of the official BLMC launch made to its workforce.

What became apparent very soon after the merger, soon after Stokes had lifted the proverbial drain covers, was that BMC had been in the middle of a mess – and BLMC made the mess worse. An obvious lack of strategy and a total lack of strategic command amid the myriad tribes, brands, factories, managers, union leaders, conveners and competing political ideologues became evident. Stokes had inherited more than a poisoned chalice and the sales figures were a false grail, a mirage. Stokes was told that 30,000 jobs needed to be cut from the newly merged brand's workforce in 1968. He demurred – and tried to raise sales well beyond one million cars per year. Why did Stokes avoid 30,000 redundancies? Simply because he lacked the political support and thus the power to enact them.

BMC's top designer the maverick Issigonis would have to go – he had ruled his roost for too long and Charles Griffin took over as chief designer and technical director with Harry Webster acting alongside him. After all, Austin may have been a fount of all things front-driven but MG, Rover and Triumph were paragons of rear-driven cars of great excellence – why should they be sidelined by Issigonis obsessions? Webster was latterly forced to save money on engine design which affected the crankshaft design of the vital O-series engine. This rendered the engine a rough runner.

Here lay a design, brand, sales and marketing schism inside the merger – one often forgotten.

All that Stokes found in the design studio pipeline was the Maxi – which he likened to a 'hen coop' and ordered to be slightly restyled without major tooling changes. Apart from a few ideas for what would become the Marina, and facelifts for ageing Issigonis designs became a temporary marketing device, otherwise the cupboard was bare.

Maxi was very clever, but in its early cable-operated gear change, synthetically moulded fascia (soon to revert to the conventional) and appearance of an angular greenhouse, it missed the marketing 'bling' mark that the Renault 16 had landed upon – yet Maxi was tougher, more rigid, more crashworthy, roomier, and more efficient. Maxi was launched at £980 – expensive and only just below the larger 18/22 series Land Crab. Yet Maxi was a trailblazer, a really sound idea, but its lack of style and the BL 'narrative' killed it – eventually! Oil leaks from the E-series engine and electrical malfeasances afflicted the car. Maxi was also the reason Allegro was denied the hatchback it had been conceived with. A hatchback was Maxi's USP!

Stokes the salesman also knew that consistency of branding was vital and stated in a BLMC document in 1970 that, 'As a world-wide organization, it is essential that the Corporation presents a unified front on a global basis'.

Sadly time and money were not generous to such plans.

By 1970, BLMC was still strike-bound and a further strike at Triumph's Canley plant was about whose job, and which demarcation, framed the screwing-in of screws on a Triumph dashboard.

Stokes would say to the press on 23 February 1970, 'I cannot believe that this state of anarchy is what the majority of our workers really want.'

Commenting upon the daily stoppages inside BLMC's plants, Stokes stated that such disputes 'can only be planned and deliberate', and that he believed that 'insidious coercion' was apparent.

Stokes knew BMC and BLMC had quality problems – the warranty claims and reputational profile proved that. Latterly inside BLMC there was a Specialist Car Division Advisory Board (SCDAB) that was tasked to look at warranty issues and their cause – a lack of build quality and a lack of quality from external parts suppliers (such, nearly killed Jaguar). But Stokes did not have urgent success in tackling the quality problems and it is a shame we cannot question him as to why not.

Was Stokes a villain or a hero? Unless you experienced what happened to MG after the merger – where the workers *did* blame Stokes for his decisions – then Stokes cannot be called a 'villain', and in some ways he was a 'hero', but his motives might not have been quite the act of selfless sacrifice at the altar of national good that some suggest.

By most accounts, Stokes was rational, ruthless, yet often considerate. But we have to ask why he allowed so many allegedly inept product planning decisions and a confused management structure to persist within BLMC from 1968 into the 1970s. He had power and he often used it, yet the problems of an over-stuffed and inter-tribal middle-management are obvious by the outcome of events. Maybe BL *was* too big for one man to effectively manage?

Of relevance, for example, in its post-merger BLMC iteration, Triumph of the 1970s had over fifty lead engineers. Good as they were, this must surely have led to conflict. And when this large group of men did agree and make a technical recommendation for the specification of a car, why was it turned down by a non-technically minded accountant 'bean-counter' – to the detriment of the car and its sales potential? Why were product planners arguing against the recommendations of engineers and designers? Here lay a core issue in what was wrong.

There were many more examples of confused strategy and internally inconsistent policy amid BLMC.

Of Stokes, Tony Benn would latterly suggest that Stokes had an eye, an inkling of the possibilities that were inherent in the merger. But that even he could not have known what would transpire. In the end he *was* the captain of the industry, but it was probably unfair for him to be tarnished by hindsight over BL. But, like BOAC and BEA, and the procurement rows, as Benn said, 'The whole thing became a mess and Britain suffered. Ultimately the BLMC merger did not succeed in achieving its objectives.'[6]

Often forgotten is that Stokes categorically stated that the amalgamated product range (of BLMC) could create a situation where the car ranges were in conflict with one another, inside the tent. He might, he said, cull the cars that did not sell but keep cars that were selling. He also referenced difficulties with new models already cast and in preparation, competing with each other.

So here is proof, absolute proof that the problems of BL were inherent at the BLMC launch, at its creation, and existed long before the era of 'Leyland bashing', the Allegro, Michael Edwardes, Derek Robinson, or Margaret Hilda Thatcher.

Yet what of Ford? As the 1960s closed, Ford was astounding and its marketing was well-funded and of significant impact upon the car buyer. Did Stokes think he could wipe out Ford? Corsair, then Cortina MKII and Capri should really have given him food for thought by 1970. Ford's 1973 Cortina MKIII made Stokes and BL sit and up and think – Ford threw hundreds of millions at the car and the selling of it and it began to approach the magical 200,000 cars a year sold on the British market alone. BL's rival, the Marina would only exceed 100,000 a year on a few occasions.

But what had really happened underneath the pomp and circumstance of BMC *before* it merged into BLMC? Did the British car industry need 'saving' as early as, not 1967, but 1960? We know it was so, we know of the horrendous costs in production terms of the strikes of 1959-1963 that had affected BMC and driven Jaguar, Triumph, and Rover into much needed saviours – BMC and Leyland respectively!

Morris Motors at Cowley had also evolved into a regular dispute and strike situation during the BMC years. Yet just down the road at Abingdon, the MG plant had an enviable industrial relations record.

Does the evidence trail show clearer light on the error of the entire 'blame' being attributed to the cars and the workers of the 1970s and the 1980s? In case you do not know, Britain was heavily strike-bound from 1959 onwards. Even the seamen went on strike in the 1960s!

That other great almost-state-owned corporation – the national airline that was BOAC – had been brought to a global standstill in 1959 by a walk-out and protest and strike of its tradesman over the treatment by BOAC of just five employees. An airline it may have been, but BOAC was an implement of British policy and strength across the world and it was stopped in its tracks by a major and globally publicised strike as early as 1959.

Agreements made between unions and employers according to Mr Justice Lane, commenting upon a dispute in law, were perhaps only bound by being 'made in honour'. The reality of Britain at this time was that unofficial strikes could easily become 'official' without due process, diligence or structured mechanism of agreed escalation, let alone arbitration.

Was a 'strike a day' a BL reality? The answer was yes – if you counted a walk-out or shop floor dispute leading to a 'down-tools' as a 'strike'.

Ford's workers were also on strike on a regular basis at this time. While we can see the Ford female workers' 'sewing machinists' dispute had merits, other strikes were less securely anchored in their claims.

Clearly, with the evidence leading back to BMC, the known pre-merger issues and the political contributions, we have proof that men, not just cars, created the BL affair. There followed much confusion.

6
The 'Fordisation' of BLMC
Merely Matching the Opposition?

From the 1950s through to the early 1970s, BLMC's brands under the BMC-to-BLMC marquee created advanced and clever cars that were proudly built by a dedicated workforce – however much the entrenched ideas of working class-to-upper management class behaviours and psyche may have been within the mix. But then, reality and the accountants took over, and then circumstances and politics led those same accountants to try and rationalise and amortise BL and its cars into a fiscal reality that saw 'badge engineering' and parts-bin concoctions become cars intended to represent the great marques of Britain.

That, as we know, did not go well. And instead of stepping back from the brink and selling cars by design, BL went with short termism – 'instant' fashion as consumer durable cars that could be replaced cheaply and quickly, not least by re-skinning old cars into new ones by the cheapest means possible. This was something Ford was good at, but they made it work. BL would be unable to copy the idea to completion.

So, for some car makers, notably Ford, underneath the flashy trim, new paint and new badges of new front wings, outer doors skins, and modified bonnets and boots, there lay a decade old car, its original suspension, its original floorpan and structure, all with the development and production costs and tooling costs paid for! Re-skin an old car, 'trick' it up to be 'new' and the route to sales and profit were guaranteed – providing the build quality was average and the breakdowns and warranty claims were average. No *real* advance in technology, design or engineering was offered. True you could add a small aerodynamic improvement to the new outer body panels, and some new seat fabrics, and a vinyl roof, new paint colours, and new trinkets, but underneath there lay the old.

This sort of behaviour was of course not in Issigonis' mind and he hated such tactics.

Therein lay the seeds of commercial problems – stopping the Issigonis design research psychology and 'process' inside BLMC, and changing the course of the cars and their marketing was a huge problem that few wanted to address. Issigonis was in charge and few dared challenge him. In a sad and paradoxical way, Issigonis the design superstar was to become part of the problem. He would, for entirely understandable and 'pure' engineering reasons, resist 'Fordisation'. Issigonis was a purist, the idea of car design by marketing and fashion was something that horrified him.

And facelifted cars or tame new design did little for advanced design. Of structural improvements, significant passive safety improvements, increased torsional strength, better handling, new engines, better aerodynamics, or some great advance inside *re-skinned* old-model range cars? Forget it. Re-warmed cars became the 1970s mass-market menu, where the car buying public were fed the least 'new' that manufacturers thought they could prescribe to a brainwashed car-buying public. Only the AlfaSud, Citroën GS and perhaps the VW Golf bucked that trend at the time.

Yes, there were honourable exceptions to this practice but in the main, prescription-by-marketing became a car manufacturer behaviour that became 'normal'. Was Ford its master? And given Ford's success, would you argue?

Perhaps the greatest exponent of 'new-for-old' sold as totally new, was indeed Ford. Across the Cortinas, Corsairs, notably in the Granada lineage, and across its smaller offerings such as Escort (and also Capri), Ford was the master of making money by re-tailoring old cars into new cars simply by clothing the old underpinnings in sharp, fashionable new suits of outer body panels and some clever trim and colours. Give the car buyer and driver just enough, wrap it up in gift wrap and watch it all sail out the showroom. This was the Ford tactic. Uwe Bahnsen's re-skin of the curvy Granada Mk1 into Granada MkII without changing any inner metal panels was a masterpiece, yet doing the same to the Capri MkI to create Capri MkII was a touch more constricted around the front windscreen and doors.

Ford took costs out of car design and manufacture too. And why not. After all, that is how it arrived at the Pinto fuel-tank saga was it not? Pinto saved steel and thus money by using the top of the fuel tank as a steel panel in the car's rear cabin and it cost Ford hundreds of millions of dollars in legal cases that resulted from the fiery effects thereof.

Ford's costs per car-designed, tooled, and manufactured were very low indeed, BMC and BLMC costs were very high and spread across a landscape of marques, factories, and practices most of which wanted to argue with and compete with each other from boardroom to dealership.

As the late-1970s gave us the 'mini-car' hatchback boom, even Ford's new 'revolutionary' front-wheel drive contender, the Fiesta, was fashionably styled but under its skin, contained as much 'old' paid-for metal as possible. There was reputedly even a plan to use a steel pressing from the Ford Anglia in the new car to save money! The giant Ford parts-bin could contribute much and save millions for Ford and its Fiesta.

But that was the late-1970s; Ford had previously been following a finance-driven, cost-cutting creed for years and to great effect and corporate and fiscal effectiveness. Ford could move quickly, create new models, new trims, new sales-orientated badges, trims and advertising. Ford could re-skin an old car without spending a penny on what lay underneath, then proclaim a 'new' car.

Perhaps the Ford Capri was the greatest example of Ford in Europe being so *very* good at what it did. Capri was, despite its style and ability, utterly agricultural underneath in engineering terms, and it too would be re-skinned on the surface as a 'new' car, yet actually be one that was many years old underneath. No major advance in safety, design, emissions, handling, packaging or aerodynamics was offered by the re-skinned versions of the earlier-series Capri, Granada, or Escort. Even the Cortina Mk5 was a re-skin of its originator but with an extended roof height. It would be the 1980s before deeper, fundamental engineering and design changes manifested in 'new' Ford cars such as the front-driven Escort. Even then, the Sierra retained rear-wheel-drive, a fuel tank at the rear end and other antediluvian ingredients. It was a game of smoke and mirrors.

Ford knew how to take money out of a car's design and build costs. Ford knew how to give the buyer just enough. Couldn't BL try the same? Enter the Morris Marina – the last Morris-branded car ever made, if you accept that an Ital was a Marina.

We might ask how and why the Morris Marina came into being. After all it was hardly an advanced car in the 1960s tradition of Issigonis, the Pininfarina-influenced ADO16 (Austin-Morris 1100-1300), or BMC design studies for a new future. From where and why did the entirely average Marina stem?

The answer was, from Ford. But it also underlined something that Donald Stokes had said at the time of the 1968 BMH-Leyland merger. Stokes stated that the new BLMC had to do something to rival the Ford Transit for the commercial division and that BLMC had to do something to rival Ford's new saloon cars. Interestingly, Stokes also stated that he could not 'stop' new models in the pipeline that he inherited in the merger.

Stokes therefore had a hand in the 'Fordisation' ethos that was to grip BLMC.

Little known is the fact that Fordisation inside BLMC did indeed extend to BL's commercial vehicles. Stokes' comments about the Ford Transit saw BLMC frame the Sherpa van – the corporation's own 'Transit' – just as Stokes had promised in early 1968. But Sherpa was typical of BMC and its badge-engineering and parts-bin mentality. Incredibly, Sherpa was constructed, powered, driven suspended, steered, seated and trimmed using existing old BMC and BLMC parts! Even the new body re-used some old 1960s Austin van pressings. Ford's accountants would have been very pleased; if only the collection of parts had been appropriate.

Just as with the 1970s 'wedge' 18/22 series that was quickly relaunched as 'Princess', the Sherpa was originally launched under another name! First launched in 1974 as the Leyland Van but marketed as 'from Austin-Morris', more money was then spent relaunching it as Sherpa. Think of the costs and who allowed this state of affairs. In the end it became the 'Morris Sherpa' – so that was three name changes for one vehicle! More madness. Sherpa would live on under other names too, as a Freight Rover then under LDV!

John Barber (Captain N.J.R. Barber, no less) was in the 1960s Ford's ex-finance director and is a man who is so often said to have led the Fordisation of BLMC – reversing decentralised BMC multi-brand structure – but he actually had a far more detailed and nuanced position. In 1968, long prior to his 1974 appointment as managing director and deputy chairman of BL, Barber joined the new BLMC as a finance and planning director. He was deputy managing director by 1971 – at the time Donald Stokes really started to realise just what he had taken on and let it not be forgotten, co-created – even if that was within the then government's desire and decree.

Intriguingly, Michael Edwardes would soon decentralise BL, but Graham Day would, in the later 1980s, centralise it around a 'Roverisation' – which was as mistaken a strategy as Fordisation was in 1968. The proof of that lies in today's reality, does it not?

Barber gets the 'blame' from many for Fordisation, yet this misses the nuances of the situation. Yes, he was ex-Ford, and yes, there was tribal and trench warfare inside BMC and thus BLMC across the brands, and a confused model range and marque strategy existed. But the facts about Barber's position are as proven by Donald Stokes' own statements in 1968 – that one of the biggest supporters and movers of a Ford-like BLMC policy was Donald Stokes! This paradox is rarely referenced amid the 'Fordisation' of BL story. Stokes wanted to ape the Ford corporate-marketing model and he admitted that, yet Barber is always cited or 'blamed' for this and the ensuing Marina. George Turnbull also preferred the Ford-type plan. Turnbull would fall out with Stokes and depart. Barber would then be promoted. He would also oversee the Italian Innocenti operation.

According to internal BLMC sources, Barber actually believed in pitching BLMC slightly differently to Ford's place in the market and yet knew that, whatever cars it produced, BLMC had to adhere to a 'normal' model replacement cycle – like most major car manufacturers. Is this where the ensuing confusion and erroneous claims lies? Barber was Stokes' de facto deputy. Did the Jaguar-Rover-Triumph (JRT) upmarket brand/marketing section idea come from Barber? Many think so.

BMC and BLMC did not have Ford's economies of scale and volume production and never would – Barber must have known this, so his claims seem to have logic and veracity. Barber, of course, tried to reduce workforce numbers (by up to 30,000) and factory sites in 1968 – long before Edwardes was allowed to succeed in such, post-1977, through government support and union manoeuvres.

Barber would face the unenviable task of BLMC's 1972-74 record of strikes, lost production (over 150,00 cars per year) and the unfeasibly rapid Ryder enquiry and subsequent report. So badly did Barber feel over his termination of employment after the Ryder report, that he took legal action. He was succeeded at BL by Alex Park.

Barber stated to many, and to the media,[1] that he felt it was vital to understand a business rather than the techniques of finances – which might be imposed upon a business. Again this shows that Barber was *not* as dogmatic a follower of imposing Ford's financial structures upon BL as some have suggested. Barber *did* understand BLMC.

By the late-1960s, BMC was increasingly staffed by corporate planners and sales and marketing orientated staff poached from Ford. BMC/BLMC's own leader was the sales-orientated Donald Stokes and as we know, Ford's sales-led specifications and regular model-cycles appealed to him. To the old school, Issigonis engineering specification-focused men of Austin, let alone those of Triumph and Rover, now within the BLMC/BL tent who had to adapt their thinking and the cars, life was not easy.

Soon, some Ford designers would move to the Midlands alongside Ford managers, too (notably Roy Haynes and Harris Mann). But it was the sales-minded senior managers who came into BLMC from Ford who decided to move it and its marques away from their respected and defined outputs and to create a range of cars that were not just badged-engineered, but envisaged as cheaply engineered fashion leaders to deliver the basic ingredients in a short-model cycle series of money making packages. And after all, making money was rather important to keeping the show on the road and the workers employed. Stokes of all people knew that, providing that the product, its identity and its abilities, were clear.

The problem was, however, why would BLMC's traditional customers go to their friendly dealership and buy a Cortina clone with an Austin or Morris badge? Surely, if they wanted a Cortina or an Escort, they would have already bought one – from Ford. No one seems to have asked the obvious question: if you are going to make and sell a car almost identical to its pre-existing rival, and to make the s*imilarity* the paradoxically unique selling point, how and by what means are you going to persuade an ever-increasing number of car buyers to buy it? Offering brown soup when brown soup with a garnish is already selling, seems to involve a fundamental misunderstanding of the 'USP' – the unique selling point concept. Merely keeping up with the competition was not a recipe for advancement, was it?

So 'Fordisation' was not, nor ever could be a panacea for BLMC, because BLMC's internal issues and practices prevented its application – witness the Morris Marina as a proof.

Ex-Ford product, accounting, and marketing managers inside BL preached a new mantra – money and costs before all else. If it worked for Ford (it did) it could work for BMC as BLMC – but it could not. None of the applied Ford techniques of styling and gimmickry overcame the underlying issue and problems of the BMC and BLMC cars – nor the change from Issigonis' 'genius' design credo to the 'standard' design in the cars or their customers' minds.

This utterly demoralised the engineering and design talent within the company.

Keeping up with opposition (just) became the new BL, 'Fordised' thinking – but by re-purposing its old parts stock!

The Maxi which came out in 1969 was deemed to be BLMC's first car but it was not – it was BMC's last car and the last Issigonis piece of applied 'pure' design. Even Maxi was constrained by an old engine and parts-bin thinking. Soon it would get the new E-series engine and revised interior and gear change. It was the one new car due down the BMC pipeline at the time of the 1968 merger. That it would span three decades (1969-1981) would seem irrational! But it was the Morris Marina that was BLMC's first 'Fordised' car.

There were in fact sound reasons for creating the Marina – if you thought a certain way. But such thinking was at the expense of the Issigonis ethos and his cars that then dominated Austin and Morris. And the customers' mindset.

'Clever' marketing men thought that the BMC range had become too defined, too closely tied to the Issigonis output and domination of design. So, widening the product base, opening up the brand was not without foundation as a decision.

Sadly, this move went no further than a decision to try to do nothing more than keeping up with the opposition (Ford), and this was not going to ensure long term survival via massive sales appeal either – especially when the car was the ADO 28 or the Marina. It seems BLMC went from the Issigonis extreme, to the other, far end of the spectrum without considering the middle ground.

Marina would use a 1950s Morris front suspension arm and trunnion joint, rear leaf springs from an antique emporium, old Austin engines, old components – including a Triumph-sourced rear differential, Triumph gearbox, side mirrors off a Mini and possibly the worst front seats seen in a so-called 'modern' car – all of it hiding under a topping of chrome, vinyl, black trim paint, spot lamps, shiny wheel rim 'finishers' and utterly 'standard', if clean, styling. Haynes and Mann had created a cleaned up contemporary Cortina – hadn't they?

Marina was styled to deliver exactly what was asked for. You cannot blame its stylists for what lay underneath. But where was the unique selling point likely to make Marina a star?

It did not have one, it simply mirrored the competition.

Marina offered BLMC customers a step backwards into a new present – a rear-wheel drive car from a brand so famously associated with front-wheel drive cars that had worn Austin and Morris badges and found and 'converted' many customers. Indeed, Morris stopped selling its Morris-badged version of the front-driven 1100, 1300 or ADO 16 when Marina entered the showrooms. Somebody assumed that loyal Morris customers would make an easy and willing switch from ADO16 as a small family car, to the much larger, 'booted' rear-driven Marina – a car of altogether different type, class and price. Here again were product planning and assumed outcomes that led to trouble.

Oh, and if Marina had not captured them, wait a few years and sell them an Allegro! Another differently configured, differently classed car – that went *back* to front wheel-drive!

So poor was the Marina's front end handling (understeer), especially in the heavier 1.8-litre version, that *Autocar* and its rival *Motor* both made representations to BLMC after driving pre-production press test cars. Of note, it was *Autocar* Technical Editor Jeff Daniels who went to see Harry Webster to tell him that, unless changes were made, the magazine would have to say something in print to potential Marina buyers. Some small suspension changes were agreed and the matter was contained. Yet it turned out that a few unmodified cars did get out and bad press headlines appeared. The nascent Consumer Association proved its worth with its coverage.

What was not seemingly discussed was the issue of the even more powerful and heavier six-cylinder Marina to be offered in Australia.

Worse was to come in the Marina experiment; Ford kept such 'fashion' cars on the market for four or five years and then churned out a re-skin, or a new model as a quick replacement to generate showroom visitors. And if Ford did make an error, as with Escort (and latterly Sierra), it threw vast amounts of men and money at the car to solve the problem. BL did not!

The Marina as a 'Fordised' stop-gap car built to such a 'Ford' psychology, should have been quickly replaced, but was not. Instead, BL kept tarting it up, over and over again until it was a decade and half old; the toolings were flabby, the car shoddy and the car buyers gone elsewhere. Why would you, in say, 1980, buy a tarted up Marina facelift of a facelift of a car originally designed in 1969? Wouldn't your money go to what was a really new car (or in Ford's case, what *looked* like), a totally new car as in a new design?

The influx of Ford managers in BL as BLMC and its Austin-Morris division gave rise to a view that what had worked for Ford, would do the same for BLMC.

Existing BLMC cars were 'facelifted' with shiny new grilles and dashboards – think Mini Clubman, or Maxi Mk2. And, as we know, Marina just kept on getting re-titivated. But of course, it was hamstrung by less-than-average engineering ingredients, notably that woeful front suspension, and a general air of Birmingham in the rain on a dull November day. Marina was Marina until it became Ital – which meant it was still a Marina minus £10 million. Quite why the excellent 'free' in-house revamp of the Marina drawn up by Harris Mann was not used, is beyond understanding. Maybe it was the lure of a badge that read 'Ital' or even 'Ital SLX'.

Marina was utterly contemporary and, crucially, was rear-wheel drive. But hang on, hadn't BL's customers been *educated* into front-wheel drive, Issigonis engineering and then into Pininfarina design? Let's forget the rear-wheel drive version of a front-wheel drive car that BMC made called the Austin Three Litre, or the mix-and-match, front and rear drivetrains of the baby Triumph. So far from keeping up with the opposition, Marina took BLMC backwards and contradicted the preference that the customers had been inculcated with by BMC in its Issigonis years!

At its birth, Marina, that first true BLMC car and set to be the last Morris car, had to react to not just Ford and its Cortina, but also the fact that the Cortina was getting bigger as it was being reinvented across its variants and Escort was creeping in a class below. Triumph's brilliant engineer Harry Webster was tasked with launching an Austin – the Maxi in 1969 and then a Morris – Marina in 1971. Webster had the unenviable job of making Marina a reality via a costly new factory revamp at Cowley and new processes – no easy task. Later fitment of O-series engines and some very Ford-like expensive-looking wheel trims could not hide Marina's failings as a marketing-based car not an engineering one.

Marina did sell, but mostly to patriotic British buyers. Marina did not last long at all in Australia, nor in left-hand drive form in parts of Europe. Incredibly, Marina scraped along for well over a decade. It marked the beginning of the BLMC era and the beginning of the end, but it was not the sole cause of failure. But it was and remains, a talisman of much that went wrong.

In Marina, the designers, the engineers and the cars the workers built, were thus not just a step away from the company's previous ethos, but a step backwards from advanced engineering identity as a product and brand that its customers had become loyal too. Marina had a 'live' rear axle, leaf springs and axle tramp – even as 1.3-litre Ital!

Marina was not just hobbled by its suspension and parts; it was offered as a two-door fast-backed car.

Bizarrely, this base model two-door 'fast-backed' car was not initially marketed as a coupé but instead as a sort of 'value' or base trim model two-door in the intended range, perhaps to rival the basic Ford trim of 'L'. But the two-door base model Marina then became a Marina Coupé, notably twin-cam 1.8TC with potential.

Whatever its badging, the truth was that this coupé Marina looked all wrong because instead of following normal practice for two-door or three-door cars, especially fastbacks, by having newly tooled, *longer* front doors to make it look 'right', BLMC's management worked out that they could save many hundreds of thousands of pounds by *not* having new, longer front doors for their Marina two-door or Coupé. Instead, this car was forced to use the existing very short front doors from the four/five-door Marina saloon and estate cars. This saved BLMC much in terms of design, tooling and production costs. Yet it resulted in a coupé of a car that looked long-tailed and with weird, short little front doors. Latterly, lashings of thick black paint around the window line and pillars (a late-1970s styling trick), made Marina Coupé look more modern.

It sold of course, but only domestically and sales of the up-market, torquey and well-performing 1.8TC, suffered, once drivers found out about its reluctance to corner as well it should have done.

Imagine if they had got Marina two-door right. It might have replaced the MGB GT (no!); surely that would have been logical badge-engineering taken to its heights! As it was, Marina, across all its incarnations, even with new O-series engines and myriad trims in black rubber, chrome, vinyl, velour and other tweaks, signified the confused thinking of BLMC out of the BMC parts-bin amid the threat of Ford.

A Marina 'Special' saloon looked modern but was very old indeed underneath. The best car in the Marina range may have been the five-door estate. It achieved a loyal following (notably amongst 'lefties') and respectable sales figures. Overall the Marina range's best sales year was in its third year on the market in 1973 with 115,041 cars sold in the domestic market. But from then on, it declined downwards towards 50,000 a year – hardly viable at under a thousand a week.

We might argue that if Marina had properly played Cortina at its own game, that would have been both good, and bad enough, but Marina stumbled (literally). Years later, as an example of how it should be done, Vauxhall's Cavalier would beat Ford and its Cortina at its own game, across two model cycles and over a decade. Cavalier unmasked the ancient, hidden underpinnings of the 'new' Cortinas. What was BL's competitor to the Cavalier and Cortina a decade and a half later? The ancient 1969 Marina as an Ital of the 1980s. It was supposed to soldier on while BL waited for Montego.

Marina was launched in early 1971 and by the 1980s in its Mk 15¼ iteration, an Ital – the old Marina with new front and rear lamps and a chrome window trim at the cost of £10million wasted; it simply was beyond even being outclassed

This was the bizarre and paradoxical outcome of the 'Fordisation' of BL and its thinking. And it was not even as though the brand defining the product was bad enough, because the product was poor.

So, trying the Ford recipe within BL and across its marques, might best be described as a reasonable idea carried out the wrong way, with the wrong ethos through the wrong product. Marina, seen entirely from a domestic British mindset was *not* an abject failure, yet seen globally, seen in design terms and in terms of fighting Ford at home and in Europe, it did fail.

Meanwhile, Cortina sales leapt ahead, at one time recoding an amazing 82 per cent increase in sales in the period 1971-72.

Perhaps even curiouser was what happened decades later to the Morris Marina. The defunct Morris was reincarnated after 1998 in China as the Huandu Cac or CAC. An unfortunate name for a car of the Ital's provenance. However, these Chinese-built cars, notably the estate variant, were given Sherpa van-derived suspension of increased ride height, revised floorpan tooling, and lower side-panel plastic cladding to keep the vulnerable lower door skins dry and damage free, and expensive, modern full-width front and rear one-piece bumper valances – again to provide protection to the metal from rural road assaults. Quite how the car coped with the increased ride height and roll-dynamics is anyone's guess. The Cac was popular in rural areas as a sort of car that could be used as a van or a bus, indeed it was officially categorised as a bus! So Marina became Ital became Cac!

But before there was a Chinese car industry, how, we must ask, did BLMC have a weak model range with limited appeal, just as the great 1970s car sales boom arrived? Why was BLMC so unprepared, so ill-equipped to offer the cars the customers wanted – or were told they wanted.

Surely it all came back to *before* that merger of 1968 and the hidden confusion that lay below decks. Management, and government, not workers, had charted this design course. But, back with the workers, trouble and far-Left activism was more than brewing. There could only be one outcome. In 1969, just as the Marina, was being readied, something else was being framed – a report about British industrial relations in the form of White Paper sought by no less a figure than the Prime Minister Harold Wilson, who was about to make himself very unpopular with Labour's biggest backers – the trades unions.

7

'In Place of Strife'

Left-leaning paradoxes

As a direct result of the reality and impact of the motor industry strikes and the other dire 1960s union-led disputes, the governing Labour Party issued a report as a White Paper entitled 'In Place of Strife: A Policy for Industrial Relations'.[1] This was launched in January 1969 and was a blueprint written by a Labour team headed by no less a figure than former Secretary of State for Transport Barbara Castle, now Secretary for Employment and Productivity. The clue was in the job title – productivity!

The paper was designed to frame how to *reduce* the power of the trades unions. In fact Castle drafted it with Harold Wilson's full agreement. The pre-existing workforce problems at BMC and now BLMC were pivotal to Barbara Castle's thinking. Strikes were still occurring, by the thousands of strike days per-year per-worker. Even Labour's own – even fighting 'Red' Barbara – had had enough. Surely this suggests that a deeper mechanism than 'just' workforce and union unhappiness was at play within Britain in the 1960s? There was little consensus underneath the veneer of party politics.

The Labour Cabinet was divided and a row broke out resulting in the Castle paper being discarded and its recommendations ignored. Workers went out on strike in protest at 'In Place of Strife', and its recommendations. The Morris men at Cowley certainly made their feelings known.

Principal amongst those opposed to such union reforms as suggested in the paper, was a certain Cabinet member, James Callaghan – who went on to be prime minister at the height of the later, 1970s BL strike era. Perhaps if he had endorsed and not opposed the paper, things might not have been as bad as they got, say some – of the Right. Indeed, for by 1977, Callaghan himself was having to stand up to union power at BL and beyond; in fact union power had destroyed his premiership by late 1978. So his 1969 victory over the White Paper 'In Place Strife: A policy for Industrial Relations', paradoxically actually influenced his later defeat. He had tolerated the Left of the unions (who funded him and Labour) and opposed Castle's 'In Place of Strife' in 1969, yet a few years later, was electorally punished by the consequences of that very action.

Labour's history is also deeply carved with the effects of Castle's suggestions because from the reactive process to her paper, stemmed *more* not less strife, and as an unintended consequence, the Thatcher revolution. Some of the hard-left argue that the unions as the people who went on to 'collude' with the employers, thus bear some kind of paradoxical blame for Thatcher.

Only when such massive forces are considered can we begin to appreciate just how toxic and how powerful the union and (sometimes politically separate) workforce and sociological issues inside Britain and especially inside BLMC were. If a Labour government could be taken to crisis by such tactics, what hope for a business, company or capitalist?

Yet how did Barbara Castle arrive at such an 'anti-union' position *before* the severe and disastrous 1970s BL disputes, before BLMC was nationalised in 1974? Was she externally influenced or advised? How much of a 'reaction' to then Conservative proposals, let alone union or worker power, was her White Paper? Yet surely, this was a scenario where even Labour had to do something, was nearly brought down by the sheer power of the immovable trades unions, workers and their might? Were 'Reds' really under the bed?

Castle got to her position with 'In Place of Strife' as a direct result of the strikes and strike culture that manifested in Britain from 1959 to 1967 – long before Benn, Wilson, Stokes, and Harriman, 'agreed' the BLMC merger in 1968. She knew that such strikes were close to destroying Britain. She may even have known about Soviet-linked philosophy and its infiltration of the unions and the workforce.

Surely the cause and the effect of the machinations over 'In Place of Strife', notably the factors that led to it, never mind the reactions too it, might suggest that consensus had not been achieved by Labour? And were not Cowley, much of BLMC, and Whitehall itself, riven with far-Left, the Left, the Centrist, the names of Benn, Callaghan, the TUC, et al, all fighting for their patch of internecine turf as Harold Wilson smoothly glossed over the surface of it all with his apparent competency? Had not Macmillan's and Douglas-Home's old gin and tonic Tory toffs made way for Wilson, beer and sandwiches in Downing Street? Yet underneath lay unresolved factions and continuing strikes across many industries.

What of the far-Left and their view that BL was a microcosm of the British Class Struggle? Where did that fit into consensus politics and Labour policy and government, let alone the day-to-day management of BL itself?

Incredible as it may seem today, given its Left-leaning author Castle amid an 'old' Labour government, 'In Place of Strife' clearly suggested the re-drawing and re-structuring of union powers, workforce rights, arbitration, and was set to reform the whole process of industrial relations. It suggested the use of ballots prior to strike action and an independent board with legal power to enforce decisions and penalties for non-compliance. The existing voluntary collective bargaining mechanism was to be thrown out and replaced by state intervention amid a formal industrial relations mechanism. Radical stuff.

The Trades Union Congress (TUC) opposed the paper and the bill that it proposed. TUC General Secretary Victor Feather tried to negotiate with Castle and Wilson but the TUC was unwilling to entertain such change. It is suggested that Wilson threatened to resign over the issue of refusal to reform by the TUC and that union leaders Jack Jones and Hugh Scanlon offered Wilson a face-saving route out of the situation with a commitment from the TUC to make a 'solemn' agreement to try and resolve unofficial disputes internally. But that meant Labour men had to tackle Labour men who were militants inside their own unions, did it not?

As a brief foray into a post-1969 future, after his defeat by Edward Heath at the next general election, few imagined Labour's Harold Wilson would return to Number 10, but in 1974 he did. Wilson had had time to do deals with the unions and mend the fences that 'In Place of Strife' had created in 1969. With the TUC's new liaison group under Jack Jones and Hugh Scanlon, a 'Social Contract' was created by the new government. Did this influence Labour's next prime minister, the union-sponsored James Callaghan – the man who had crushed 'In Place of Strife'?

Within three years, Callaghan, struggling with BL and with union action and militants, brought in Michael Edwardes to BL in a move that still seems utterly bizarre of a socialist Labour prime minister who had defeated union reform in 1969.

The failure of Castle's suggested 1969 reforms was a pivotal moment and in hindsight may be said to reveal just how serious the situation was in Britain at that time. Who would run Britain, the Labour government as elected, or the TUC? Or forces further to the Left than the TUC? How close were we to crisis and how much was BLMC part of it? The answer to such questions may be the same – very close indeed.

Lord Rochester, a man with years of business experience, stated in a rational and largely non-partisan speech to the House of Lords in 1969 that unless better industrial relations were achieved, Britain faced collapse amid anarchy. Freedom of work and rights at work were one thing, but had the strikes now become a mechanism for something else in Britain?[2]

Many people openly began to ask this question. Was the country in the grip of something undeclared? Today, ex-BL men still suggest just this very scenario – the same one as Lord Rochester uttered in the House of Lords in March 1968.

But were such opinions nothing more than a right-wing reaction of 'anti-worker' sentiment? Or were they devoid of politics and just the rational, common sense views of many across all classes who could see something was going on?

Was it all what today we might call a conspiracy theory? Perhaps, but perhaps not. British social science was clearly implicated in what went on at this time. So, once again we have evidence of a societal problem, and maybe even a growing social 'disease' that affected BMC long before BLMC and BL were born.

Some observers implicate Castle's 1969 suggestions of union reform as a betrayal of her origins and of the Left-wing. The Castle white paper was re-written in weakened form and some years later became the basis of the Trade Union and Labour Relations Act, upon which Thatcherite policy would expand and claim much credit for 'reform'.

The de facto cabinet split that Castle's paper caused may well have impacted the result of the 1970 general election and the defeat of Labour to Edward Heath. Labour lost the election of 1970 and the toxic issue of industrial relations, notably at BLMC, passed to Edward Heath the new pro-EEC Conservative prime minister. His attempt at union reforms via his Industrial Relations Act, led to ultimately to his downfall via the miners' strike and also in 1972 the dockers' strike that framed the case of the 'Pentonville Five' and their case at the National Industrial Relations Court.

The TUC and its General Council had made it clear to Heath that unless the Pentonville Five were freed, it would bring the country out on strike in July. The five dockers were immediately released. Numerous unions then left the register that they had joined under the anti-union legislation and within which they had been bound in relation to taking action.

Problems in industry and at BMC and BLMC clearly influenced the course of the nation and its government. With 2.25 million unemployed, a three-day week, power shortages, unions in open revolt against the Industrial Relations Act, the National Industrial Relations Court, soaring prices and inflation, Heath – obsessed with joining the EEC – lost control and if the miners had not brought him down, there is little doubt that BLMC would have. The 1970s were far more of a national crisis than today's viewpoint can convey. The country was on the edge, but no one had clarity as to what lay beyond the precipice and who was funding it. Heath knew how finely balanced society was in the 1970s – he had the offices of the *Morning Star* bugged (as revealed by later Cabinet Papers).

Heath found himself enmeshed in the problem and 1970 saw significant workforce and union unrest across Britain – this lasted for several years and had the motor industry at its core. Heath's ailing regime pressed on with industrial reform and re-structuring of union powers and rights. So the miners took him on in the 1972 miners' strike which they 'won'. Britain was divided and in chaos long before Margaret Thatcher ruled.

Heath made this general election about 'who governs Britain' – the unions or the Government. The bizarre answer from the people was to just about a elect a minority Labour Government – one sponsored by the unions! A second general election at the end of 1974 gave Labour a tiny, three-seat majority, but it opened the way beyond Wilson to Callaghan.

So the Conservatives were soon to be thrown out of power and Labour, briefly under Wilson, then under Callaghan, returned to power. Wilson and Labour were subjected to internal hard-Left activism at this time, and he and his government are likely to have been under 'watch' by forces of the British establishment.

Yet still the toxic problem of so-called union power and damaging strikes remained. Callaghan's prior-1969 refusal to embrace Castle's suggested union reforms, came back and not only bit him in 1976 as it opened the doors to a series of new union negotiating acts, but it also saw him lose patience with what was going on at BLMC; yet still he refused to recognise the role of the hard-Left in what was occurring.

Callaghan, the man who had defeated 'In Place of Strife', a man whose career was union-sponsored, turned his position around in 1978 and said to the BL workers, 'Do not look to Government for any more solutions. We have done our part. Now it is up to you.'

Some suggest that if Callaghan had not lost to Thatcher in 1979, the TUC may well have directed the government on a de facto basis. Yet it seems that this had already *happened* in 1969 when Barbara Castle's 'In Place of Strife' was defeated by Callaghan and the union bosses, with direct national policy outcomes.

BLMC's pay-by-piecework system in all its layers of confusion and negotiation had to go, and it did. A flat rate, and in 1970 a 'measured day' payment system, was brought in and many disputes followed amid centralised negotiations and the issues of the 'closed shop'. Was the introduction of Measured Day Work or rate into the BLMC plants in the 1970s the fulcrum around which union power was divided and management strengthened? Some say it was just this, a mechanism that management used to weaken the ever growing union shop stewards ranks. Persuading union members to 'participate' also divided the workers – creating divisive internal hierarchy.

Ultimately, Castle's 1969 paper may have helped re-frame the debate to the point upon which Thatcher latterly forced through her 1980s union reforms and did 'win' against the unions. But all that lay in a future as yet to be cast. The underlying social, worker and political unrest, bubbled on and between the 1960s-80s era strikes and management and political contradictions, there were cars to build.

Yet the nation's chronic strike-bound condition continued. BL strikes would not stop, and by 1986, Rupert Murdoch would be embroiled via his News International, Wapping plant, into the 'reform' of the print industry amid allegations of an alleged plan to encourage the very strike action that he was determined to eradicate.[3] It all sounded very familiar.

How chronic, how endemic was the national strike bound condition? In case the reader is any doubt, let us recall that just as the new Rover SD1 V8 was finally making its mark in early 1978, the SD1 production line was brought to a standstill by a few workers of line-inspector grade who were annoyed that their standard issue white overalls were substituted by brown overalls without due consultation. Half a dozen men complained and downed tools. Three dozen more stopped work in sympathy. Before you knew it BL managers had a dispute on their hands and had to lay off over 3,000 Rover SD1 factory line workers. The great new car with vital orders building up, was stopped dead in its tracks. Strife still existed: customers would go elsewhere. Just before such events, BL's personnel director Geoffrey Whalen had resigned amid the unmanageable mess, and who could blame him. 1970 to 1978 was to frame BL's own strife and that was all long before Margaret Thatcher arrived on the scene.

8
1970s Numbers Games

(Warning: contains vital statistics, but not pretty ones)

'Do not look to the Government for any more solutions. We have done our part. Now it is up to you.'

James Callaghan, Prime Minister. January 1978

In case you have not realised, or do not wish to realise, the BL tragedy was serious. Serious not just for British engineering and design, and its workers but also for Great Britain PLC and its economic situation. As an example of the BL tragedy, let us recall the 1970s to 1980s truths of BL – topped off by Sir Michael Edwardes' very real warning that he would (and could) close down BL. BL needed to reduce its workforce from 143,000 to 100,000 by 1983. That was about 43,000 working men and their livelihoods.

Of note, Edwardes would create a senior team of BL management leaders, three of whom were ex-Ford. 'Fordisation' was still an undercurrent.

The early, original 'Fordisation' of BLMC in the late 1960s failed because it was not fully enacted, not a true revolution, it was hobbled by some unwilling managers, parts-bin ideas, stifled practices and what today we would call 'legacy issues'.

Change, the new, was only *partially* allowed to take place. What could have worked, did not. Too many people were entrenched in the BLMC bunker of a mindset. Stokes' lead was lost. Those that tried to escape were hobbled by the realities of corporate thinking. 'Group think' started to take over. George Turnbull had a senior directorship at BL at this time and he too had to juggle all the competing themes, tribes and funds. He saw that better opportunities lay beyond BL. The forgotten name of James Slater (as in the well-known Slater Walker) as BLMC director was also part of the 1970s BLMC story – having been asked by Stokes to perform due diligence on BMC's accounts in 1968! Slater accused BMC of a lack of model and product planning, early on.

For BMC and thus for BLMC it was not just the workers who were tribal – the dealers who sold the individual BLMC brands were in open competition with each other – often trying to sell identical cars with nothing but the badges changed, to customers in the same town via dealerships that were not very far apart. If not in an Austin Morris turf war, they were trying to sell Rovers or Triumphs that competed with each another, or with a rival, yet still BL, marque!

Rover 2000 or Triumph 2000 or Land Crab 1800S? Rover 3500 or Austin 3.0-Litre? Triumph 2.5PI or Land Crab 2200? Wolseley 2200 or Austin 2200 – with or without a 'Princess' badge? Triumph 1500 or a Toledo? MG1300 or Austin 1300? The confusion was badge madness. Meanwhile back at the factories, design teams were competing with each other too. Here lay the psychology of what went on.

On the factory floor, productivity and build quality were suffering.

Author Jeff Daniels,[1] citing BL's poor production rates, specifically stated that it was in 1972 that the BL workforce started its own self-destruction. This is questionable, based on the record of disputes, and strikes within Rover, Jaguar, Triumph, BMC, and BLMC, as evidenced from 1959 onwards. In fact, the number of man hours lost at BLMC per year rose from 5 million to 10 million between 1969 and 1972. Evidence of far-Left activism at Cowley and Longbridge before 1972 also tends to prove that the trouble began prior 1972.

Things may have escalated in the 1970s, but it was long before then that the rot set in.

By 1974, BL was almost bust and by 1975, Sir Don Ryder and his Ryder Report looked into the just-nationalised British Leyland Ltd. This framed its own reality and guaranteed BL becoming an 'unbreakable' concern that would apparently suffer few job losses and go on to sell an ever-increasing numbers of its existing cars and new models; such projections may have bordered on the delusional.

Gone were Donald Stokes and John Barber, in came Alex Park as chief executive. Of factory closures? Little was said. Of operating costs? Even less was mooted. Stokes is a figure of blame for some, but this must more widely be seen as unfair, unless one is ex-MG. He took on a sinking ship, a poisoned chalice of a car company amid a society and a company riven with class conflict and far-Left infiltration. Stokes took difficult choices, and was unable to take some choices that he preferred. But many argue he was in error with his MG strategy. And of course Stokes was co-architect of BLMC, so cannot be wholly without blame.

The suggestions of the Ryder plan, which made various strategic recommendations for BL (though not everyone agreed with its suggestions), was to make BL a global player with all the brands under the one over-arching all-knowing body. Others thought that separating off the marques into autonomous brands or brand groupings and giving them free rein was a much better, sales and product orientated idea.

The chances of BL reinventing itself in the manner of which the previously ailing Volkswagen AG car manufacturing concern had just been turned around in very short time with very good new cars, was receding upon the wings of many factors.

The Ryder Report assessed that there were 246 separate bargaining units across the entirety of BLMC and in the Cars division there were 58 bargaining units and 324 pay rates. Rationalisation was needed.

Of note, the TGWU's assistant general secretary Mr H. Unwin and an NEB member stated that the factory floor machinery being used by BLMC was a 'disgrace' to the industry. And the truth was that BMC and BLMC had not updated their factories in decades.

Ryder's report was hastily written, many felt it lacked depth, nuance or forensic detail. John Barber challenged it and paid the price, but was proved correct in the end.

In 1973, BLMC issued a guide to dealers about the new 'BL' branding and it categorically stated that:

'In the past, British Leyland distributors and dealers, by having to relate themselves to certain marques only and adopting a specific marque signing policy, have lost entirely the benefits of a country-wide impact which a corporate image can give to some 6,000 British Leyland sales outlets in the U.K. As well as to the many hundreds in Europe and overseas.'

So was enforced a 'rationalized identity programme'. It took years and cost a fortune, only to be quickly torn down as BLMC became known by its later names. Down came Austin or Morris signage, up went BLMC signage which often read 'Leyland', thence to come down again and become Leyland Cars, Austin-Rover, Rover, and MG-Rover. Incredibly, a few private remaining original dealers finally put up MG's Chinese signage!

But in the 1973 BL branding document was the proof that what had gone before had been a mess.

Back in 1967, BMC had achieved sales of £467 million, but lost £3 million. By 9 December 1974, BL ran out of operating cash. The government had to step in. Who got the blame – Stokes of course! But Stokes *had* actually engaged in dialogue with the unions, and he had tried to rationalize cars and the costs of their diverse ranges and manufacture. But Stokes had had to bend to the whims of government. Some say he was not ruthless enough, too nice, but that was easy to say. For Stokes, one wrong word, one wrong move and an all-out national strike could have resulted.

At this time (1973-74) Volkswagen (VW) was in real trouble – requiring a state bail-out. VW's new small car to replace the Beetle was still rear-engined and a bit of a contraption. Just as occurred inside BL, this prototype upon which money had been spent, was binned. The difference was that it was a bad car, whereas some of the prototypes binned by BL were very good and might have saved the company!

BLMC was quietly terminated as a trading name on 27 June 1975 and officially became British Leyland Ltd. But in lay terms it had been 'BL' for a long time, yet had suffered from the confusions of blending all the differing brands together in 1968. It would be as late as 1975 before all the old, separate Austin, Morris, and other signage would come down from dealership buildings.

British Leyland Ltd was divided into separate divisions at Government's order:

Leyland Cars;
Leyland Truck & Bus;
Leyland Special Products;
Leyland International.

Of cars, vans, buses and trucks, there was much to offer – at its best there was the Leyland National bus, at its worst there would come the Leyland van or Sherpa – one of the strangest collection of old BMC and BLMC parts ever to be amalgamated into a 'new' vehicle. Soon, a new Rover would rationalise the internal competition between Rover and Triumph by the simple act of wiping out Triumph's claim to and production of, the 2.0 and 2.5-Litre sporting saloon. To coin a phrase, things could only get better.

Within two years, the strikes resulting from attempts at resolving these internal issues and others at BL had reached their peak and did so under a *Labour* government. 1977 was critical. Even Leyland's profitable truck business was out on strike. BL nearly went under again, but BL was being overseen by the National Enterprise Board (NEB) and dependent upon its advice to government as to whether further funding from the tax payer should be forthcoming for BL. Remember, at this time BL was 95 per cent owned by the State and paid for by its taxpayers. Then came the BL toolmakers' strike and its effects upon the company and upon politicians.

BL, with only enough money to fund selected new model developments, had to make almost impossible choices about its next new cars; they were crucial choices and inside BL, arguments raged about which model choice offered the best chance of a quick delivery of cash through sales success. Outside the factory gates, the very fact of BL's survival became a threat racing towards reality. But the end of BL, the giving up on BL as a closure, would have taken at least five years to negotiate and it is said, could have cost the nation £10 billion to sort out. BL employed around 150,000 people, was responsible for the employment of 150,000 more via its suppliers, and contributed about £450 million a year to the exchequer through all its works, not least the tax its workers paid – tax that they probably ended up paying back into BL at the rate of just over one penny in the pound in the late 1970s.

BL employed over 12 per cent of the workforce in Oxford, 100,000 people in Birmingham and its environs – approximately 3 per cent of the West Midlands workforce. In 1979-80, BL's sales made a massive contribution to the UK's gross domestic product – over 1.5 per cent of the total GDP figure. What government, Labour or Conservative, could tackle that without trouble?

It is conservatively estimated that BL was responsible for the direct and indirect second party employment of a million people. BL was also shifting around half a million cars a year, including export earnings. But in 1977, BL was in massive trouble and needed regular injections of state aid or your cash (by 1981, BL sales would slump to under 400,000 cars per year for the first time, at 396,400).

Curiously, the unions and their shop stewards' committees' main issue with the 1978 Edwardes plan was that it did not project to build enough cars! The unions wanted BL to build one million cars per year. Yet such a figure could not be achieved because of strikes and low productivity – overseen by guess who – the unions! And did they forget that in order to build one million car per year, they had to be purchased by customers who wanted to buy them in the first place? Looking inwards, navel-gazing, the unions demanded a one million cars per year plan and even drew up their own strategy to make one million cars a year. The only problem was that they did not work out a way of *selling* those one million cars!

Surely in 1978, what the 'workers' wanted was their rate of pay restored to an industry-competitive level and recognition of their skilled trades through pay and to-be-agreed incentives. But what of actually building cars? What of productivity? Without that, no pay rises would be possible as BL's titanic struggle lurched onwards.

Despite BL's losses, its suppliers – the external people who manufactured the parts that the cars consisted of when built – were making a profit. Their employees were by the 1980s less minded to strike – unlike those at Lucas, whose 1960s strike had paralysed BMC car production. More cars would mean more pay. Unless of course, no one wanted buy the cars due to either poor design, or poor build and even worse reliability.

Prior to 1978, Labour and its Minister Eric Varley had offered BL a fixed £1.4 billion to restructure itself and save the car making future of the Midlands. But costs, including the costs of strikes and inflation, let alone problems with the cars and the dealers trying service and repair them, began to mean that if no more money was allowed, then the new model cycle – the key to BL's future profitability (even according to Ryder), would become a 'Catch 22' situation.

Just as with the Concorde project, or the Nimrod military airframe fiasco, each further investment in the ever-deeper pit of BL's cash requirements, would take the project closer to potential disaster, consequent political intervention, tax payer protests, and the delays and constraints that would adversely impact the actual subject of the investment and its chances of ever working properly and of earning back any money.

In purely automotive terms for BL, had not this scenario been proven on a smaller scale recently before, with the BL Allegro affair? Cost-cutting had ruined the car's original design brilliance, its chances of success and a decent fiscal return. Had lessons not been learned?

Remember, Allegro had had its original hatchback design and low-line front end *removed* on costs grounds related to being made to use parts-bin toolings and engines, yet the management had previously authorised the *adding* of a hatchback to the Austin Morris 1100-1300 range in Australia as the Nomad, and the fitting a larger engine! An Australian market large saloon, the P76, had been paid for too! Yet back in Birmingham, the penny-pinching was rampant.

Across the 1970s, BL's market share fell, from 33 per cent in 1974 to 27 per cent by the end of 1976; few people ever considered that market share falling to near-15 per cent within three years. Ryder had suggested a strategy based upon a BL market share of 35 per cent. *This* was the delusional mirage. Ryder's misplaced faith in BL's cars and the public's 'buy British' tastes were soon exposed.

A series of strikes, a series of poorly made cars, amid a series of poorly designed models, meant that BL's customers had walked away. But was the poor build quality solely the workers fault? Not entirely, and let's remember that the need to meet production targets saw BL managers as 'quality inspectors' overrule line-men and force the approval for despatch to the dealers of cars with known manufacturing issues that should have gone to the rectification area (every car maker has one). That way the 'numbers' were kept up, and the problems left to dealers to resolve.

This is the perfect example of how 'workers' and 'managers' were both involved. And if the externally supplied parts were of poor quality – such as Lucas electrical items – did not BL bear some responsibility for that and the direct consequence of cheaper, lower specifications being set by the supplier in order to meet BL management's price stipulations?

This was how the cars suffered before they were even built.

A rocky corporate patch for BL had occurred in 1976-97 which saw BL's new leader, Professor Sir Ronald Edwards, die unexpectedly in 1976. Into the BL hot seat came ex-Spitfire pilot Sir Richard Dobson. Derek Whittaker ran the cars division.

Dobson, (with no car knowledge but a global leader of the tobacco industry) warned as early as spring 1976 that he could foresee a time when he could no longer advise the investment of any more money into BL. Appointed by Lord Ryder with little consultation, Michael Edwardes knew Dobson and cautioned him about getting involved with BL! There soon followed more strikes and the infamous toolmakers' strike. In 1977, Lord Ryder resigned from the National Enterprise Board.

Dobson was an old fashioned type, whose conservative views seemed as entrenched as the union leaders' leftist views. Dobson had to go, so said many people after a speech he made was described as racist and anti-union. A 'Dobson out' movement and petition was started. He resigned on 21 October 1977. BL's leadership was in crisis – it had shades of BOAC in the 1950s and 1960s.

But wait, Allegro Mk2 and MK3, TR7, Lynx, Maestro, Princess 2, Marina Mk 4⅔, O-Series engines, Hydragas, Montego – all were due down the BL birth canal. And curiously, the name of the man who allegedly warned Dobson to steer clear of BL soon turned up as a consultant to BL at the highest level – Michael Edwardes.

In 1978, Leyland Cars Ltd became BL Cars Ltd, and was split into Austin-Rover and Jaguar-Rover-Triumph divisions. Yet by now, Britain was a net importer of cars for the first time.

Things could only get better. Metro would soon arrive to open the floodgates of a tide of new BL models. Drive the flag! Wait for it, soon would come the legend, 'A British car to beat the world'.

A British car to beat the world? And why not? After all we were a nation of engineers, designers, builders, bodgers, artisans, men in sheds, brilliant at making great aircraft and great cars – as well as great ships and great railway locomotives.

Oh, and BL's Special Products division based in Leicestershire which sold trucks, military vehicles, and construction equipment, sold nearly £200 million of its products in 1977, and made a quiet, un-headlined profit of over £10 million. Led by David Abell (who had overseen Leyland Australia's enforced run-down), as the BL Board's 'youngster', BL Special Products sold its wares on a global basis and was ripe for being cut away from BL and sold off.

BL's Truck and Bus division sold £480 million of its wares and made a £43 million profit. But these highlights were absorbed inside the great BL money-devouring monster – even if all its cars could dip into the parts-bin of 'shared commonality', a significant money saving factor. Unipart? A useful profit centre originally set up by John Egan before he left BL. He would later return at Edwardes' invitation.

In the 1970s, Jaguar made money, even if declining 1970s quality control was putting the warranty claims costs up. But creating Jaguar-Rover-Triumph separated off the more prestige end of the BL brand. It allowed these brands only limited autonomy, and of course would make them easier to sell off if push came to public outrage and political order. Land Rover could be 'isolated' as a brand and be used to milk cash via basic models and the increasingly upmarket Range Rover.

As 1978 closed, BL had a small, overall trading surplus of about £10 million after tax, yet had received nearly £400 million in funding, grants and schemes in 1978 – so-called 'equity' finances.

It was as early as 1977 that BL had explored a tie-up with a large car making brand. Peugeot S.A., had from 1974-1976 completed its purchase of Citroën and some minor French marques, now, as the 1980s were due to dawn, Peugeot was rather surprisingly scooping up the British arm of Chrysler and creating a new marketing arm – Talbot. Talbot, an old brand, would in name only build modified Peugeots in Coventry, or it would until it was killed off. Peugeot would then build its own-branded cars in Coventry until it closed down its British car making activities – all the while with Britain as a full EEC/EU member and with the British Government citing EEC/EU rules in its refusal to further bail out Peugeot at Coventry!

BL meanwhile was talking to Peugeot's great rival, Renault, and had agreed to jointly work on some small-scale engineering projects, but as for merger or collaboration talks, they went nowhere – Renault had enough problems with the French workforce and unions. But there were discussion about BL licence-building a Renault in Britain. This did not transpire.

So started BL's discussions with Volkswagen, which were to bear only small fruit.

Michael Edwardes reckoned BL needed a partner, even it meant licence-building their car with BL badges on them for a short period. As early as 1978, Edwardes sought engineering and manufacturing efficiencies for BL. He talked to American friends at Chrysler and he had excellent contacts in Asia. But after 1979, Europe was inviting – notably for political reasons.

Despite an agreement with Volkswagen, Edwardes cleverly decided to box clever and also look east, to find a car maker that needed the lever of a toe-hold in Europe and as a way of circumnavigating trades rules, tariffs, and the protectionist policies of 'little Europe'.

For a while in late 1977, it seemed that Volkswagen were seriously interested in buying Jaguar from BL and creating their own upper-crust arm. BL also talked to Datsun, and, it is suggested, to Toyota. But Honda? That lay in the near future. Meanwhile, BL had old cars to facelift and new ones to design.

What could possibly go wrong?

The answer now lay in something beyond good or bad car design. The answer lay in build quality, or rather in BL's case, an absence of such a vital factor.

Poor, actual hands-on build quality (as opposed to technological or financial limitations upon manufacturing processes) *was* a 'worker' issue, no one can deny that, surely? The lack of pride, the demoralised men, the distant upper management, the on-off nature of the production lines amid daily 'walk-outs' and agitation and argument, here again is the behavioural psychology ingredient of the BL story, one that is so often ignored. These cars were built under a cloud of mass-discontent, maybe even a group depression. Is *this* why they were as it is alleged, 'thrown together'.

But we should not forget that the 'line' moved fast, jobs had to be completed in an allotted time, and that little margin for error or problem was factored in. Supervisors were keen to hit target numbers and get cars despatched to dealers, irrespective of flaws or build quality requirements.

Stop-start production lines and cars left in limbo, perhaps even outside in the rain, it all happened.

Yet the BL workers did not specify the material's quality, the paint, the tooling, nor the trims and parts. All *that* was down to penny-pinching measures ordered upon the cars and those that made them, from on high amid their tribal squabbles of marque mixed up with marque.

BL skimped on prices to its suppliers so items submitted were of low quality. But why did the bonnets wobble on the likes of Marina, Allegro and Princess? Why did they twist when you propped them up? Answer – because BL skimped on steel to save money. Steel was not as thick as it might have been, hinges soon went loose. Shut lines and panel gaps were inconsistent. Paint was thin. Then all the parts were 'thrown' together.

Some BMC and BL loyal customers would return. But many *would* not. BL's 3,000 dealers had a hard life and many quite understandably were tempted away by foreign marques and a regular stream of new models every four years. But BL still needed to lose at least 1,000 of its dealers from an over-stuffed dealership layer where many old family concerns were to be swiped aside by the shock of the new.

In 1979, Margaret Thatcher and her policies would arrive with not an ounce of sympathy for the old ways, instead, ruthlessly culling vital aspects of Britain's industrial heart. Thatcher was from a poor family, yet became an intellectual of elite thinking and married into money. She must have been in terrible internal conflict, yet maybe she never knew it. The 'old toff' Tories of her Cabinet were singularly ill-equipped to deal with her personality construct and resulting behaviours, neither were BL's workers, the miners and the NUM!

But *before* Thatcher of 1979 is where we have to seriously begin to ask, was BL brought down by politics? Thatcher's subsequent arrival into Downing Street simply upped the ante on an existing disaster.

Prior to Thatcher, there lay deep within BL truly experienced and knowledgeable men like Harold Musgrove and George Turnbull; both men would become exasperated with BL and the meddlings of external bodies. Turnbull had joined the Standard company as 14-year-old apprentice and worked his way up to become joint managing director of British Leyland by 1973. Turnbull, despite his elevated status, was popular with the workers and the unions; his departure in 1974 removed a key figure who perhaps had had the potential to avert the series of 1970s and 1980s strikes at BL. Turnbull left because he could see the vital factor of ensuring BL's volume car production was at risk under the machinations of BL, government, civil servants and the strategies inherent within the affair.

A colleague and friend of Turnbull's was the BL salesman with the amazing name of Filmer Paradise (Director of Sales, Austin-Morris). He reckoned the Marina would be a best seller and that BL could shift over a quarter a million of them a year! Paradise did his best to flog BL's cars abroad, but as the 1970s matured, the writing was truly on the wall and when Turnbull went, so too did Paradise.

Cutting the model development funding for volume car production at Austin and Morris, and diverting funds to specialist vehicles and trucks, was a mistake said Turnbull – who resigned. He would go on to lead at Talbot UK and beyond, but he proved his point by leaving BL and as a next step, setting up the reality of the first Hyundai car to threaten the British domestic market – the Pony. From that, Hyundai went on to the success it now enjoys. Turnbull also ran the Iranian state car production conglomerate and might have used that as a springboard for cheap imports into Europe, but it did not happen.

As for BL's outdated cars in 1978, well, if you swapped an Allegro or a Triumph Toledo for a new VW Golf, it is unlikely you would return to BL – however strong your patriotic vein. There is no doubt that BL's car range was the most outdated in its market.

At this time, the giant Ford Motor Company had, despite all its headline sales figures and great PR, entered its own period of strikes, build quality issues with some models, and productivity problems. Yet somehow, Ford avoided the worst 'BL' type headlines, or blame and opprobrium as a brand. Ford was still loved even if its 1970s fare were on occasion rust-prone, soft-skinned, facelifted, 1960s-origins cars tarted up with style and often built abroad but 'imported'.

But BL's 'problem' cars were real.

In 1975, the West German Auto Club had awarded the venerable Triumph Spitfire a 'Lemon' award. Lemon as in more faults than any other car they had appraised or tested. The German-run Spitfire on long term twelve month test had got through two engines and a gearbox as well as numerous other items.[2]

In July 1976, BL would sell sixty-six Allegros in Germany! Yes, sixty-six examples of BL's rival to the vital new VW Golf. The Golf soon sold that *per day* in Britain, let alone Germany, and that was on a bad day! Guess how many Golfs VW sold per day at its 1977 best in Germany alone? The answer is a staggering 3,300 a day.

1977 was a critical year for BL. By the summer of 1978, the sales figures for July of that year were scary beyond the white cliffs of Dover.

So BL sold sixty-six Allegros in Germany in July 1978, whereas VW sold 100,000 Golfs in March 1977 in Germany. In Britain, Allegro once sold over a thousand in a month. In its life, Allegro sold just over 630,000 cars, yet less than 25,000 were exported. Apart from the French, who liked the gas and air suspended ride, few Europeans took to the car. Innocenti, however, produced their own branded version of the Allegro – the Regent – complete with the almost-square steering wheel!

BL sold just thirty of its new 18-22 'wedge' Princesses that July 1978 to the Germans – thirty of the Passat rival! It gets worse. July 1978 saw eighteen Austin Maxis sold in Germany. Eighteen of the BL hatchback!

So, BL sold 130 cars in Germany in July 1978 at the height of the new era of car design and marketing as the 1980s were about to dawn! In the first half of 1978, BL shifted just 7,590 cars in Germany. Many of these were the then new Rover SD1 range with three engine variants, and the revised Jaguars which just about retained a loyal yet increasingly annoyed following in upper middle class German buyers' minds. They were annoyed because their Jaguars and Rovers kept breaking down, or bits broke off.

In stark and vital comparison, Renault sold nearly 10,000 of its superb R20 in those first six months of 1978 in Germany alone. 10,000 of just one French model – to the *Germans*. That is hundreds every day! VW, Renault, Saab, GM all sold their mid-range hatchbacks by the tens of thousands in Germany, Britain, and the Netherlands, beyond their home bases of France, Sweden, or Germany.

BL's market share in Sweden in 1978 was 0.4 per cent. It had twenty-five dealers! Yet in Denmark, BL's 1978 range sold surprisingly well. So the cars' quality issues cannot have been the sole factor, can they – perhaps the dealers and their warranty repair qualities must have been 'better' in Denmark? We cannot suspect that Danish BL cars were better or less worse than those sent to Sweden or Germany.

As for late 1970s BL sales in Italy or France, things were so bad that even the potential of the new range of 1980s cars from BL – the Leyland Cars coded LC (or LM) 10/11 that became Maestro and Montego – seemed questionable as the customers would have long deserted the BL dealership in favour of a car that, if not perfect, at least would run and resist rot for more than six months. But Maestro and Montego *did* bring great improvements in quality and reliability.

European nostalgia for the Mini, wood-lined Rovers and sleek Jags, was by 1978, a myth rudely shattered by Allegro, Princess and Marina, while Triumph, Rover and Jaguar, lost their quality and started the slide down the reliability stakes. Even a wood and velour-lined Wood and Pickett Rover SD1 failed to revive any fortunes.

In 1978, German BL dealers had to take five Morris Marinas by order off BL, in order to qualify for each single Jaguar XJ6 that they would order as intended stock to sell from their showroom.

Imagine trying to sell Marinas to hard-charging, autobahn-storming German drivers! Just how long would a Marina survive such high-speed and hot running? Not long at all, and anyway, one winter in the Alps would kill off a Marina; who would risk a Marina 1.8 with its lurching front end handling on an icy Alpine road? Only a brave soul. Or an Australian, who could buy a six cylinder 2.6-litre E-series engined Marina in Australia as the Leyland Marina! Imagine trying to get that around a tight bend in the rain. It had 123 bhp and a hot running three-speed autobox; failure was designed in.

The stylish and futuristic Princess 2200 ate driveshafts in Germany and ran hot when exposed to continuous higher-speed running on roads that were not congested British routes. The Triumph Dolomite Sprint lasted just over a year on the German market, breakdowns and ruinous warranty claims being a death knell.

By 1979, Jaguar sales in Germany were collapsing at the altar of build quality – or the lack thereof. German Jaguar dealers were offering thousands of deutschmarks off the XJ6. How about £3,000 off a new XJ-S in Germany at just £12,000!

Even Range Rovers needed discounting to sell, so bad was BL's reputation in Germany.

As men toiled at Longbridge, Cowley, and Coventry to churn out BL's finest fare, BL sold just a few thousand cars for the entire year of 1978 in Germany, and 130 cars that hot July.

130 cars. Go on, read it again:130.

It got worse. At home, in Great Britain, in 1978, BL had sold just 468 Triumph 2000 and 2.5, and 675 Stags. By the following year, BL's market share had dipped below 20 per cent to 19.6 per cent.[3]

It had been only eight years earlier in 1971 that the market share of *all* imported cars into Britain was 19.3 per cent. BL's market share at home had been 40.2 per cent. Less than a decade later, BL was 19.6 per cent and the imports at 56.3 per cent.

This was more than a reversal, it was a national disaster, yet was largely invisible to the British public – the taxpayers that funded it all! All they knew was that BL's cars were either old fare, or new but broke down or rusted, or both.

Now it could hardly be that the British public had become so utterly infatuated with foreign cars that they would abandon the home marques to such a degree by sheer fashion or conversion, could it? There had to be an underlying reason and there was, it was about the *product* and little else other than its build quality, or lack thereof.

BL's product was failing. It's brand was damaged.

Foreign cars could break down too, but less often. Foreign cars also rusted – even the new wave of shiny, vinyl trimmed, chrome encrusted, thin-steel skinned Japanese ones. Rusty VW Golfs were not unknown. Renault's great white hatchback hope was the modernistic 14. But 14 lacked build quality or decent rust protection. It soon scabbed its way to an early death – even with a hatchback, a good engine and a modern style.

But many BL loyalists *did* indeed favour the BL offerings over the modern competition. But, for BL, the fact was that its cars were still mostly 'old' cars. Austin Morris, JRT, and all, was incorporated into Leyland Cars Ltd in 1975 and then the mixed messages really took off. By 1978, the incoming Michael Edwardes could see the error of this policy and took them apart!

This then was the depth of the BL story. Yet Britain's governments of all political persuasions were prepared to pour hundreds of millions into BL – well beyond £3 billion in total. Soon after 1979, Margaret Thatcher's newly-elected Conservative regime would have no option other than to pour another £350 million-plus into BL, and then more, another £1 billion-plus.

Michael Edwardes had been employed in 1977 as a 'consultant' to BL (yet still contracted by his old company Chloride) as a chief executive-type strategic figure – *before* the 'golden' contract with which the new post-1979 Conservative administration under Mrs Thatcher (and Sir Keith Joseph) lured Edwardes into a named leadership role – one actually paid for by BL, or should that be the taxpayer at up to £100,000 per year.

Edwardes – remember he was previously appointed into BL by the Labour Party and was a member of its NEB and voted onto the NEB by union leaders, so was not known as 'union-basher', had to wield the knife beginning in 1977. There would be workforce cuts and the Labour Government knew it.

On the day Edwardes started work at BL, a new union agreement came into force which should have curtailed the 'wild-cat' strike mentality that had pervaded. BL's then 120,000 plus workers would adhere to a strategic industrial relations plan in a pay bargaining structure. In the decade since the departure of Donald Stokes and the arrival of Edwardes, many of BL's senior men (Turnbull, Barber, et al) had been sacrificed at the junction of its policies and its plans, not to mention the strikes and the consequent lack of build quality in it cars. Intriguingly, Edwardes as executive chairman had far more power than past leaders of BL and he did not have to go through the weird diplomatic process of

Civil Service administrative machinations to get his decisions ratified. He also kept on BL's last leader Alex Park in an advisory capacity.

So BL had been run by Donald Stokes the buccaneer, then with others and Alex Park carrying out the role of BL's chief executives but dancing to a government prescribed tune. There also came the Dobson affair. Did BL's complex management structure need culling? Edwardes, with little sales experience, but huge experience in corporate and man-management and the psychologies thereof, would put his trust in what he called 'high-calibre' managers and actually recruited those he wanted into his court.

The truth was that BL was in chaos, a mess spread across many layers of the company from shop floor to senior management. BL's thirty-plus factories were scattered across the nation and the industrial relations were appalling and the cars often not much better. Yet Range Rover existed inside BL! Jaguar still had allure and the Rover P6 was old but popular. And Mini just kept on going.

Great marques had been brought together under the BL banner, but their engineers and designers competed against their colleagues in the same stable. The operating costs were massive. Dealers competed not just with each other but internally within the Austin and Morris badge-engineered empire. Triumph's potential new cars were emasculated or culled to avoid clashing with the one and only new Rover, the SD1. The SD-2 of 1975 was a prototype Triumph that was designed to come in several versions with mildly differing styles and trims. It had huge design and marketing potential but was cancelled after five years work and millions spent – dumped, only then for money to be poured into the dubious Honda-Triumph Acclaim 'Bounty' code-named project.

MG was denied its new sports car – because Triumph got it.

Could, or even *should* BL be turned around and saved? Some thought not. BL did not even have financial consistency from the NEB who could pull the plug on any day they wanted. And where was the normally vociferous Tony Benn at the height of the BL debacle in 1978? He had been moved to a post in an unrelated government department. Meanwhile, even patriotic commentators thought that BL was holed below the water line – in 1978. Graham Turner, the esteemed Midlands industrial correspondent, let rip; BL was, he said, in fatal decline and if it was salvageable in 1971, it was not in 1978. Old models and a workforce who did not believe that the new models could save BL and their jobs, were key issues.[4]

Turner opined in *Car* magazine in November 1978 that in his view there was not one single part of BL that had a long-term future. And the workforce could, suggested Turner, be responsible for some of their own troubles. He added a 'farewell' to BL. But why was an expert like Turner to be proved wrong, as he was? The answer was because he did not take fully into account the politics of the affair. BL *had* to survive.

BL was beyond recovery opined Turner. Perhaps a few choice elements might be sold off, but BL was terminal said the journalist who had his ear to the ground. In truth, he *would* belatedly be proven to be correct, but before that happened another decade of delays, delusions, hard cash, and political issues would occur for BL. Another billion pounds plus and over 500 million deutschmarks would go up in smoke before the *same* old reasons as Turner cited would finally explode into a long delayed reality of something more than head gasket failure.

In 1976-78, every BL crisis put back the vital new cars that were desperately needed to earn money through sales. A refusal by the unions to work a night shift (with pay!) to produce extra Rover SD1s to make the most of its new car and 'Car of the Year' order book, meant that thousands of order and customers were lost. Who, even amongst patriots, would wait six or more months for a car when they could buy a Renault 30, Ford Granada, or even a Citroën CX, off the shelf?

Intriguingly, the Transport and General Workers Union welcomed Michael Edwardes' appointment in 1977 as a consultant to BL. Few people on the Left recall that! Or that it was a *Labour* government that hired Michael Edwardes and a Labour prime minister (James Callaghan) who let Edwardes cull BL jobs, firstly at Speke and then at Bathgate in Scotland.

Did Edwardes accept the BL challenge off the back of Denis Healey's promises of jam tomorrow amid a 'boom' that would not bust? After all, he had little warning that Thatcher would lead the Conservatives and then form one government, let alone three. In 1977, over two decades of Thatcher was not visible.

Bathgate was interesting, for it was one of the biggest factories in Europe and turned out car parts, engines, commercial vehicle parts for bus and truck, and notably, Leyland tractors. Edwardes first ordered its slimming down in 1978 under a Labour government which seemed willing to acquiesce but which was unwilling to let him close the plant instantly. But under Thatcher, by 1985 Bathgate was finally closed.

Callaghan was union sponsored, loyal to the unions, and had defeated union reform around a Labour government's Cabinet table in 1969's 'In Place of Strife' as a union reform plan. But at Bathgate and beyond just a few years later, here was Callaghan appointing Edwardes and giving him the power to close factories, cull jobs and confront the unions. This huge inconsistency in Callaghan's behaviour and policy has an explanation – yet it is one rarely cited.

If you tackle old BL employees, and even politicians of that era, today, they clam up and refuse to discuss, deny, or confirm anything on the subject. The narrative rules.

The explanation lay in a subject that was to be left side-stepped for years. The issue was the reality of the far-Left infiltration of the BL workforce (way beyond 'Red Robbo') and certain structures within the Labour Party. Therein lay the elephant in the room as the unspoken issue. Instead, the media portrayed the unions and their leaders and conveners (such as Derek Robinson) as the cause and the definition of the 'workforce' or 'strike' problem or 'disease'. But this was not the full story, not all the case – something far more extreme was hidden under the BL bed.

A report by the Central Policy Review Staff, said that amid BL's management and its workforce, there was 'trench warfare' at this time. Management were at odds over their brands and their cars and the Stalinists and Communists in the workforce believed in different outcomes and the two factions were to argue inside BL.

Callaghan's post-1975 new revisionist view was that his government had done what it could for BL and that its workers now held their fates in their own hands. Such a position rather took the argument away from Mrs Thatcher's position as Leader of the Opposition – that Tory ideology would be tougher on BL and its workers and their unions. It also shows that blaming Thatcher, 'the milk snatcher', was not to be wholly accurate. She even allowed a reformed National Enterprise Board (NEB) to briefly survive, despite its Bennite origins. Quite what she thought of Michael Edwardes having been a union-approve NEB member we do not know!

The truth was that even for Thatcher, (love her or hate her), the BL narrative was set. This now includes the oft-repeated mantra that Thatcher divided society. Surely, the facts outlined here prove that society was divided long before Margaret Thatcher took it a step further? Conversely, the narrative says that Thatcher (with Edwardes) 'tamed' the unions, yet the evidence proves that a significant part of her legislation had its roots in the work of prior governments including Labour ones.

Utterly bizarrely, it had been Labour and Barbara Castle in 1969 who had come up with the union reform White Paper, 'In Place of Strife', and although crushed by union power, it opened the door to reform in 1976 and Callaghan's reversal of his previous pro-union position because he insisted on union reform and brought in Michael Edwardes who was *not then* known as a union antagonist.

Thatcher would get the 'credit' for 'her' union reforms, but the facts were that their origins lay, utterly paradoxically, within the Labour Party in 1969...

With Edward Heath briefly elected and then gone, and the post-1974 Labour government's economic position facing questions, a loan from the International Monetary Fund under its belt, and Chancellor Denis Healey promising the delivery of an upturn, there was no way in which BL was going to be abandoned by Labour in 1978. But what of any new government?

Curiously, as Labour was reluctantly agreeing to giving BL billions, it was also inducing Chrysler to stay put with state aid (£150 million plus) for its British factories. Little did anyone know that Margaret Thatcher would soon give state aid to Japanese car makers to set up in Britain as partly state-funded competitors to state-funded BL.

This was the price of politics.

Harold Wilson, so often portrayed as highly efficient, a true leader and consummate political player, has a conflicting record over union reform, BMC and BL and over 'In Place of Strife'. He may not have been as 'in control' as perceived wisdom and the 'spin' of history would have us believe. But he got out when on top – before he was got rid of – the fate of even the strongest of Leaders, and of a Prime Minister yet to come.

Triumph's Stag was brilliant but had engine issues. These sadly diverted attention from its design brilliance and global popularity. A 'fastback' was built but not produced. Stag was another 'hero' of great British car design that was contaminated by what happened at BL.

1970s Numbers Games • 163

MGB GT – in white and scuttling away from Prescott in the hands of young owner in 2019. A time-warp of MG experience. Often credited to Pininfarina in this fast back GT guise, it might be fairer to describe it as inspired by a lovely Pininfarina prototype and taken to production design by Hayter, Thornley, and Enever of MG.

Rover's SD1 of 1976 was innovative and trend-setting. It's interior was a as radical as its exterior. Bache's car was a landmark design.

Above: Rover as part of BL – advertising for the smaller-engined SD1 twins

Left: Austin Metro became Metro and Rover Metro/100. This is the 'GTa' model in all its glory. A brilliant little car, but outdated and outmoded.

Car magazine was a supporter of BL and its engineers and designers and directors. These covers capture the essence of the era. (Author via Bauer Media).

166 • *British Leyland: From Triumph to Tragedy. Petrol, Politics and Power*

Right and opposite: *Maestro. BL got this right, despite a few hiccups. It was safe, modern, and sold well. But build quality remained an issue. This is the 1.6 Austin version, but MG variants soon arrived, the Turbo being fun, but the brilliant Perkins-diesel version was much more sensible.*

Below: *A Honda interior with the addition of a Vanden Plas badge on the steering wheel. This was the reality of Roverisation. Marketing madness.*

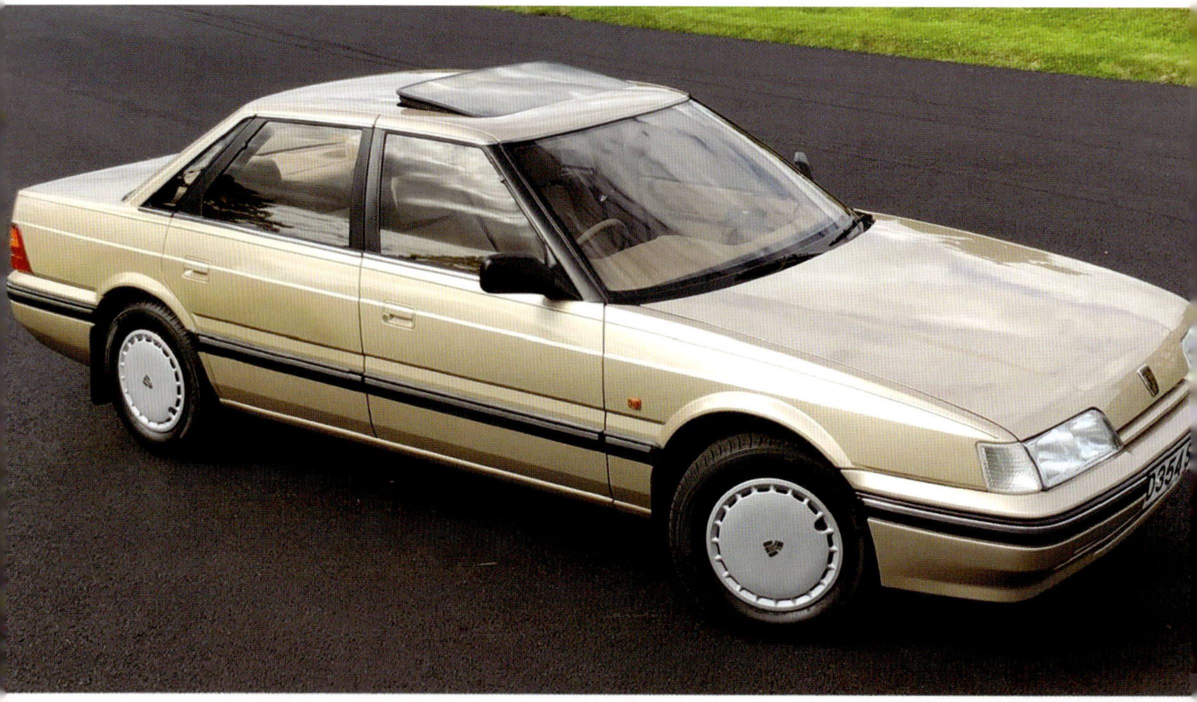

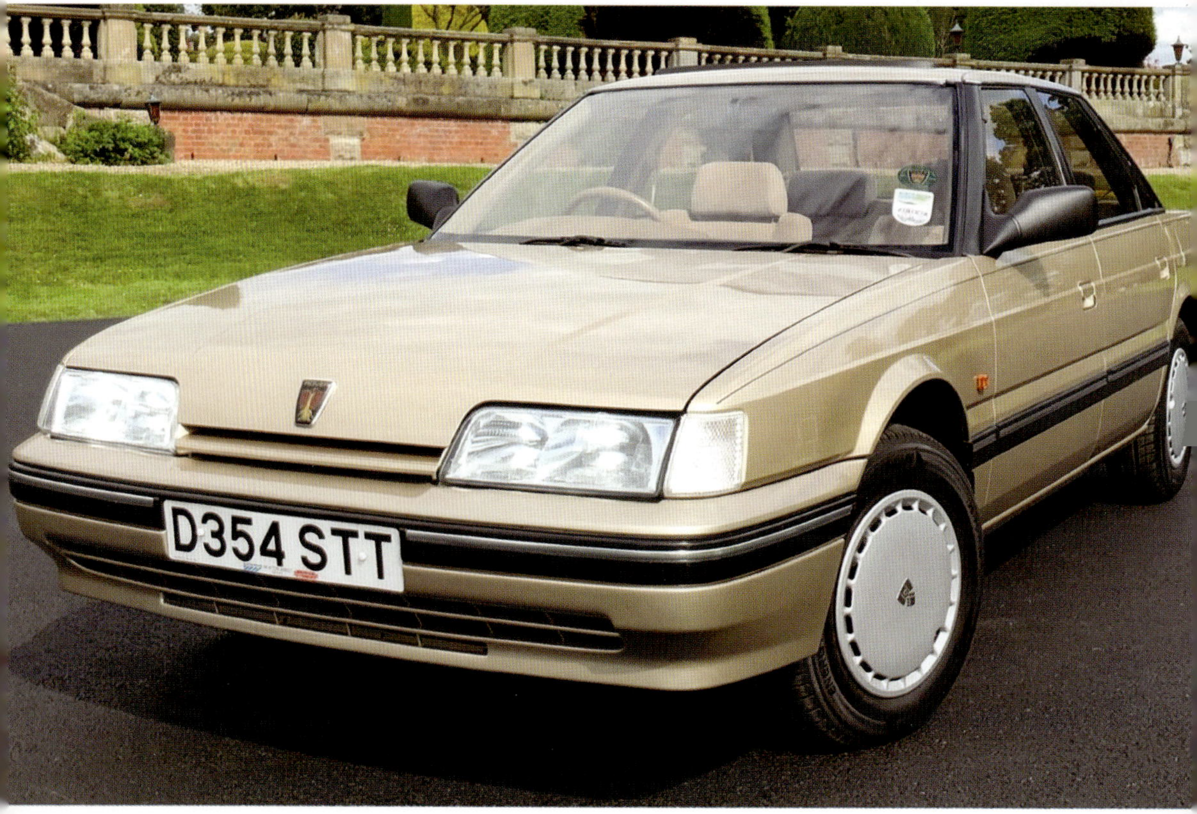
D354 STT

Above and opposite:
Rover's 800 in a rather conservative gold and beige yet still looking sharp. The styling from Gordon Sked made 800 look up to date and very smart. The Honda version of the same car was decidedly dull to look at.

9
1980s
The Edwardes Effect

'If revenue and costs cannot be balanced by 1983-84 there would be no point in putting more money into the car business... The directors are in no way so emotionally involved in the business that we would not close part of it – or the whole of it.'

Sir Michael Edwardes at the BL Annual General Meeting, May 1981.

Michael Edwardes' early moves as 1978 dawned had to be dramatic; the strike-bound Triumph factory at Liverpool Speke was closed and TR7 production shifted south-eastwards. Bathgate was tackled. A new Mini – the long overdue replacement which many managers in BL knew was key to its future – was scrapped despite much expensive development, killed off at just the moment it was most needed to become sales reality. There followed the second bite at it that became the Metro.

Edwardes threatened 15,000 redundancies at what he saw was an over-staffed BL. Closing down loss-making outposts of the old empire and 'rationalising' the model policy was what Edwardes planned in very different vein to the mid-1970s Ryder Report and its own recommendations for BL. He would soon cull 30,000 jobs form BL's total global staff of 196,000. The British BL head count would go from 150,000 down to 100,000 across Edwardes' tenure.

In two years after Edwardes took up the BL appointment, the Thatcher Conservative administration would be in place. And despite its ideology of privatisation, the truth was that there were three things it did not then *dare* to privatise – BL, the NHS, latterly to be privatised by New Labour, and British Rail (latterly to be privatised by the Conservatives). And after all, one good question was, who the hell would buy BL anyway? One quick look at the Rootes/Chrysler UK/Europe situation and the reinvention of it in the UK as Talbot after being sold off on the cheap made much clear about the realities and the costs of British car building in the Midlands.

To gain an idea of what did go wrong, let's continue the depressing economics of BL's entry into the 1980s.

In April 1980, 19,000 BL workers went on strike against Michael Edwardes' 'ultimatum' to accept the 5 per cent pay offer. Refusal might result in sacking. Yet the strike was broken by union leader Moss Evans of the TGWU, who reached an agreement with Edwardes that ended the threat of a mass BL walk-out. Yet Evans had initially supported and encouraged action against the 5 per cent pay policy and imposed terms. Within days, Evans and ten other union leaders had agreed to Edwardes' demands. He said he thought he and the union had 'saved' BL and many agreed – but not the Trotskyists, who accused them of a 'betrayal'. They saw the struggle a different way.

That Chrysler was nearly bankrupt and Ford deeply in debt, seems to have been seen through a reverse-angled mirror by the far-Left.

Edwardes made a very important point that is often ignored in the BL narrative and the anti-Edwardes narrative.

He said:

'My actions, my strategy may have seemed severe to some, but the point was that things had been let to go so far, that drastic action was the only answer. I was fighting against years of accumulated problems that were now a huge barrier and required massive action to solve. This is why we had to do what we did. If not, collapse was the inevitable outcome of what had built up behind the dam.'

But Edwardes key point was thus:

'We were always reacting, rarely did we have the chance to strategically plan and when we did, it was constrained by what had already happened. Our hands were on many occasions, tied. Given the hand we were dealt with, we did well.'[1]

Cognisant of such issues, a secret 'no-strike' plan was being envisaged by union leaders and BL management for the 1980s. It came to nothing and was battled against by the far-Left as an act of ultimate union 'betrayal'.

But BL wages *had* slipped. Instead of being just above the national average as they were in 1973, factory floor manufacturing wages at BL in 1980 were around 20 per cent below the national average. Inflation was rising, but BL workers' pay was not just static, but static at a rate far lower than the national scale. A production worker at average grade earned £88 a week at BL, yet the national average was £122 per week. With two million unemployed, was this the moment to strike?

'Workers are pricing themselves out of their jobs,' said Margaret Thatcher in response.

Meanwhile BL was paying just under £100 million a year in bank interest on its recent loans.

The new Metro was about to be launched in 1980, yet Edwardes latterly recalled that when he was about to give the car its local Birmingham launch speech, he was in fact armed with *two* speeches – one announcing Metro and one announcing not Metro, but the total closure of Austin Morris. His choice as to which to read out fell to the decision of the workers as to whether they would vote to strike to support Derek Robinson's dismissal, or not. This was the famous February 1980 'Cofton Park' Longbridge open air union meeting. Robinson was not supported by a majority of his fellow workers; BL and its new Metro lived![2]

And despite its excellent working record (no major strikes), MG at the Abingdon plant was soon to be utterly terminated, closed down and turned into a badge-engineered brand. Sadly, the 1979-80 plan to sell MG, or the rights to produce MG-badged cars (initially based on the existing MGB) to an Aston Martin related, Curtis-led consortium, failed.

Completely separate from these factors were the BMC and then BLMC motor sport legends and the motor sport budget. Racing, rallying, especially rally had taken BMC and then the BLMC name across the world and to great victories. From Paddy Hopkirk to Pat Moss Carlsson through to Easter, Pond, Culcheth, Buffum, Soper, and more, great names framed the BMC and BLMC competitions department and its budget – which was soon to be cut. Yet in 1982, the newly branded Austin Rover Group (ARG) fired back with the Metro6R4 Group B rally car.

There then came the BL blip – the temporary bubble of hope over financial fact – the Metro, a car like so many BL cars in its basic genius, yet tainted by having to use hand-me-down parts-bin components that included an antique engine and a four-speed gear box; did they learn nothing from the Allegro affair? Why use such parts? Because of politically imposed funding restraints.

Metro was BL's most 'political' project at the height of the late 1970s affairs of BL and the state. Yet Metro was a good car – with few glaring errors. Edwardes and BL *had* produced a winner. But development and improvement inevitably in the tide of all things BL took years.

How do you replace the irreplaceable – that was BL's Mark Snowden's view on Metro replacing Mini and he had a good point.[3] Snowden turned ADO88 – internally known as 'the shed' – into LC8/Metro, with the styling department's help. Metro took on and beat most of its ageing competitors, and matched the newer ones except in its lack of a fifth gear.

Metro performed, despite its forced compromises. It was four inches longer than its ADO88 precursor. Yet Metro was engineered on a £250 million shoestring and left talented engineers 'with one hand tied behind their backs' – according to some of them.

Men like Metro engineering leaders Fred Coultas (Chief Project Engineer) and Peter Harris (Principal Development Engineer), Robert Jones (Executive Engineer), worked miracles – Metro contained many carry-over Mini parts and the design team were forced to work around the very tall engine and air filter configuration – hence the high scuttle and sloping nose. An overdrive unit for the four-speed box was to sadly remained unfunded and unfitted. Fred Coultas' Metro team created magic from many old parts and many new ones. His team also innovated Metro's deep, interlocking sills and doors to create much better side impact performance. Metro, by the way, had a torsional rigidity/stiffness rating at a high 5,800lb ft/dg compared to Ford's Fiesta having a weaker 4,650lb ft/dg. Also of note was Metro's better beam deflection performance at 0.034in compared with Fiesta's 0.057in.

Furthermore, Metro displayed minimal steering wheel intrusion/deflection at 0.74in compared to the ECE 12 regulatory maximum permissible 5.0in. Crash energy deceleration and force loadings were near ideal – not bad at all for a short nosed car. Metro in its original form performed well in the regulation 100 per cent head-on frontal crash test at 30mph. BL's crash research programme (ESV) and its ECV2 which was based on a prototype metro had proven how good BL's engineers were.

But none of the team ever thought that Austin Metro would be made to last from 1980 to 1990, then as the Rover Metro and then from 1995 onwards towards 2000 as the Rover 100. By then, the industry's engineering efficiency and safety design improvements rendered Metro as Rover 100 utterly pointless and its EuroNCAP offset crash test results spoke volumes for how far car safety has come. Somehow, Ford's Fiesta Mk1 and Peugeot's 205 were not pilloried for their equally appalling offset frontal crash test performances, or such in real-life, but by the time Metro as Rover 100 was exposed, those two 1980s cars were long dead.

Compared to the original 1970s Mini replacements (such as 9X), Metro was minimal and late to the market. Yet it *was* a clever car, and even a good one. It also had good aerodynamics for a short stubby car at C_D 0.41 – again better than its competitors – latterly reduced to C_D 0.39. Remember, Mini had a C_D 0.48 and the later Mini Clubman had a C_D of over 0.54! This was a truly appalling aerodynamic value, even for a 1970s car. Metro's front grille offered aerodynamic function – not just styling – it controlled airflow according to airflow speed. Metro's low wind noise, notably around the A-pillars, proved how much thinking had gone into its aerodynamics. Metro's coefficient of drag was also lower than Fiesta's pointless C_D 0.46.

Metro cleverly reduced ride harshness by damping its front wheel and front suspension subframe interaction by mechanising the telescopic damper between the suspension and the bodyshell, not the suspension and a sub-frame.

Metro was roomy, more comfortable than a Mini, perky in 1.3 incarnation, handled well and truly was 'Tardis' like. Yet it needed regular servicing and had many build quality issues. But Metro's secret was even cleverer advertising (of Ford-proportions) and patriotic fervour that put it on the podium as a sales success – temporarily. Who could have suspected its afterlife as the Rover 100!

Of little reported interest, the improved efficiency A+ 1275cc engine which was created for use in the Metro, was initially developed in the BL South Africa (LeyKor), 'Apache' variation of the ADO16 1100/1300. The revised casting being tested there and in the Ital. BL resisted breakerless electronic ignition in the name of simplicity and reliability. £30 million went into improving the A-series engine and quietening down the transmission workings. A+ and the base 998cc engines also got nimonic coated exhaust valves. Metro used BL's first aluminium radiator too.

BL spent money on Metro.

Despite all the strife and the strikes, BL's engineers and designers went to town on making Metro great. Harold Musgrove watched over the new baby like an eagle with a chick in the nest.

The later Rover Metro and the Rover 100 were in fact very stupid things to do to the Rover brand, yet Metro as Rover 100 rode fantastically on its Moulton-inspired suspension redesign. Add a five-speed gearbox, a K-series engine and 'proper' seats and Metro as a Rover was a very good little supermini – except for its now compromised cabin and its terrible offset frontal crash test performance. As a result of the car's very poor EuroNCAP offset frontal crash test result in late 1997, Rover 100 sales collapsed and the car was withdrawn. The original Mini had however, 'got-away' with its terrible front, side and rear impact crash performance despite the sterling efforts of Professor MacKay at Birmingham University who tried to tackle the Mini's lack of passive 'safety', Issigonis having dismissed his concerns.

But the *original* Metro main buyers were Brits who had previously owned BL cars. A few of the French liked the Metro, but in the end it was another BL car with build quality problems. However, with a 1990 revamp, five doors, and added 'refinement', Metro remained competitive despite its origins.

Renault's ancient 5 still had its benefits and VW's Polo was just so much more complete; Ford's 'flimsy' Fiesta won fashionable approval and made the company many millions, yet it had two major issues – a terrible ride and handling compromise that was bad in the base and luxury models but utterly unacceptable in the S-model, and a very poor offset frontal crash test performance – not dissimilar from Metro/Rover 100. The wacky yet very popular 'pure' supermini choice was not Metro five-door, it was the Citroën Visa in twin-cylinder or four-cylinder guises. If Visa was too wacky, then try the car it took its underpinnings from, the brilliant Peugeot 104 in 1.4-litre S or ZX form, as a real Metro beater.

By 1981, under Edwardes' knife BL had indeed been rationalised into separate operating sectors – Cars, Unipart (spares and parts), Land Rover, Jaguar, and the Leyland Vehicles arm that sold buses and trucks. Perhaps splitting off the parts *seemed* a good idea.

1981 was a crucial year for BL. Metro lived. The four-door Range Rover arrived. The automatic gearbox for that car was deliberately delayed until its abilities had been proven, thus avoiding customers doing the development – a familiar BL issue. Land Rover's new boss Mike Hodgkinson was firmly steering that marque towards better productivity and quality, as was John Egan at Jaguar. Jaguar had a new more economical petrol engine due and Perkins diesel developments were in the pipeline for Land Rover and even for Jaguar and Rover via V.M. Motori. The new LC10/11car series were in development. And there was the arrival of the Honda-Triumph Acclaim which would at least create showroom footfall however dubious its heritage. Edwardes had clamped down on rogue BL suppliers too – upping quality and sacking those who were 'passengers'.

But ultimately you could purchase a shining, chrome encrusted 1980s British legend of engineering – a new Japanese 'Triumph' car!

The Acclaim, advertised with a 'Best of Everything' strapline, was beigeness and boring banality personified yet it sold simply because it worked and was more reliable than the ancient BL and BMC legacy cars that it replaced; such tells you just how bad the old BL cars had become, so bad that a small, flimsy Honda wearing Triumph badges, was seen as an *improvement*. This ancient old Honda with a terrible drag coefficient of CD 0.46, a car tweaked up from a Japanese domestic market model that was structurally soft, devoid of even the Honda version's more aerodynamic slanted nose, and had had to be fitted with new front seats for big-boned Brits as the original Honda seats were too thin and flimsy (the new seats came from an old Ford by the way and were ill-tuned to the Honda-Triumph suspension behaviours and harmonics).

This, an 'anti-car' consumer durable, from the company that gave you the TR sports cars, Spitfire, GT6, and the 2000-2500 saloons and the Stag. Was it not a despicable thing to do to the Triumph name? Hail the 'Acclaim CD' – the 'worst of all worlds'. But they sold! They also proved the British car worker could build, trim paint and finish a car to decent standard. But it was all too damn late. The abandoned SD2 (even with its rear-wheel drive) would have been a much bigger money earner and a better car, for it was *designed*, and engineered with advanced thinking – and proper suspension.

By 1981, John Egan (latterly Sir John) had begun to reorganise Jaguar and stamp the mark of firm strategy and solid policy choices onto the ailing Jaguar with stunning results. Improving the quality of parts supplied from external suppliers made a huge difference. Memories of Jaguar winning Le Mans five times were just that – memories. Commercial reality ruled. American dealers loved the revised XJ6 series 3 and raved about better paint and better quality of the new Jaguars. XJ40 was also due! Sadly, the proposed new F-Type – Pininfarina-shaped – was axed. But XJ-S was re-evaluated and improved.

Egan had entered Jaguar in 1980 after the likes of Frank R.W. 'Lofty' England had retired, Geoffrey Robinson would resign (he became an MP) over Ryder's suggestions for Jaguar and the 1970s fuel crisis had abated. Interestingly, three former Ford men were to be found inside Jaguar that had been subsumed into BLMC but quality had suffered by 1975. Indeed, Jaguar had to send out teams of mechanics and fitters to fettle new car stock that lay at dealers. Use of BL parts and cheaper supplied parts allied to strikes into 1980 weighed heavily on the quality of the big cars.

With Geoffrey Robinson gone, there was to be a regime change. The Ryder Report of 1975 had also suggested that Jaguar should not be a stand-alone brand. 'To hell with that' went up the refrain at Coventry. Peter Craig the Brown's Lane plant director did his best to continue the 'ethos' of Jaguar.[4] Yet Jaguar was swallowed up into Leyland Cars and the BL 'super-brand'. Jaguar had even lost its board of directors. But at least time-served Jaguar loyalist Robert 'Bob' Knight had also had his effect inside Jaguar's management team, rising to rank of Managing Director of Jaguar. But then came Edwardes in late 1977, who had the sense to usurp Ryder and give Jaguar its head within a Jaguar Rover Triumph (JRT) brand grouping – this lasted less than three years before Jaguar finally got to stand alone again.

As Ray Horrocks made his mark at Austin, an American was now to lead Jaguar – the little-cited William P. Thompson who would last only as long as

JRT branding itself. Interestingly, although not immune from strikes, the Jaguar workforce were less militant, less political, and when they realised that Edwardes could close Browns Lane and built Jaguars somewhere else if he felt he had too, the Jaguar workers grasped the facts of reality.

Then in 1980 came the man who proved to the workforce he was a Jaguar man – a local Coventry man – John Egan. New, more economical engines for the XJ-S (soon to be a facelifted XJS without the hyphen) were on the way. XJ-6 Series 3, and plans for new cars all helped. Jaguar's turnover for 1983 was £500 million. Egan proved that good management, strategic vision and tenacity, and newly willing workers could save a car company's global reputation. Almost 30,000 Jaguars a year would be built at this time. The rest, as they say, is history. Jaguar Cars Ltd was reborn as were its cars and their build quality. Finally, they were once again painted properly! Egan and his men saved Jaguar, yet what tragic irony that Jaguar then off the back of its own success, passed to Ford and thence to Indian ownership. And will the Germans eventually get their hands on it?

There is no doubt that Jaguar and the then separate Land Rover were the profit centres, the jewels in the crown of BL. But both would suffer at the hands of the BL affair and yet curiously, via Ford and BMW ownerships respectively, they would eventually be re-joined under today's ownership structure.

Land Rover began its revival under Mike Hodgkinson. There came much – from V8 and turbo diesel TDi Land Rovers, to Discovery and more. The development of Range Rover into the vehicle it is today proves that product integrity trumps brand marketing, although we can only cite the Evoque as a fashion statement and reaction.

In the early 1980s, the new Austin and Rover model ranges were due. BL and its cars began to recover, yet redundancies, closures and cost-cutting were vital, yet so often portrayed as negatives, despite being critical to the survival of BL.

Edwardes was clear headed about cars in one sense too. He knew Metro was a collection of old Austin parts, brilliantly masquerading as a new car in a new body, so he knew that the totally new LC10/LM11 series project car that was to become Maestro and the Montego was far more important to BL's survival. Yet Edwardes discovered this vital fact quite late in the day. He needed to be made to realise that for any mass market car manufacturer, the majority of its sales lay not in a super mini class car, but a medium sized family car – especially a useful five-door mid-range hatchback type. So much money had gone into Metro, and Maestro was delayed and late to a market that Golf, Astra, Escort and others had tapped into already across Europe.

Maestro used the 'bought-in' gearbox for a quick and cheaper solution than a £50 million in-house BL design and tooling. And guess where the new gearbox came from? Off the shelf from, wait for it, arch-rival Volkswagen! BL had talked to VW just four years previously about a possible collaboration and this gearbox deal was the only fruit those talks would produce. The EEC did not seem to object either – the Germans were getting paid for their gearbox, so that was all right. Imagine if VW had tried to buy in a British gearbox for a German car!

Some later claimed that the Maestro/Montego projects' finances were 'undermined' by having to buy in VW gearboxes due, it is said to BL's own engineers not being able to produce their own. The engineers dispute this, and say that there were several in-house BL gearboxes readily available for development. The engineers say it was an accountancy decision to buy in the VW gearbox – a straight case that the £50+ million or so required to get the BL gearbox into production could be better spent buying one off the shelf from VW. The immediately available VW gearbox saved time too – and time was critical in BL's survival plan under Edwardes. Maestro was needed urgently. It has also been suggested that political pressure to source the gearbox from Germany came from Thatcher's government. Given that funding came from government, it was an easy stick with which to beat BL.

Anyone unclear as to the power of government over BL needs to recall that Edwardes had to make an annual appearance before the Industry Committee of the House of Commons and explain himself and BL's actions to the assembled MPs.

Edwardes' proposed 1979 link-up agreement between Honda and Austin Rover had followed earlier attempts to negotiate co-operations with Chrysler, VW GM, and Renault, all of which foundered. A suggested Toyota link-up was also rumoured.

Edwardes had realised in 1978, just a year into his so-called consultancy at BL, that the model range was so old and the new cars so far away, that BL may not survive the interim 'bridging' period. His idea was to do a deal with a car maker to quickly licence-build mildly re-worked BL 'copies' of an existing model. In return, that car maker would gain a foothold in Britain and a gateway into the EU. So a Japanese manufacturer that might feel constrained by the voluntary sales agreement that kept Japanese car imports to around 10,000 per year, would be ideal.

Curiously, the strongest interest came not from Japan but from Germany's Volkswagen. Talks were held but came to nothing, other than links that would soon allow BL to purchase VW gearboxes for Maestro and Montego. So Edwardes looked East and the Honda talks began. There was however to be a curious future to the BL-VW talks, because over twenty years later, as BMW bid for the remains of Rover, VW put in a higher bid! That too stalled due to problems with brand ownership rights.

So it would be Honda who would soon yield up its existing, Civic-based car as the basis of the 'new' 1980s Triumph Acclaim. Honda would also have access to BL's design technology – which despite BL's reputational profile at the time, was of the highest order.

The willingness of Honda to enter into the agreement with BL (as Austin Rover Group) had its roots in the realisation that such would give Honda wider access to then restricted UK market beyond the then voluntary import agreement (agreed in 1977), and of course ultimately into the tariff-protected EEC/EU.

The arrangement with Honda, across a major cultural divide in the workplace, was a tough challenge but was well managed by a British team headed by Mike Carver as Group Executive Director Strategic Planning. There were many hurdles to overcome and many technical issues to be resolved.[5] This was about more than stick a new badge on an old Honda; ultimately it was about ARG developing a new car that led to the Rover 800 alongside Honda as they developed the new Legend in a joint production initiative. Remember, Rover might build UK area market Legends for Honda – even if Honda would then have to put them through its own 'final' checks at its new Swindon facility – soon to be a manufacturing plant.

With stage one of the Honda relationship as the Acclaim, for ARG the agreement was a saviour, but it did mean less profit on each Acclaim because a royalty had to be paid to Honda. Rover 800 was a more involved, more technical affair. 800 was a good car, but underneath still lay the early 1980s underpinnings of Honda's 'questionable' structure and if you saw the results of the 1980s German *Auto Motor und Sport* magazine and Allgemeiner Deutscher Automobil Club (ADAC) funded crash test of the original Honda Legend – 800's brother – as published in *What Car* and beyond, the elephant in the room got louder, as it did with EuroNCAP's crash test of the Honda Accord-based Rover 600.

The Thatcher government pumped hundreds of millions of pounds in BL and its new 'Austin Rover' branding. Over £900 million underpinned LC10-LC11 (sometimes referred to as LM-series) projects that were Maestro and Montego. These were the cars from which a whole new range of cars were *supposed* to stem – precursors to LC14 and model ranges beyond.

Edwardes told the media that BL needed Metro in 1980 to survive, and to convince the new Conservative government that BL could deliver and to secure the next tranche of funding. Neither were there the resources available to bring Maestro forward for earlier launch. These were the bare facts of BL's fiscal reality and explained why decisions were taken as they were. BL needed to build Maestros at a rate of at least 5,000 a week. Ford could built fewer Escorts if needed, yet at greater profit per car because Escort was, according to insiders, at least 15 to 20 per cent cheaper to make, not least as it contained less steel.

In pure marketing and financial terms, the car that Edwardes should have got into the market first was not Metro, it was Maestro. But his hand was forced by circumstance and severe political pressure from the new Thatcher regime to do something that showed that BL could deliver a return on investment and quickly. So Metro came first and helped keep the company going until Maestro materialised. But as Edwardes always advised, it was indeed a close run thing in terms of BL's survival.

At this time there lay within BL two ex-Ford managers (remember there had been the 'Fordisation' at BL in the preceding decade). These were the little-known BL deputy chairman David Andrews who had been within the empire since the late 1960s, who would peel off to run Land Rover and the Leyland truck division. The better-known Ray Horrocks was an extrovert newcomer who would be deputy managing director of the Edwardes-restructured car operation. He should have become Chairman when Edwardes went, but politics intervened.

With the subsequent resignation of the managing director David Whittaker amid Edwardes' plans, Horrocks rose to power within BL cars. It was Horrocks (as managing Director 1978-81) who wisely stopped the ungainly Mini update as ADO88 in its tracks and ordered a restyle that eventually led to LC8 directly as the Metro. It was design leader Harris Mann and his team (including Gordon Sked and Roy Tucker) who turned the flat-sided 'wardrobe on wheels' that was ADO88 into the better looking, more curvaceous LC8/Metro.

The Mini was recognised as unviable other than as an antique 'niche' product, but was now economic to produce as the toolings were long since paid for, and had a willing market. But its all-new replacement had been canned and then reincarnated as the Metro, a car which was actually the sum of its very old Mini parts. The Mini meanwhile, represented 1.5 per cent of BL's sales. And an early-1980s car sales price war raged, small hatchbacks, lightweight and with five-speed gearboxes and great handling were all the rage.

But BL could not squander the old Mini's 1.5 per cent when its own total market share was hovering around a mere 18 per cent, no matter how outdated and dire the Mini was.

With Harold Musgrove as Austin Rover new chairman (a man who had worked his way up through the ranks), Mini nostalgia was unlikely to be a vehicle for sympathy. Getting rid of the Morris badge was also on the cards;

consigning a historic and nostalgic marque to the parts bin of history, except for commercial vehicle output.

Musgrove made a public statement about Morris:

> 'Market research showed that the name Morris is synonymous with commercial vehicles. Austin with volume car production and Rover with style and quality.'

'Austin-Rover' was a brand name soon to be dubiously deployed for the 1980s.

BL's productivity was still poor and Musgrove worked hard to improve it. The average BL worker had a productivity rate of about 30 per cent less than his European counterpart and less still than the Japanese counterpart. Things needed to change, but as Musgrove knew, quality should not be compromised for quantity.

Regretfully, the early Rover 800s were to be rushed off to dealers before the factory had fettled them – numbers targets had to be met.

Rover was also soon to be amid a row with its new engineering partner at this time. The Triumph Acclaim badge-engineered Honda was now in the showrooms and a more substantially revised Honda-Rover project was on the go. The question was should the collaborative Honda deal, an early example of platform-sharing via the Honda Accord into Legend-becomes-Rover 800 (then known as the 'XX Project') use Honda's expensive double wishbone front suspension, or a cheaper and stronger conventional MacPherson strut design favoured by Rover? Would the project implode over such a row?

There was much the two companies could learn from each other, but time and money meant that a fully re-bodied Rover variant of the Honda was not possible. Rover did a re-skin of the Honda.

So in the end, Honda had won, with Rover simply 'Roverising' the cars' outer skin panels and interior and even accepting the Honda 2.5-litre and then the better 2.7-litre engine. Meanwhile, Honda's Japanese-built Integra was to be sold as Rover in Australia with nothing but the badges changed. Honda opened its Swindon facility to 'check' and, shall we say, 'rectify' its Honda-badged but Rover-built cars that were part of the deal. So began Honda's foothold in the EU.

But 1981-82 saw the closure of several Austin plants, not least the engine factory at Coventry (600 jobs lost) and an expensive move of production from Cowley to Longbridge for the ageing Marina-based Ital – truly a car on its last legs of facelifted agony. The forthcoming Maestro and Montego saw the BL board pump money into Longbridge and £250 million into Cowley for this future model production. But projects for cars as LM14 and LM15 as new models for major

BL brands, had simply dematerialised and this included the SD1 replacement, hence the subsequent Honda arrangement. Hidden away inside BL were several design prototypes created at this time, yet, despite large amounts of money being spent, they were binned just prior to being pre-production ready.

Replacing cars across the BL range with rationalised, badge-engineered types was still a product policy. Re-engineering Hondas as Rovers, and framing a future supply of cars and jobs, was the very stuff of BL's 1980s survival. Several potential Triumph cars, notably the larger SD2 saloon, had been terminated at the altar of rationalisation despite being so near to production reality at great cost already spent. The concept of spending hundreds of millions to develop a large Triumph that would compete with the Rover SD1 and subsequent Honda/Rovers within the same company was deemed pointless. And the decision may well have been *fiscally* correct. But it left many buyers looking elsewhere – *not* at the Rover offering. Then came Triumph's Honda – the Acclaim, and the end of dignity.

1981-82 saw bad consumer headlines for BL when the issue of it (and other car makers) charging far more for their new cars in Britain than in Europe came to the fore. A private individual could buy a BL car (or another make) in Europe for much less and 'import' it into the UK. This was known as 'the personal import loophole' at the time

BL's cars (in near UK-spec and right-hand drive) were cheaper ordered in Europe and delivered there, than they were at home in Britain. Domestic BL prices had to come down. A new Metro L sold in 1981 for £3,500 at home in Britain where it had been built, yet in The Netherlands and in Belgium, the same Metro could be purchased for around £2,500 – or £1,000 cheaper!

Who was making these massive margins? BL and its British dealers, that is who – and the British Government with its 10 per cent car purchase tax on top of VAT! Oh, and wait for it, British customers for new cars were charged up to £400 per car as a 'delivery charge' that was hidden in the price. Given that the dealers had to order a set number of cars for delivery per year as part of their dealership agreement, charging the innocent customer for delivery to the showroom seemed like nothing more than a rip-off. British BL dealers operated on far higher profit-per-car margins for private sales (but not discounted business sales) at 16-20 per cent, than their European BL dealer colleagues at 8-11 per cent, on cars which had a lower sales price as well!

A Jaguar XJ-S over 40 percent cheaper to buy in Germany. But a mid-range Mercedes was about 30 per cent more expensive in Britain than it was in Germany. The dealers made the most of the margin!

But BL's cars cost far more to produce due to lower productivity than its rivals, so if car prices were to be equalised in the British domestic market across the European markets' prices, then BL would lose millions. The 'personal import loophole' would soon require action from the EEC and British Government. So much then for 'free movement' of goods in the EEC.

Prior to her untimely death, Dame Sheila McKechnie (Director, Consumers Association) told me this when discussing BL in 1997:

It is a wonder, beyond even patriotism that British car buyers kept faith with British Leyland. The cars were at times dire, even the good cars were ruined by quality issues. Our files are packed with complaints about its cars across decades. Then to find out you might be paying a thousand pounds more for your car than a Belgian, well for many it was the last straw.'

Dame Sheila was also deeply shocked at the outcome of the original AMS/ADAC Honda Legend crash test and then the 1997 Honda Accord-based Rover 600 EuroNCAP offset crash test findings in 1997 (at which she and I were present). How, she wondered, could crash test and injury prevention standards between cars vary so much when the 'best' performers were seen alongside the 'worst'?

An argument over BL's non-existing bread and butter saloon; was it to be a car bigger than a Mini or Metro, yet smaller than the Cortina class of car or one smaller than even the LC10 (Maestro-to-be) or the Ford Escort? In effect, this was the car to replace the brilliant 1960s Austin/Morris 1100 and 1300 ranges which Allegro had failed to adequately replace in terms of ability, style and sales. BL's failure to reinvent this formula, its failure to keep loyal Austin/Morris 1100/1300 customers within the BL tent, saw massive sales go to competitors cars. Ultimately, the deliberate decision to abandon this vital car type and market sector, would lead to many loyal BL managers taking the decision to quit the BL ship.

Even that time-served old BL hand Musgrove would quit his stellar role as BL model policy became stretched too far. Edwardes took tough decisions, some were his and imposed by him, others were forced by the fiscal reality of the place he found himself in under government edict and control.

But that lay in the near future as, by 1982, BL did not have its leadership marked out for the future. The Conservative government, paradoxically wrapped up in the Union Jack of patriotism, was meanwhile selling off every national asset it could, even to foreigners. Sir Michael Edwardes, the man who had re-structured

BL would soon be off. But the Thatcher regime had stuck with Edwardes and had backed his fight with the unions, and had just given BL another £1 billion (£700 million in 1980, then more) – a contribution of nearly £20 from every British taxpayer! Thatcher's Sir Keith Joseph must have known his hands were tied behind his back.

No wonder that 'Returning British Leyland as quickly as possible to the private sector', was the terminology used by Mrs Thatcher's newest Industry Secretary Patrick Jenkin. In his subsequent book, *Back from the Brink*,[6] Edwardes castigated Jenkin for a lack of understanding of a structure such as BL and how it operated. Jenkin intervened too much, thought Edwardes, but Jenkin had Thatcher breathing down his neck. Jenkin also became embroiled in Peugeot's closure of its West Midlands facilities and a lot of EEC-related argument went on. Peugeot – which lost £550 million in under 36 months at this time – wanted the Thatcher government's help keeping a British factory open during the Iranian crisis which had stopped Peugeot's British Chrysler/Talbot arm earning from its Iranian car building contracts.

The government had refused help – citing EEC rules as justification for such – to the French!

Privatising BL ignored the reality of BL, its history and its practices, that had not truly been in private hands for decades and which had been fiddled with by Labour, and Conservative politicians and their governments and civil service for years amid the dead hand of the state and the imposed strategy upon BL. It sounded almost Marxist – which is what some of the workers aligned themselves with.

Except of course that a Marxist or socialist state might not have tried to force privatised reality upon an endemically state-supported and chronic body like BL.

Edwardes sold off over a dozen key parts of BL and completed the closure of the Triumph and the MG factories. Edwardes had to make regular statements to the House of Commons Industry Committee to explain BL's latest position and to justify its needs for more cash. The fact that BL had been losing £1 million a day never *seemed* to weigh heavily upon the pin-striped Edwardes. Could BL break-even by 1984 or 1985? Edwardes suggested so. But BL had just absorbed £990 million and needed £150 million more to keep going. In 1981, Edwardes had asked government for another £1 billion to bridge BL until its new models and their earnings came through in the mid-1980s. It sounded a lot of money, but it was probably less than a tenth of the cost of closing down BL and the resultant devastation of the Midlands motor manufacturing crucible.

Edwardes enacted factory closures and workforce redundancies and he got them through despite the protests and strikes. He also built around him a team of men who were highly capable and many of them had come up through the ranks from the factory floor as apprentices who had risen into management. These men were not extremists and not anti-worker, but they were anti-stupidity and anti-industrial suicide. Edwardes built a 'Core' model policy for BL's phased survival 1977-83. But the problem was surviving just to the next phase to get there!

In the end, BL's own in-house designed and engineered core model range based across three ranges that shared many cost effective components, failed and was replaced by the outcome of fate rather than strategy. By the late 1980s, the new-design core models, which had been envisaged as the real, true heart of a revived BL, had effectively been replaced by Rover models entirely derived from the Honda-Rover varietals – which were not totally new cars at all – they were badge engineered existing cars. As in BMC and BLMC, badge engineering ruled. But this time the cars were not self-created. As soon as the supply of Honda models to re-model and re-market dried up, Austin Rover would have no new models due – the pipeline would be empty. This was 1968 all over again with just the names changed!

Prior to this outcome of perhaps unintended consequences, Edwardes' early 1980s top team were well qualified, highly experienced and if anyone could do it they could. The key competencies that now ran BL were:

Chairman Sir Michael Edwardes – just 50 in 1981; David Andrews (48) was ex-Ford, and became executive vice-chairman; Ray Horrocks (50) ex-Ford, as chair and chief executive (Cars); Tony Ball (47) ex-Austin, as chairman and managing director of BL Europe/Overseas; Harold Musgrove (51) ex-Austin, as chairman of Austin Morris and Rover Triumph; John Egan (41) ex-General Motors, as chairman of the new Jaguar Cars; and Mike Hodgkinson (37) ex-Ford, as managing director Land Rover.

As the 1980s evolved, Ray Horrocks would prove vital to Austin-Rover, as it soon became, and John Egan would define the new Jaguar. Tony Ball would keep the sales teams and dealers going – vitally. Key to this team was Harold Musgrove – today approaching his nineties but still telling it how it was.

Musgrove was *not* an upper middle class manager and he had served as navigator in the Royal Air Force. He had then come up through the ranks from Austin apprenticeship and a career at Leyland trucks. Gritty, plain-speaking and driven by logic, he was the ideal man to achieve high office but not forget his origins, yet to temper his loyalties with hard, sound, commercial reality in a corporate role. He also had a talent for design and quality details and few know that he contributed to the excellent interior and fascia design of the Rover 800. He also suggested changes to LC/Metro prior to final production sign off. Musgrove was and is a car man through and through.

A lot of people liked working for and with Musgrove; they knew where they stood, although alleged plain speaking might have ruffled a few feathers along the way!

Musgrove brought a rational, logical, common sense reality to management affairs at BL. He was vital to on-going survival and day-to-day management of the company and its issues amid what was to all intents and purposes, a battle. He believed in BL and AR, but in the end he had to stand his ground against strategy that he did not agree with. Some criticised his management style, but did they ever wonder if they would criticise the captain of a crashing airliner as he battled to save them? In another context, this is what Musgrove was doing; someone has to be the captain, to act with command and stand by their decisions. Others not so encumbered often stand on the sidelines and carp. BL was 'crashing', but just less obviously than an airliner. Musgrove, like Edwardes and Stokes, dealt with the hand he was given.

One of Musgrove's most difficult tasks was sorting out the union issues and 'managing' Derek 'Red Robbo' Robinson. Getting rid of Robinson was to be no easy task and reputedly, both Edwardes and Musgrove had to seek prime ministerial support from Callaghan and then Thatcher, to manage the 'sacking' of Robinson and to manage the ensuing union protests and strikes. Robinson was not finally supported by his colleagues in a ballot, and he lost and *they* went back to work. Had a deal been done behind the scenes between Leyland, Downing Street, and the unions? Possibly, but in the middle of the affair, the government changed when Labour lost the 1979 election and the Conservatives were returned to power – 1979-1997.

Musgrove would rule as Austin Rover Group chairman, yet somehow have to divorce himself from his lifetime's experience up close and personal with the cars themselves. Dealing with Thatcher's top new man for the company, Sir Graham Day and his plans for 'Roverisation' was not going to be easy either.

Musgrove would take his leave at the moment of his own choosing.

In early 1982, BL's top salesman Anthony Ball (who had joined Austin in the 1950s) and had worked with Edwardes, resigned. BL's global and European sales machines (which Ball had run) were shaken up by Edwardes and the whole BL cars mass market division renamed Austin Rover Group.

Anthony G. Ball had started out at his father's car dealership in Somerset, but was taken on as an engineering apprentice at 'the Austin' 1951-55. Voted Austin apprentice of the year, by 1959 he was running the launch of the Mini! He went on to a stellar career in the motor industry and marketing world and was Austin's youngest ever sales director. He then worked for BMC until 1967. After leaving, he returned to the BLMC tent in 1973 and put his overseas experience to good use, rising to managing director of BL's overseas division and via various roles then to be chairman and managing director of BL Europe. By 1979, he was a director of BL sales worldwide and the man behind the launch of the Metro. He latterly worked for Jaguar-Rover-Triumph in the USA and then became a director of Jaguar Cars Ltd.

Ball was a key figure in keeping BL going and enthusing its people to keep faith with the company in difficult times. He remained a stalwart BL man amid the industrial action and early Edwardes days. Ball also advised three government ministers and his contributions are sometimes forgotten in the fog to the BL story. Ball is typical of the true motor industry men who played a positive role in BL. Ball deserves special mention as the man who somehow kept BL's exasperated dealers on board through the lean years and the strike-bound years.

The new sales supremo was to be Trevor Taylor. Jaguar was granted its autonomy back as part of the re-organisation.

'Rationalisation' had meant cutting BL's dozen or so internal tribes of cars down to four key brand leaders. But who would imagine that a decade later, the Metro, tucked and tweaked, would become a Rover! This was badge engineering taken to the absurd. It soon died, and it deserved to, despite finally boasting excellent suspension.

But in 1982, despite Edwardes, BL was still a beast of the state and of the nation. Selling off its car and truck operations was not yet part of the BL plan, nor part of any contract, yet clearly this was the aim. But if you sold off the inherent marques including the best bits, surely that would make the remaining edifice's fare less worthy, less attractive to any potential private investor?

Yet appearing in front of the Industry Committee at the House of Commons in early 1982, Edwardes stated that the company could break even by 1984 – despite over £100 million in interest charges.

BL's market share slipped to below 18 per cent for 1982 – making just 405,116 cars. 1983 started badly, with the Metro production lines actually shut down for a short period due to over-large stocks building up in fields and storage compounds around the country. But BL had got to 18 per cent of the UK market which was just shy of the 20 per cent prediction under the Edwardes plan.

But Edwardes would get BL more government money before he too departed. BL would go on to post a very small profit from part of its vehicle sales; Bide reaping the Edwardes, Musgrove and Horrocks inheritances.

A £1.3 million trading profit in the first half of 1983 seemed incredible. But a 'trading profit' was an irrelevance given BL's underlying costs and just how much money had been swallowed. BL had lost almost £63 million in the first half of 1982 but with a net accounting loss of £143 million for the whole year! And BL was still losing over a million pounds a week in operational terms in 1983. Bizarrely, the previously highly profitable Leyland Trucks division made a significant contribution to the total BL losses.

So bad had been the early 1980s situation that the Transport and General Workers Union commissioned its own report into the costs of closing BL. That report reckoned it would cost in excess of £10 billion to close BL amid the effects of such a decision upon British manufacturing and society – and that it might take more than five years. Thatcher's own advisers suggested a cost of £3.3 billion to close BL, but Chancellor Geoffrey Howe suggested a lower, more palatable figure (£300 million suggested). But even Thatcher refused to undermine Edwardes and openly consider closing BL by government order. The knock-on effects across over a million, associated Midlands workers and families was not to be ignored.

By 1982, BL had yet another temporary pass from the taxpayer. The story behind this reality is also the explanation as to how that reality became just that.

What on earth could be done with BL whose losses were nothing as to the costs of closing it down. The government had a plan – sell off part of BL to a foreign investor, notably, a European one and do so in return for EEC access via BL's production capacity. But no major European car maker wanted BL – even if Renault had a quick sniff at the idea. Talks with Chrysler did take place under the Thatcher-Reagan 'special relationship' but came to nothing. But General Motors began to take note in 1983. Edwardes, meanwhile, favoured a potential Japanese 'technology'.

The axe fell on the new, three-year-old Austin Ambassador – by now the hatchback the Princess should always have been and a rewarding car to drive and own. It sold around 10-20,000 a year and bridged the gap for Austin Rover until Montego arrived. But Ambassador was economically unviable. Musgrove had chopped it in act of rational ruthlessness.

For 1983, Austin Rover built, (according to the Society of Motor Manufacturers) 219, 079 cars – nearly 220,000. But 400,000 was the more viable, accountancy-led hope.

BL needed a new small car for the end of the 1980s and in project named AR6 it had not just the answer but a glittering future, which was to be cancelled (see chapter 11). What of BL's other products – trucks, buses and light commercials? Even they got mucked up – witness the revolving door of the Sherpa van and its multiple reincarnations.

BL's commercial truck, van and bus arm had also been devastated by strikes, but these were less visible it seems, and the brand was to be hived off, although the van saga and Leyland DAF was no easy read.

For example, the 1973 'Leyland Van from Austin-Morris' soon become a relaunched 'Sherpa' and then a 'Morris Sherpa', and then became a 1980s 'Freight Rover' van!

A van with a *Rover* badge? The ancient Sherpa was re-born, re-engined (again) re-facelifted (again) and lived on. What crazed strategist thought of this? Remember this was a 1970s van created from 1960s BMC and BLMC parts – even an old, narrow, Austin J4 van roof pressing! A 1960s amalgam tarted up with more lashings of black window trim paint and new seat trims, to create a van to enter the 1990s. It was the old product planning madness again.

Here again died brand equity – the value of the inherent brand and its products. The twist in the tale was the selling off of Leyland Trucks and its Freight Rover as a joint venture between Rover Group and DAF N.V. (Naamloze Vennoostchap) in 1987. This turned the Sherpa into the '200' and '400' – not to be confused with a Honda-based Rover of the same nomenclature. This joint venture went into its bankruptcy in 1993 and a new Leyland DAF Vans corporate outcome created a 'Convoy' out of the old van.

Leyland DAF's failure in 1993 would also precipitate the collapse of John Shute's International Automotive Design (IAD) who were owed £500,000 by Leyland DAF amid IAD's losses of over £12 million in 1992. IAD was purchased by the Mayflower Corporation which owned Motor Panels, Land Rover's body supplier. IAD had also been involved with Montego and Rover design projects.

What of BL's competitors? Ford we know about, but what happened at Vauxhall was really rather interesting – another tale of one lead figure saving the day.

Strangely, BL's 1970s-80s other rival in the home market, Vauxhall, seems to have got away with it in PR and brand legacy terms despite several years of bad press stemming from strikes, low productivity and a confused era of Opel badge-engineering in the early 1980s. Indeed, Vauxhall's over-stuffed workforce of 73,000 in the mid-1970s was soon culled to around 25,000 by late 1981 after a loss of around £40 million in 1980. A disastrous, long strike at Vauxhall Luton in 1979 and disputes at other plants saw productivity fall. If Vauxhall did not sort it itself out, said GM, investment in new models would not be forthcoming and the company would simply become an off-shore builder of Opel-based kits sent over from Germany.

Yet by doing deals with the unions, amalgamating the Opel products (upon which many of Vauxhall's cars were based) and rationalising not just the model range, but also the dealer network, General Motors (GM) brought sense to ailing Vauxhall. GM also unveiled a vital class-leading car in the 1.6–litre-2.0-litre mainstream family saloon and rep-mobile company car market. This was the initial rear-driven Cavalier, soon to be eclipsed by the even better and frankly brilliant Cavalier MkII of 1981. This car, the front-wheel drive Cavalier MkII range of four-door and five door models redefined the class sector and did so before Ford launched its rear-wheel drive, agricultural-under-the-skin Sierra – a sheep in shark's clothing if ever there was one (yet soon 'improved').

Montego, front-driven and middle of the road, sufficed for BL and was good, but Cavalier was better. The GM Cavalier was a global car platform too – the GM J Car type was highly economic not just to manufacture, but also to modify for each marketplace. Even GM-Opel designed cars built and sold in the UK had a high UK parts content (50 per cent) and Cavalier reached 70 per cent.

There was a dominant personality driving all this design and direction – a straight speaking Aussie, John Bagshaw. He and his team, and great design from Luton under director Wayne Cherry, gave GM Europe and Vauxhall/Opel a new beginning and a rising market share. Vauxhall – a British brand going back to the Edwardian mists of time – was saved and made great again. GM poured over £100 million into Vauxhall in 1982 (but £1 billion into GM Europe across manufacturing and design) and turned the marque around by creating cars with design flair, good economics and sales appeal.

Meanwhile, until Montego took off, BL still put its old Marina-as-Ital up against the Cavalier, and the four-speed Metro up against the new Vauxhall Corsa supermini. Rover's SD1 took a punch on the jaw from the Royale/Senator prestige saloons and the coupé version (as Opel Monza/Vauxhall Royale Coupé) were real stunners – a true GT tourer of real ability to rival the best names in the business.

Across the transition from the 1970s to the 1990s, the freedom for GM directors to direct with decisive moves gave GM a huge advantage, as it did for Ford. But poor old BL was hobbled by its state control, 'civil service' political regime, legacy cars and heritage attitudes, and the winds of realpolitik.

But here lay a question. If the unions were prepared to deal with Vauxhall's management and do deals to save the company and their jobs, why were they so recalcitrant to do likewise at Cowley and Longbridge?

The answer lay in politics, the power of membership, and the strength of the far-Left between Oxford and Birmingham. Surely the Midlands were not 'Red' to the point of revolution?

10
'Reds' Under the BL Bed?

'BL is a microcosm of the British Class Struggle'
>As stated by the Workers' Socialist League in
>'Car Industry Crisis: A Policy for BL Workers'.
>17 September 1980. Workers' Socialist League/Folrose Ltd.

'If we could bring down BL we could bring down the government and the system'
>Communist Party of Great Britain member

'We believed in replacing British society and government with a Soviet-style society'
>Former Trotskyist BLMC worker

'I cannot believe that this state of anarchy is what the majority of our workers really want'
>Sir Donald Stokes 23 February 1970

Any suggestion of 'Reds' at BL leads to accusations of a 'rant' or a paranoid condition. People of certainty, people who know what they know and refuse to know anything else, often state that a discussion that contains views contrary to their own, must by default be wrong or paranoid or a rant.

Such are the common human techniques which prevent debate outside of the fashionable or expected narrative. This is why so few people have been prepared to forensically discuss the politics inside BL other than to praise or attack Derek Robinson – the media's figure of 1970s 'Reds under the bed' fun.

Derek Robinson was the not the first communist union convener at Longbridge – he had been preceded by Richard Etheridge who retired in 1975, the year BL was nationalised. Robinson was a member of the Amalgamated Engineering Union (AEU), which is now within the UNITE movement.

Robinson, who started work in the Austin in the 1950s, was at the forefront of the era when car workers challenged the establishment. But *Robinson* did not engineer nor market the cars did he? But he did instigate or oversee a process of confrontation, refusal and interrupted build that cost BL a great deal in the design and selling of its cars.

Many say that he and others went far beyond a fair, rational union remit of protecting workers' rights against management and its cost-cutting and share dividend payment strategies. It became an endemic and epidemic 'them and us' war didn't it? Up to two or three down-tools or walk-outs a day became an abnormal normal. Yet there were those inside BL who thought Robinson too tame, too weak and too 'Right-wing'!

Michael Edwardes arrived at BL in a consultancy capacity in 1977 with claims he would encourage 'participation'. Robinson indicated he would *agree*, not least as it would give the workers some degree of control – or so he thought. But participation did not last long and Edwardes imposed his plans. This included a 5 per cent pay policy which mirrored Labour's own prior anti-inflationary policy. His alternative was to sell off and/or close BL and certain unions accepted this as a truth despite being under a Labour government, soon to be replaced by no less a figure than Margaret Thatcher.

Edwardes tried to weaken local union leaders and Robinson, who together promptly issued a protest pamphlet to the workers and operated through the shop-stewards. It was this predictable act of publication that was used as the lever to sack Robinson. Indeed, many suggest it was a trap set by Edwardes (who allegedly knew what the unions were up to internally) into which Robinson leapt. Jack Adams (who would eventually replace Robinson) and Mick Clark, both officers of the BL Combine Committee, were also disciplined for being cited within the pamphlet. Over 30,000 Midlanders walked-out in defence of Robinson – who Thatcher would later label 'the notorious agitator'.

Ironically, Robinson was, in the final vote over the action, let down by his union bosses and fellow workers who voted by a massive margin, *not* to strike to secure his reinstatement after he had been sacked by BL. So Robinson was not, in the end backed by his own union superiors and colleagues – just as Labour's power waned and the new Conservative regime was due in. They preferred a safer route and those that did not wanted revolution far beyond even Robinson's dealings.

Oddly, Jack Jones of the Transport & General Workers Union (TGWU) and Hugh Scanlon Amalgamated Union of Engineering Workers (AUEW) – both antagonists against 'In Place of Strife' in 1969, then said in 1977 that they would *stop* the strikes and stop the militant tendencies within BL – notably the Trotskyists of Cowley. These acts were in contrast to their 1969 position. Yet the Far-Left suggested that this was a form of 'collusion'. Jones was latterly alleged to have had Soviet links as the media portrayed him as a 'Leftie', yet there is clear evidence of his actions in participating with senior BL management and its plans in the late 1970s and early 1980s as well as his commitment to tackle militants inside the trades unions for the Labour Party.

In 1979, the AUEW (at war with itself say some) would want to avoid to be seen to be actually supporting Derek Robinson. So it set up a committee of inquiry that kicked the issue down the road to 1980, thus allowing time for a strategy to be arranged and the 'right' people made to think the 'correct' way.

It is reputed that Michael Edwardes had received a copy of the minutes of a meeting of the Longbridge communist leaders. It was suggested that they were drawing up their own competing plan to restructure and 'save' Longbridge. In fact, Robinson's sacking was opened by the 'participation' and his own role within it. It was 'participation' that led to Robinson's downfall despite his early willingness to actually participate. In fact, Robinson became a victim of his own union, didn't he?

Robinson's sacking was a significant event in the trades union movement nationally. Many BL workers distanced themselves from Robinson's so-called Left position and actions. Yet the true far-Left, the Trotsky and revolutionary socialist factions also failed to support him – on the grounds he had compromised and perhaps even 'colluded' with the 'right-wing' unions! The far-Left thought that Robinson was not Left enough.[1] It was inside the 'revolutionary' arm of BL's workers, that such far-Left activism was strong, and set against the unions and their leadership! Yet the headlines in the national newspapers portrayed Robinson and the unions as the Left-wing 'communist' agitators and strikers who wanted to bring down BL. Trotsky got less of a mention.

Some suggest that in there was a large proportion of the workers and union men who were less-Left than the media said, but were they in fact, not Left enough for the revolutionaries within their ranks who saw BL as a 'microcosm of the British class struggle'[2] and were actually intent on a social and political revolution leading to a Soviet-type State of Great Britain?

But why did so many of the non-hard-Left union members *not* support Robinson? The answer lay with alleged behind-the-scenes deals between Downing Street, the unions, their leadership, and a possible government guarantee via a secret deal to BL that BL's sacking of Robinson would *not* result in the shut-down of the company by strikes; that the unions would, after a show of strength, yield. This is exactly what is alleged to have happened across the end of the Labour government and the incoming Conservative government of 1979. And Robinson was gone within months of Thatcher arriving. Was this point proven?

Thatcher in her memoirs[3] called Robinson 'the notorious agitator'. Others, notably fellow Left-wingers, insist that Robinson was simply doing his job and protecting workers' rights in an age of rampant capitalism and appalling unmodernised factory conditions. In an act of ultimate irony, his union would soon agree to 'no-strike' deals with the Japanese car makers whose new factories had been set up inside Britain by Thatcher's government using taxpayers' money to create an internal competitor to BL – itself taxpayer' owned.

If you thought it was just BL who were endemically strike bound in the 1970s, think again. Ford, Vauxhall and many European car makers experienced strike action. Even Porsche faced union hostility and strike threats in reaction to plan to close its Neckarsulm factory. But the BL narrative dominated the headlines.

'Blame Edwardes' was an easy chant to make. But no one cites his predecessor, Barber, even though Barber's closures came before Edwardes' plan.

At Longbridge, a subsequent post-Robinson strike ballot went through for action, yet the unions did not implement the ballot. Edwardes saw his chance and offered them all a 'back to work deal' and those that refused it would be sacked. Without solidarity, the 'brothers' were doomed and the strike soon broken. BL quickly withdrew from the Engineering Employers Federation and the fog of 'war' again descended.

Robinson was also reputedly convinced that the Conservatives were intent on destroying British mass market car design and manufacturing (actual car building not CKD 'kit' type assembly) in order to keep factions within the EEC/EU ruling bodies happy. After all, Germany (and to lesser degree France) would greatly benefit in economic terms if its single biggest car making competitor (BL and British car making) was to be killed off.

We can if we want, dismiss such claim as a paranoid or politically blinkered conspiracy theory typical of an extremist. We can also opine that Thatcher's anti-European mindset contradicted such theoretical thinking. However, we can also see that today, Britain has no mass market car design and manufacturing facility – just German, Japanese and French owned assembly plants. And London rules the global financial roost – not Frankfurt.

So Robinson's claims, however fanciful, have seen a proof of event – but probably by a different route to his suggestion of a big European financial conspiracy.

Robinson's biggest error of belief and claim was to divorce the issues of BL's cars from the workers that made them. In his comments in 2000, when BMW were losing £1 million a day from Rover, he told the media that he did not think his actions of the past had any significant bearing on BMW's decision to abandon Rover's troubles in 2000 – a £1.5 billion loss in 1999 – the worst in BL/Rover history. Apparently the past strikes has a minimal impact, according to Robinson.

He categorically blamed the cars and the types of cars that had been designed and built for BL's problems and then claimed that management had then sought 'scapegoats' to excuse or explain away the cars' problems, by blaming the workers. This blinkered position of Robinson's vitally ignored the fact that (a) the strikes impacted upon the build quality of the cars – which then did not sell, and (b) that management could not afford to develop and manufacture all the cars it wanted too, because they did not have the money to do so – and they did not have the money because government refused to fund all the schemes because of past records. Limited state funding stopped many new car developments in their tracks, such as AR6 for just one example. Why was government funding limited? Because of strikes, low productivity, and poor sales stemming in the past from poorly built cars. State funding would only be of limited scale.

Robinson somehow convinced himself that his and his colleagues' actions did not impact the cars that they built or did not build.

This then was the delusional 'reality' that was allegedly in evidence from Robinson and others.

What of import controls on foreign-manufactured vehicles? Nothing. In fact the state's *encouragement* of foreign-built vehicles and then the use of taxpayers' money to build foreign car makers' factories in Britain to build British-made but foreign designed, badged and owned cars was soon to be imposed as Thatcherite policy. And what if buying a British-built Japanese car converted a British car buyer from buying a BL car into a new loyalty to the Japanese marque? What if having owned a British-built Japanese car, that buyer then went on to buy a model not built in Britain, but in Japan?

Couldn't Thatcher see that this was then an outflow of money, profits and jobs to Japan, actually encouraged by building Japanese cars in Britain at the expense of British jobs and the British economy? And yet in another paradox, Thatcher would support limited scale State funding of BL, despite some members of her Cabinet demanding otherwise.

No 'protectionism' in the British car market was to be allowed, yet across the world, other countries, notably the United States of America, were framing protectionist automotive policies. It would be the likes of BL which would have suffered in a UK v. US trade war over cars in the 1980s. And what on earth would Ford of Dagenham but controlled in Detroit have done? Or GM's Vauxhall?

Thatcher was, therefore, unlikely to 'save' BL with such protective measures, preferring to play a bigger game, whatever the cost.

Yet incredibly, the far-Left decided it *opposed* import controls that might protect BL and its workers' jobs! Apparently this was protectionism for BL! The far-Left explained this by reasoning that such a policy would require the workers to collude with the employer, and to act against workers in *other* countries and that was not to happen amid the wider picture of the great 'class struggle'.

So on one hand they shouted 'save us' and on the other the rejected the aid offered!

Protectionism would also, said the far-Left, lead to demand for higher productivity and lower wages! Such were the complexities and ideological machinations of politics and the British motor industry at this time. Here the reader needs to remember that whilst Communism believed in mother Russia and the Soviet State, Trotskyism believed in a global struggle and revolution in every country. Workers in one country had to support workers in another, irrespective of any harms likely to the workers in a country as they helped those in country and beyond.

In 1977-79 there were the legendary '523' individual industrial disputes of varying degrees of action and impact within Longbridge and cited by the media to be under Robinson's aegis. The costs in lost production are said to have exceeded £200 million. But many of those 523 disputes were minor and of daily discourse, say the Left. However, the 523 also include the massive disputes and strikes that cost BL so very much.

Edwardes' plan was to cut 15 plants and receive £500 million in state funds in exchange for this 'cost' saving. Robinson decided to thwart the plan and any union agreement to it.

Yet Robinson *had* gone along with the earlier Ryder plan for near bankrupt BL and co-operated with management, as had union bosses. It was the very far-Left of 'revolutionary' belief that had made the most of Robinson and his profile and influence and been active in the factories to upset car production. Remember, the far-Left stated that BL was the 'microcosm' of what was effectively the British class struggle – a war.

Those who knew Robinson say that on a personal level he was personable and kind. Clearly he was a communist, but it seems he was not enough of the revolutionary Left for some.

Far-Left Trotskyists buried within BL's workforce worked *against* union co-operation with imposed or agreed plans – they were further Left than Robinson himself. Yet Robinson publicly threatened to destroy the Labour government's social contract with the TUC, a policy that would have implemented a wage policy in exchange for beneficial employment legislation. It would have also brought down a Labour government and could have opened the doors to a state of national emergency – civil unrest and the opportunity of revolutionary protest, or a right-wing coup.

Somewhat bizarrely (when viewed from afar) there was a schism inside the Left-orientated workforce and in the union structures. Communists, Trotskyites, and socialist revolutionaries existed within the BL workforce and their openly admitted aim was the restructuring of British society (it still is). Workers' rights and militant action to protect them was Robinson's position and he claimed he never betrayed the workers. But some on the far-Left said that so-called 'Red Robbo' was a man who had 'colluded' with centrist or right wing union leaders. However incredible this may seem to those unaware of the schism, it is an example of the layers within layers of Left-wing politics at work within BL.

Far-Left wing commentators on Robinson's legacy still categorically state that the job of union activists is not just to 'fight' the bosses and the system, but also to create industrial strife, political struggle to fight capitalism and to fight for a socialist society. The critical phrase 'the enemy within' was uttered inside BL in the 1980s, but not by management and not by Thatcher – instead it was spoken by union leaders in reference to the far-Left.

Here then lay the still-undeclared 'truth' about BL. Former senior BL men, and former politicians are absolutely clear (as long as it is an anonymous attribution). Britain *was* on the brink of civil instability. Soviet infiltration (with funding?) or even insurrection was mooted. Government and society were at risk and BL – and it seems the miners and the dockers – were the chosen instruments of the revolutionaries.

Sensible rational, non-politically extreme men, today say that the far-Left wanted to use BL as a vehicle to revolution and that this was the 'something else going on' so often hinted at, yet never declared in the ensuing years. Sabotaging the company was the aim and to do so, were the cars sabotaged during their build in order to ruin their reputations? It's an extreme suggestion but not one without alleged evidence.

Imagine if Wilson, or Callaghan, had actually closed down BL? There is little doubt that mass protests on the streets could have led to civil insurrection and national crisis deeper than that of 1977-79. Was this how close we got to the British revolution, or the alternative, a British Right-wing coup, both cited so many times by historians since? Thatcher of course did sell off BL as Rover in a context that left the state's hands all over BL. New Labour effectively had to sell it off for a second time and announce its death.

Jack Jones, the union leader so curiously cited in recent accounts as Soviet-linked, was in fact to be a Centrist in the union movement and in Labour. As part of the 1969 'deal' to defeat 'In Place of Strife', the unions, and notably Jones as new General Secretary of the TGWU, had agreed to tackle union militancy, on an internal, in-house Labour Party-unions basis. Does this meant that the far-Left's view that Jones was in their eyes, a 'Right-wing' union leader, is logically evidenced?

Tony Benn's diaries (*Against the Tide*) and comments he made to me in an interview, categorically state that he had discussions with Jones about BL and strikes, and that Jones had suggested the sale of BL – as opposed to nationalisation. This seems even more incredible when one considers recent claims that Jones was an alleged instrument of the Soviets.

The scapegoat of much in the 1980s became Michael Foot MP, whom the mass media portrayed as a Leftie typical of the 'Reds under the bed' headlines. Yet despite his socialism, he was also a pragmatist of huge intellect who could think his way around problems. Contrary to much popular hype at the time, Foot the intellectual was *not* the fulcrum of the BL workers 1980s' unrest. Was he out of touch with what was really going on in the party? Perhaps, but the truth was that the political Left had within it factions that were beyond its control and Foot knew this and said so to me.[4]

BL was, said Foot, 'out of control, a crazy situation. So many people were at fault.'

Foot would in 1986 go on to make some very pertinent observations about the proposed BL sell off. But in 1979, as Thatcher arrived in Downing Street, there was much that was rumoured behind the scenes of British politics.

In *The Frolik Defection*,[5] it is cited by Josef Frolik that British trade unionists were alleged to have been deeply involved in Soviet tactics within Britain in the 1960s. Several leading British trade union figures were cited as Soviet Bloc contacts or allegedly in receipt of payments from the KGB.

By 1977, over a dozen Communist Party of Great Britain members were reputed to have been on the Transport and General Workers Union national executive. By 1979, Labour (union-funded) itself may have been penetrated by Soviet-linked union officials say some observers.[6]

Yet Right-wing observers often failed to detect the political nuances between the unions and the actual workers as a membership; the 'workers' often contained men much further to the Left than their union leaders were. The account of militant roles within the workforce authored by ex-Morris Motors, Cowley union chair (TGWU branch) and shop steward Alan Thornett in his book *Militant Years: Car Workers' Struggles in Britain in the 60s and 70s*, might shock the Right-leaning reader, but it reveals many truths about the internal politics of BMC and BL's workforce. It also reveals the reality of the very poor conditions inside BL's ancient factories.[7]

Yet these factories were latterly modernised. BL spent nearly a third of its 1970s £1 billion from Government (the taxpayer!) updating and modernising its factories – rather than solely spending that money on design and development of actual cars. BMC management had surely been at fault for letting things slide in terms of factory conditions.

Thornett had joined the Communist Party of Great Britain at Morris Motors in 1960 and went on to join the Socialist Labour League in 1966 and thence the Workers' Revolutionary Party. He later renounced Trotskyist groups and focused more on workers' rights than revolution.

We are forced to ask just how far the pendulum had swung inside filthy, draughty factories dating from before 1939. Yet BL *would* spend hundreds of millions of pounds modernising Cowley and Longbridge. But would the union accept the new factories and their new practices?

Thornett also authored *Inside Cowley: Trade Union Struggle in the 1970s – Who really Opened the Door to the Tory Onslaught?* Readers who (like me) are *not* of a far-Left persuasion, might read Thornett's politically open works to grasp the full 'facts' as seen and openly stated from an alternative far-Left viewpoint seemingly seeking social and political change or revolution.

Ultimately, the collective desire must have been to influence government policy and seek to utterly change British society.

Cowley had 100 per cent union membership of its 12,000 employees and a 300-member shop stewards' committee. Over 250 'actions' or 'strikes' per year were at one stage recorded. In 1969, Cowley made its feelings about the Labour government's 'In Place of Strife' White Paper very clearly known. The far-Left blamed not just capitalists and employers for attacks on trade union power and militancy, but even identified 'right-leaning' enemies *within* the unions structures.

One Socialist Press pamphlet[8] ran a 1980 front-cover strapline saying that a BL plant had been closed by Michael Edwardes *and* the Confederation of Shipbuilding and Engineering Unions (CSEU)!

This came about after the period in late 1979 when Michael Edwardes projected his next stream of closures and redundancies – needing to 'lose' 25,000 workers. The CSEU not only supported Edwardes' plans but called for a 'yes' vote at ballot. The outcome was that Edwardes' plan was supported by the unions and many of their members. Hence the Socialist Press claims that the CSEU had supported Edwardes.

It becomes very clear that the unions so often blamed by the Right, Thatcher, and those of Conservative Party persuasion, *were* in fact seen as too 'right-wing' by the comrades and blamed by them for a collusion with BL's management. Inside this intriguing, contradictory schism, we find the truth that what went on at BMC and then BL, truly was a mechanism upon society, part of a class struggle by the far-Left. It was also to see manoeuvres and manipulations by the Labour Party, the TUC and the trades unions to manage the situation internally.

However hard it may be to grasp, there *were* people within British society who sought total political and sociological change to a socialist or communist state and they were active inside BMC and BL. There is also much logical evidence that certain union leaders and unions, did 'participate' with BL management in agreements that went against some of their members' wishes and claimed best interests.

So were BL's cars just the pawns in a greater political game?

There really were 'reds' under the bed. Which ought not be the shock to the conservative minded that it seemingly remains to be. We also know that M15 was 'watching' certain MPs, trades union leaders, and workers. Indeed, claims of MI5 involvement with BL workers have been made.

The later abnormality that was New Labour, has seen a return to 'real' Labour and the lifting of the duvet of radicalism to reveal that the forces of socialist or Marxist change still run deep in Britain's society. The British class struggle, now layered with a camouflage of diversity rights and religious division, still exists, just as it did in 1970s Britain. The only difference seems to be the decision of the Left to abandon its traditional anti-EU stance and to wish to support and remain within the EU amid its privatisation and private banking hierarchy that relies on and encourages low-wages, poor employment contracts, economic migrant workforces, and tariffs.

But was it true that the 'workers' developed an endemic condition of anti-productivity?

The figures, the stories, the facts and the photos do speak for themselves. Who can forget Birmingham newspaper photographs of BL workers asleep on the Longbridge night shift – asleep in the back of the cars they were supposed to be building. This then was the other side of the coin seen from just one example.

By 1979, the state deal was that BL could have another £500 million provided that it closed twelve factories. Edwardes had already demanded 15,000 men redundant and Speke closed. The unions *had* agreed, yet we would see via Robinson and via far-Left activism, more resistance to more change.

Whatever the truth, Margaret Thatcher and Keith Joseph can hardly have been compassionate negotiators over BL, but note that they did not come along until 1979. Many of BL's original, production-crippling strikes occurred beforehand under a *Labour* government – just in case you forgot.

By 1984, the venerable and ancient MG dealer, University Motors, which had been founded as a garage in 1917 in London, closed down and sold off its dealer sites for supermarket developments in London's lucrative new 'boom' property market. Cars – BL's cars – no longer paid. Staff were sacked and lives were affected. It was the story of the early Thatcher years. But don't worry, it was, we were told, all worth it. Fiscal realignment and paying your way and living within your means, were truly worth it, whatever the cost amid a pre-existing subsidised mechanism (one like BL), so said Mrs Thatcher, who forgot that keeping the Midlands at work was, to coin a phrase, a price worth paying. Instead, she gave the Japanese car industry millions in cash and benefits to start internal, British-built competition to BL.

The idea of living within your means might sound good as a starting position in life, but applying it retrospectively to a near bankrupt company and a workforce and society not used to such edicts, was going to be far more difficult. The process did not start with a clean sheet. People's livelihoods were at stake.

This paradox presents deeper problems than simple market-force economic policy can cater for. Mrs Thatcher's Cabinets wrestled with such contexts and logic, but *she* refused to accept any deviation from dictated opinion *whatever* the cost to the country, to BL, its workers or people in general. The market must decide, effused Thatcherism, which boded ill for BL and its offering within its market.

If the Falklands war had not come along, and if a global upturn amid a service and banking resurgence had not started in the early 1980s, it is unlikely that Mrs Thatcher would have survived in power amid the hyper-inflationary years of the early 1980s. Yet she did, and the effects, good and bad, of that upon BL (and more) are with us today.

Were there really 'Reds' under BL's bed?

Isn't all that just a rant and a conspiracy theory, as those who wish to deny or obscure the facts so often state?

Of course there were, and no it is not.

11
BL Brilliance
ECV3 to AR6 and Beyond

The Spen King-engineered, Harris Mann-styled, ECV 3 was futurism personified and a world-beater in all but production reality. ECV 3 was a glittering future, yet one cast to the winds of a fate that was so damn British in its tragedy.

There was much genius inside BL – real brilliance. Some of it got through into a few of the cars, but the reality is that the best bits of the brilliance got stopped – sometimes just before series production was about to begin.

Precursors included the Rover P8, P9, P10, projects – excellence ingrained in a saloon and coupé that was packed with advanced technology and 'active' ride. Triumph's Stag Fastback was another missed opportunity, as was 1975's Triumph SD2, hobbled by internal conflict and spending restraints. Harris Mann's designs for a new MG 'Magna' sports car for the 1970s saw management turn it into the TR7. All MG eventually got was shut down prior to the Roverised MGB that was RV8 as an exercise in cynical nostalgia marketing – even if it was a very good car!

The Triumph TR7 was totally new and much under-estimated and as longer-wheelbased Lynx coupé not just as V8 but with several smaller engine (2.0-litre) options could have taken Europe and America by storm – not just as a Stag replacement, but as wonderful car in its own right. A 'sports hatch four-door coupé' at just the time such cars became popular. Its potential of half a million sales was so stupidly binned at the moment of its birth, just as pre-production cars were due on the lines. A Lynx 2.0-Litre 'sportsback' might have sold to the world. Donald Stokes would have loved selling them if time had not intervened.

Much of the Lynx was already tooled, tested, proven and paid for, because underneath it was a TR7. This was a new car but it fitted into the parts-bin ethos – but successfully. Development of the body did cost money, but the essentials of the floorpan, inner wings, bulkhead, doors and A-pillars, windscreen glass, front lamps, bumpers, and interior fittings were all pre-existing TR7 items requiring often minimal modification and re-tooling.

Although planned to be launched with the SD1's Rover V8 mated to a five-speed gearbox, the fact was that a wider market lay in the planned 2.0-Litre versions. Several in-house BL engines would have fitted into the commodious engine bay – not least the TR7's 2.0-Litre engine and the 2.0-Litre high-efficiency, tuned-up Dolomite Sprint engine which would have matched the V8 for torque and speed, yet greatly reduced the fuel consumption.

Was the cancellation of this car BL's biggest 1970s blunder? I and many others believe so. Think of it – a V8, then a 2.0-Litre sports hatch at the height of the market. Yet one with four seats, a massive boot, and much more room than even the Ford Capri or Vauxhall Cavalier/Opel Ascona three-door. This car could have competed globally with the likes of the later Audi Coupé, the Saab 900 three-door and numerous American offerings of the same size but of far less style and efficiency than Lynx itself.

Strong, ultra-safe, stylish, fast (and fuel efficient as a 2.0Litre), with room for business people or country types to load up, Lynx was the greatest 'nearly' car of BL's true era. American sales would have been massive, for this car would have fitted in with their needs *and* sporting desires. It could have relaunched Triumph or MG in America with huge success. Sales in Europe and Australia would also have been very strong.

Lynx truly could have been BL's saviour, the car to relaunch the British motor industry on the world's stage. Instead, it was binned just before birth after so much brilliant work had been done. Was this the craziest decision taken at BL in the era? Without doubt. Instead, the money went into more dubious projects, to little acclaim. We were denied a so-called 'Lynx' effect!

If ever proof was needed of the genius inside British engineering and inside BL, we need to look no further than 1983 and BL's Energy Conservation Vehicle 3 – ECV 3 project car. True it was not a production car prototype, but it was a stunning precursor of today's technology and potential. As such, ECV3 was a remarkable advert for BL brilliance. It followed on from the ADO 88-based ECV 2.

ECV 3 was one of the best designed, best engineered, concept car-cum-prototype visions ever seen in the modern era. Indeed, its genius has been proven by several subsequent cars that have incorporated part or all of its advanced thinking.

British Leyland Technology – the incongruously named 'BLT' – was set up within BL to create an advanced design research facility to promote a design research culture and a strategic direction for the future. Few could have predicted the brilliance of the ECV 3 car that manifested from BLT.

In a project led by the legendary Spen King, BLT created a low-drag, medium-sized family car for the future that was aiming at being 60 per cent more efficient than the norm of 1983. The design and engineering details were stunning. Spen King put all he had learned into ECV 3 and it was a testament to the man's genius. The futuristic, holistic and completely authentic styling was by Harris Mann in what many think was one of his cleverest designs.

The body design featured a high, domed, teardrop-shaped four door two-box coupé shape reminiscent of Citroën's GS yet with an identity and graphic all of its own. A sleek, glazed, low frontal panel rose back into a flush-glazed cabin turret with exquisite detailing of the science of aerodynamic flow. Much attention was paid to airflow off the sides and rear off the car, as well as the underbody flow and the 'CSP' or critical separation point of that airflow.

If Citroën or Mercedes, or the Royal College of Art Vehicle Design Unit, or the Los Angeles Art Center studio, or Stuttgart University, had produced ECV 3's body, the publicity would have been global in its hailing of car of the future. But it came from BL! Boring old BL.

The 'aero' target was to get down to CD 0.27. ECV 3 got to CD 0.25 and for high speed running with its thermostatically controlled nose cooling inlet vents closed, CD 0.24! Class average figure for coefficient of drag was in 1983 was still CD 0.41.

The body's construction saw a composite of synthetic panels, alloy parts and sub-chassis members complemented by larger moulded plastic panels that included the doors and roof. Special chassis members, subframes and rear suspension members kept the weight down to under 700kg/1,470lb. In fact, the body weight saved well over one third on a comparable steel shell. The car's total all-up weight was just 664kg. Such figures had never been achieved by any manufacturer or design house prior to ECV meeting such targets.

Today, welding of aluminium is a known art across several car makers, but back in 1983 it was still a rare aerospace-related art and racing car technique. So BLT glued the ECVs alloy frame together – the first-ever bonded aluminium car chassis/frame – then clad in non-structural plastic parts and in aluminium panels. This was huge technological achievement.

The excellent unladen-to-laden weight ration of ECV 3 gave it compliant suspension, ride and damping characteristics. Noise Vibration and Harshness factors, as the NVH factor were superbly achieved.

The clean, low emission 1.1 Litre engine of 72bhp with 72lb of torque in a pent-roofed design multi-valve head, was a future-proof three-cylinder injection unit – they are all the rage now! A true 60 mpg in combined driving cycles was achieved from this petrol unit. A 100 mph top speed came from the efficient cylinder head and from low drag. The K-series engine has its origins in this very efficient three-cylinder engine design. A VW-sourced gearbox (as with Maestro) provided slick manual control, but a CVT was the final intention.

This car chased efficiency not performance. It achieved it and in fact beat its target of at least a 60 per cent improvement on the then industry norm.

ECV 3 was stunning, a world class concept car that shook up several lead engineers and designers with the major auto manufacturers who really had been caught napping!

Spen King told the media in 1983 that although ECV 3 was a concept, or a show car, he would never have been given the money to develop it if it had not had the potential to create or influence a production car as a knowledge transfer outcome for a future as yet unshaped. This was particularly true of the advanced body construction materials and process. And of course, Jaguar, Audi, Toyota, and so many others now manufacture aluminium and plastics composites chassis and bodied cars.

Seen up close and inspected, subject to questioning by the media (including me) ECV 3 and its creators were proven. Here was an advanced, cheap and easy to manufacture, cheap and easy to run and own car, that could have had a massive future as a resultant mass production British car. ECV was a true 'Concorde' moment – proof of advanced British genius. Sadly, fate did not allow it to be translated in to a production car. But its influence is significant.

Remember, this was 1982. Today, we have seen the Audi A2, and a rash of subsequent aero weapon, composite construction cars (think Smart) with fuel-efficient three-cylinder petrol engine all wrapped up in cars with details of construction, suspension, drivetrain, etc, that are hailed as today's genius for a new future. Can we not cite the Honda Insight as having been part-inspired by ECV 3?

In ECV 3 there was a smallish car with medium-sized car room in the cabin, and advances in all the key areas. ECV pre-dated all today's similarly engineered and designed efforts, as a precursor, a pathfinder. Just imagine if BL had survived and presented a productionalised version for 2010's marketplace, and an electrically-powered advanced variant for 2020 and the decade beyond?

What if Citroën, or VW Audi, or Honda, had produced a production car like ECV 3 for mass sales in the new millennium? Imagine the fuss. The Audi A2 was a pretty close ECV copy was it not – but not as adventurous.

Who knows, maybe the forthcoming Dyson electric car may be a sort of ECV 3 reincarnated (or will it be a cross-over instead)? Whatever happens, ECV 3 was one of the best pieces of engineering and design to come out of Great Britain in the last three decades, sadly its chances died with BL.

BL spent nearly £7 million on a new styling studio at Canley, but eventually, the new centre at Gaydon's Advanced Technology Centre would dominate (yet this would not be included in the later sale by BMW of Rover to the Phoenix Venture Holdings Group.)

BL's vital new 1980s supermini-class car was stopped by outcome of government's action. This car was AR6 – a superbly styled and engineered new 'Metro plus' design proposal It was perfect for the Supermini-plus sector and was the same size as Peugeot 205. In fact AR6 as 'new' Metro was like the ADO16 – the 1100 and 1300 re-born – pitched into the same sector and ready to sell by the millions. Here was truly the car to resurrect BL and British design leadership – flush glazed, alloy bonded, with advanced engine and combustion and it had 'Issigonis' Tardis-like cabin qualities.

The styling was fashionable yet timeless, smart yet neat. AR6 was a true design highlight and ready to take on anything the 1990s could throw at it. ARG could have relaunched the Metro name with this stunning car. But it was not to be.

AR6 was created in 1983-85, with flush glazing, aerodynamic bodywork, an advanced K-series engine, possible diesel and three-cylinder variations and absolute design mastery; it could have been the European class leader.

Designed by Roy Axe's team with lead input from Stephen Harper and David Saddington, AR6 was futuristic beyond short term fashion, incorporated some ECV 3 themes and was another 'nearly' car that could have saved BL and AR. Originally suggested as aluminium-bodied, a cheaper steel choice became obvious as the prototype was developed; AR6 could have been launched in 1989, but BL did not receive the state funding to develop it further. AR6 needed about £350 million to get it into the showrooms. It would have been money well spent, say most commentators.

Here was the equivalent of VW's Golf 'moment' and equal to any Peugeot, Citroën, Renault or Fiat.

AR6 was Britain and BL's best hope for massive sales. It lay on the cusp of shaking its competitors to the core, yet its cancellation was a direct result of Margaret Thatcher ordering the quick sell off of BL (potentially at that time to GM or Ford) and so she must be cited as paradoxically, unpatriotically responsible for stopping the car that could have not only saved BL, but met her own demands that BL asked for no more state aid! Messrs Musgrove and

Horrocks were reputedly spitting nails over Thatcher's order of a 'fast' sell off and its inherent cancellation of AR6, just as they had got BL and AR6 to the dawn of a major success. Beyond AR6 lay AR7 and more cars.

Musgrove always cites the loss of AR6 as critical to the ensuing failure of the company and as part of his decision to leave.

Was this enforced sale and enforced termination of BL's brilliant AR6, the maddest moment of the 1980s? Thrown away was the biggest BL 'winner' in years.

Graham Day was the chairman who had the task of cancelling AR6 in 1986 and his comments at the time suggest he failed to see a future for a car like AR6 – preferring to invest in upmarket Rovers – which it seemed meant spending millions not on AR6 as a new car, but spending millions on Roverising the decades-old Metro and tweaking up Hondas. This was not a clever decision. If you want to know when BL and AR as the future died, AR6 and its termination was it. If AR6 had gone ahead, it is unlikely that the fate of BL, AR and Rover would have been what it is. AR6 could have sold a million, instead it was killed.

Thatcher, and then Day, are allegedly directly responsible for the death of AR6 and all that was lost.

AR6 did however prove yet again just how great the design and engineering talent within BL and Rover truly was. AR6 contained several design/styling themes and ideas which appeared in later cars from other manufactures, but that was not the point, AR6 truly was both advanced and accomplished. Here lay one of the best, never-produced cars of its era.

'A style for the Seventies' – so said the BL press kit for the Princess. But the truth is that the Princess still looks good – timeless and not a car to quickly date – the mark of good design.

> 'Doing a big Austin was a huge challenge. I wanted to create a car that would beat the opposition, to add something. I set out to design tomorrow's luxury family car. Something to make the competition look old fashioned,' said Mann recently.[1]

Harris Mann's Princess (ADO71/Project Diablo in-house at BL in 1971) was an advanced and superbly riding car, but it was undermined by the way it was fitted out and built. Eventually it was sorted and became an Ambassador. But by then the car buying public had been the development guinea pigs for BL – again. How telling that you could purchase an after-market Princess hatchback conversion from Crayford or Torcars! By the time Princess was sorted years later, it was too late. The Ambassador was the car that the Princess should have been as one of the best cars in the world in terms of ride quality and cabin comfort. Yet Ambassador lost some elements of Princes, notably the seats. I and others view the final Princess 2, 2000HLS (O-series engine) as the best looking and most resolved Princess.

Princess designer Harris Mann had trained at Westminster engineering school, then he worked for Duple, Loewy, Ford, and came to BMC in 1967 with Roy Haynes from Ford. Mann had also designed a world famous moulded plastic watering can. His grandfather had driven the LMS 'Royal Scot' steam locomotive and Mann was steeped in British engineering and industrial design. A talented designer who seemed to present cars of great scale and stance, Mann knew that replacing an Issigonis car was no easy task.

Issigonis apparently was a touch disdainful because Mann did not have an engineering degree. This seems sad as Issigonis himself had once slated mathematics as the enemy of creative thinking! But Mann was, he says, influenced by Issigonis' ethos and he retained the Issigonis packaging but in a new, international style – the 'wedge' 18-22 soon to be re-christened the Princess range. Taking the Land Crab and making it modern was how Mann approached the Princess, but he went deeper, saying:

> 'I saw it as the third stage in a programme to get away from the sedate image of our quantity production cars. Marina's styling was clean and simple . . . the Allegro was more advanced. This (Princess) even more so... We're not trying to be transatlantic or European. There's a sharp edge to European styling that I try to avoid. The object was to be international in appeal, but to retain our own identity... this car is not a crib of anyone else's.'[2]

Mann did not follow fashion, he created it, and in the Princess, he presented a car of obvious futurism yet with stylistic harmony that nevertheless was the shock of the new. It *was* a big Austin. Superbly scaled, only the addition of the Wolseley grille was of question and that was soon stopped!

Mann's TR7 was also advanced and a trendsetter before its time. Think of Chris Bangle's later works for BMW and Patrick Le Quement's designs for Renault and it becomes obvious that Mann was the precursor of the new age of the daring. And can we see an American influence in some aspects of the Princess and its trimming and details? Perhaps – and Mann was an admirer of some American styling ideas.

Ford's Capri Mk1 now hailed as a design classic had quite a bit of Mann's pen in its design. And can we see a hint of Capri's instrument cluster in Allegro's instrument cluster and pod?

A look at Mann's 'Zanda' project car design shows a car up there with Bertone's output of that era – modern but classically executed architecture.

Mann has taken much unfair blame for Allegro, which in production form bore little resemblance to his design drawings and was interfered with by 'group think' and parts-bin mechanical requirements that had a major impact on its scale, shape and sizing.

Like so much of the BL story, Harris Mann's car designs were afflicted by build quality issues and the underlying BL story.

'Was there something else going on at BL?' Mann said to me when we discussed the often unmentioned politics and causative behaviours on the factory floor. Mann, like other senior BL people now wonders if 'something else' was going on.

Mann left BL in the early 1980s after fifteen interesting years. Latterly, he worked for BMW, MG Rover, Subaru, and lectured at Coventry University's revered transportation design unit.

Many observers (correctly) feel that Mann has been badly treated not least by the media over Allegro, and that he deserves a place at the top of the list of modern British car designers. Now 81, Mann retains the kindness and justifiable, quietly spoken pride of his work, yet his frustration at what happened at BL and to 'his' cars is obvious.

Dare we imagine if Hydragas had been made truly interconnected as 'active' with electronics just as was planned (Citroën managed it!). Alex Moulton fixed a Metro up equipped with interconnection and special damping, even if he did drive a Citroën XM! Rover had experimented with an 'active' electronically signalled oleo-pneumatic suspension years beforehand, yet events took over. The Rover 100 had super, Moulton developed, gas suspension, but the rest of it was dire. If only the real, true Issigonis-designed Mini replacement had not been killed off at the beginning of the 1970s.

The true new Mini replacement of the 1970s (code named 9X) was a brilliant piece of Issigonis thinking and also modern, yet was killed off after much development money had been spent, and the Mini as reinvented by BL partner Innocenti was ignored for Britain. Then came the new ADO88 Mini for the 1990s which was stopped, and revised into LC8 as Metro. MG Midget revivals were canned too. AR6 was killed on the cusp of international success and stardom.

Without a wider, new range of cars, BL's marques had little future – as Harold Musgrove the four-decade BL veteran and ultimately Austin Rover Group Chairman and Chief Executive always said.

He has been proved correct.

Yet there was *so* much BL potential – as the MGF later proved, as did the Discovery. But we also got the Maxi, Allegro and then the ancient and flimsy Honda Ballade as the Triumph Acclaim. And we got a multi-million pound Marina Mk15 called Ital. As for a Rover 100, and a Honda Civic turned into a Rover 200 and 400, or an under-damped Accord turned into a Rover 600, what a waste – only then to be reborn as a phoenix from the flames. And in Australia, the Honda Integra was sold as Rover 400 with *nothing* but the badges and a trim or two changed (which is what General Motors expected Saab to do with its GM-based cars!).

Inside BL there were clever men who knew how to build a safer car and BL did much work to improve its cars' passive safety. Of note, the MGB's hull had been very strong. Land Crab, Maxi and Princess all had stiff centre bodies and strength. Triumph TR7 and the Rover SD1 were much stronger and safer than of their many rivals of the day. TR7 and SD1 were superbly engineered and very 'safe' in structural, crash-test scenarios. Maestro also delivered a strong offset frontal crash test performance for its era and added expensive metal beams in the engine bay to protect the footwell. But these men had little chance of input into the Roverisation of Honda-based structures.

In the 1970s and 1980s, 'safety' was a marketing cliché and only a few car manufacturers *actually* made 'safer' cars from a crash worthiness point of view and even Ford got stung over safety via the Pinto fuel tank saga, but somehow sidestepped the Fiesta Mk1's alleged unfortunate, offset frontal crash dynamics despite the BBC's repeated coverage of the issue.

Yet 'safety' became a marcomms strapline that eventually became a 'five stars' EuroNCAP medal where adding a warning light, an electronic device, earned extra 'stars'; one might argue that EuroNCAP's excellent works might be undermined by such decisions.

The established narrative says that the Metro 'saved' BL and that is true. But Metro was a collection of old Austin parts clothed in a new body and which was then via euthanasia, to live again as the Rover Metro and then Rover100. But Maestro, as already stated, was a *completely* new car from the ground up (except for the 1.3 litre A-series+ engine used in the base model) and therefore, surely we should cite Maestro as the more significant achievement?

Maestro was achieved on limited funds in a short time and despite a few areas for improvement at the facelift, Maestro was very good but not sadly, the class leader. But Maestro *was* a very decent, contemporary car that offered BL dealers and their customers a *real* reason to be proud. *Car* magazine stated that Maestro was a master-stroke – high praise indeed from what was then the most plain-speaking motoring observer. But not all agreed.

Maestro was Rover designer and BL chief stylist David Bache's last car – and the cause of some unhappiness. Bache left BL over issues surrounding the Maestro. Neither he nor his then boss Harold Musgrove were to be drawn on the affair. But we might say that there were some alleged disagreements within the company over Maestro's design.

Bache began his career designing dashboards and trims for Austin and is credited with the Range Rover (which was outlined by Spen King and Gordon Bashford) as well several vital Rovers. Sadly, Bache's leaving from BL/ARG was less than ideal. He died of cancer in 1994. His Rover P6 and his SD1 must in many people's opinion, rank as two of the greatest car body designs ever produced.

Bache's Maestro design is said to have contained much work by designer Ian Beech and was very neat. Yet it was somewhat 'upright' and had been kept on the drawing board for some time – and styles had evolved in that period. Bache had also included a scalloped feature that many argued over. Some insiders wondered why Harris Mann's sleeker, more aerodynamic design failed to win through – especially after strong showings at styling clinics. But this was the stuff of internal BL events and the important point is that the Bache design was chosen. [3,4]

Harold Musgrove was reputedly unhappy about Maestro's styling, and this may have been reflected in several views about Bache's retirement.[5]

GM's subsequent Cavalier MkII had definite overtones of Mann's design. Given the oft-noted similarities between some of Mann's designs and those of Vauxhall under the brilliant Wayne Cherry's design direction at the time, we might wonder why Mann did not end up at Vauxhall?

Maestro had a strong range of engines, and even the antique A-series became the A-plus with numerous combustion efficiency tweaks that gave about a 10 per cent improvement in average driving. Small but worthwhile. Maestro steered well, (despite torque steer in the more powerful turbocharged variants), boasted some of the best front seats outside of Volvo or Saab seat design and had room across the back seat for three adults. The initial dashboard design was perhaps behind top standards but latterly remoulded for Maestro and Montego application.

Maestro rode well, came in diverse range of trim options (hail the MG Maestro!) and was a roomy hatchback for a family. Curiously, Maestro was neither as small as an Escort in the cabin yet not as big as the larger rivals of Cavalier or Sierra types. Rather than fall between two segments, it created its own.

The subsequent LC/LM11project – the Montego was not just a Maestro with a longer boot and nose, its wheelbase at 101.0in was actually longer than Maestros 98.7in and despite appearances, the rear side doors were not identical pressings. Created out of Maestro underpinnings by designer Roger Tucker, creating a four-door saloon from Maestro was not easy – especially with a short wheelbase, and long overhangs to consider. The old-fashioned three-piece rear windscreen and side window combination caused many a debate inside BL.

Despite the hand-me-down body, Montego had a lot of technology in it.

Maestro's R-series engine – a modified E-Series – gave way in Montego and a 1600 S-series engine itself a further modified E-series block yet with many new major components. This 10° forward-inclined, divergent valve configuration, 'thin-wall' (thus being lighter) engine was not however available at Montego's launch and was gradually introduced as production built up. The S-engined Montego pioneered the use of 'programmed' electronic fuel injection in a mass market car (a Lucas, not a Bosch system) and by 'thinking' for itself, the ignition process becomes more efficient. Montego also had advanced inlet-air temperature devices to further improve engine efficiency. A lot of this work stemmed from BL Technology's work, yet has been forgotten in the mists of the BL 'narrative'. Combustion efficiency revisions were also made to the O-series engines that powered larger-capacity Montegos.

Montego was more cost effective for BL to build and had more profit in it.

Therein lay a financial issue that had not been 'Fordised' within BL. Car makers make more money on bigger cars, providing they do not put too much value into them. Car makers make less money on small cars but they tend to sell more of them – higher volume but lower yield. Maestro fell between two classes – Escort sized and Sierra sized, and it contained more metal than an Escort but sold for less than the price of a Sierra. Throw in the VW gearbox costs, and Maestro made less money per car, per cost of manufacture, than it would have done if Ford had made it. In terms of retail price per weight, Maestro was less profitable than the Ford Escort, which like Fiesta, had weight and metal shaved off it.

Sadly, despite reaffirming the British domestic buyer base, and securing export sales, notably in France and Italy, Maestro developed a rust issue, notably at the rear wheel arch, and its trims and fittings were not as long lasting as those deployed in the rival VW Golf. Maestro diesel (Perkins-engined) was a superb car for those in the know. Ultimately, we cannot ignore the fact that it was held back at least in-part by its 'upright' styling and fluctuating build quality. Montego however, was truly competitive and sold very well.

In the mid-1990s, Rover did a deal selling Maestro (which ceased production in 1995) tooling into Eastern Europe where former Soviet satellite nations were eager for newer cars. At Varna in Bulgaria, the out-of-production Maestro (the steel bumpered base model) was manufactured in 2,000 'Roadacar' units. As later as 1999/2000, unsold Bulgarian-built Maestros were being shipped back to Britain for sale through special, independent outlets, not least via the 'Ledbury' operation. Maestro still looked modern and smart as the Millennium passed.

The Maestro's ultimate fate was just prior to 2000, to be sold off by Rover's German owner as a rights package (a British company named Parkway had built some left-over Bulgarian cars as Rhd variants) and to head further east, to China. There, Maestro became the Chinese Maestro with a Toyota-sourced engine. By 2003, the Maestro was in production with a very long badge across its tail that read 'FAW LUBAO QE6410'. Nobody ever understood this, but the rather good Maestro became Chinese car (after an initial go as a Maestro-based van badged as a 'FAW CA6440UA') via its rights passing to a Chinese tobacco company named Etsong and then to First Auto Works or FAW for series production of the Maestro 'FAW LUBAO' range. The Montego was to follow likewise and the Montego's front end was also grafted onto the Maestro (badged as the 'QE6440 Ruby') from which it sprouted in the first place nearly three decades before; the sloped nose looked really good on the previously bluff-chinned Maestro.

The Chinese Maestro lives on to date as a production car that has been tweaked and facelifted and re-badged as a 'Yema' and the incredible thing is that the Yema F-series soft roader which has been in production since 2012, looks like a Subaru copy, but is in fact the doors, floorpan, roof, windscreen of the original Maestro dating from the very early days of BL's origination of the car. The shape of the windscreen and doors and side windows give the game away in what appears to be a modern and bang up-to-date vehicle!

Ironically, even at the end of the BL story, the brilliant engineers and designers left inside Rover Group and MG Rover were offering up superb car design ideas – right up to 2000 and beyond.

Rover's turbine experiments extended to this P6-based prototype that looked more Paris than Solihull.

David Bache's personal Rover P6 based coupé, known as 'Gladys', this was a proposal for a two-door sports car that might have made the most of the Alvis badge. Built by Radford Ltd as a 'one-off'.

Above: *Looking very Austin Drawing Office or 'ADO' this 1960s idea for a little MG had shades of Peugeot 304 – surely?*

Below: *The SD2 prototype – it might have been rear wheel-drive but it could have become front wheel-drive! The lost proposal for a 'real' Triumph that was abandoned so close to production status. A huge loss and worth more than the damned Honda with a Triumph badge that became reality. This was a great modern design that just needed some final styling tweaks.*

Looking like a cross between a Glas, a BMW, and a Triumph, this is the Michelotti update design based on Triumph underpinnings. Another 'nearly' car.

Above and opposite: *Was Lynx the biggest BL 1970s loss? Take a TR7, add 12 inches to the wheelbase and add a fast-back. Offer a V8 or a 2.0-Litre and you had the Lynx – Triumph's stunning four-seat 'sports-hatch' world beater that could have sold half a million plus (notably in the USA). A nearly car and massive loss to BL. Killed by politics, power, and forced hands.*

BL Brilliance • **217**

Rover SD1 estate. It could have taken sales from Volvo and Ford, but only two were built!

Below and opposite above: Was AR6 the 1980s greatest BL loss? Here 1984-1986 was a stunning, modern super-mini with advanced design and features that could have dominated European sales and given the likes of VW, Peugeot, Renault, and Fiat a bloody nose. Bonded windows, alloy panels, an advanced engine, huge interior and style, AR6 had it all. This could have been the big one – BL Technology's world class supermini. But no, cancel it and spend the money on Roverised Hondas and tarted up old Minis and Metros. Madness, utter madness.

BL Brilliance • 219

Below and overleaf above: ECV 3 – was this the future's biggest loss? BL Technology under Spen King created the world's most advanced 'Eco' vehicle of efficient engines and 'aero' designed, composite body. In engineering terms, this design concept was a global achievement and hugely impressive. Today it would be hailed as a new beginning. Yet the company that created it is not here to reap the rewards. Another 'nearly' car.

A last-gasp 1989 MG revival idea was this DR2/PR5 proposal that was built over a TVR donor chassis. The styling by design leader Roy Axe and really captured the essence of MG. Another 'nearly' car that never was...

Harris Mann's Zanda concept wedge idea lay behind his 18-22/Princess design. Zanda was a 1970s concept that ranked up there with such concepts of Bertone and Pininfarina.

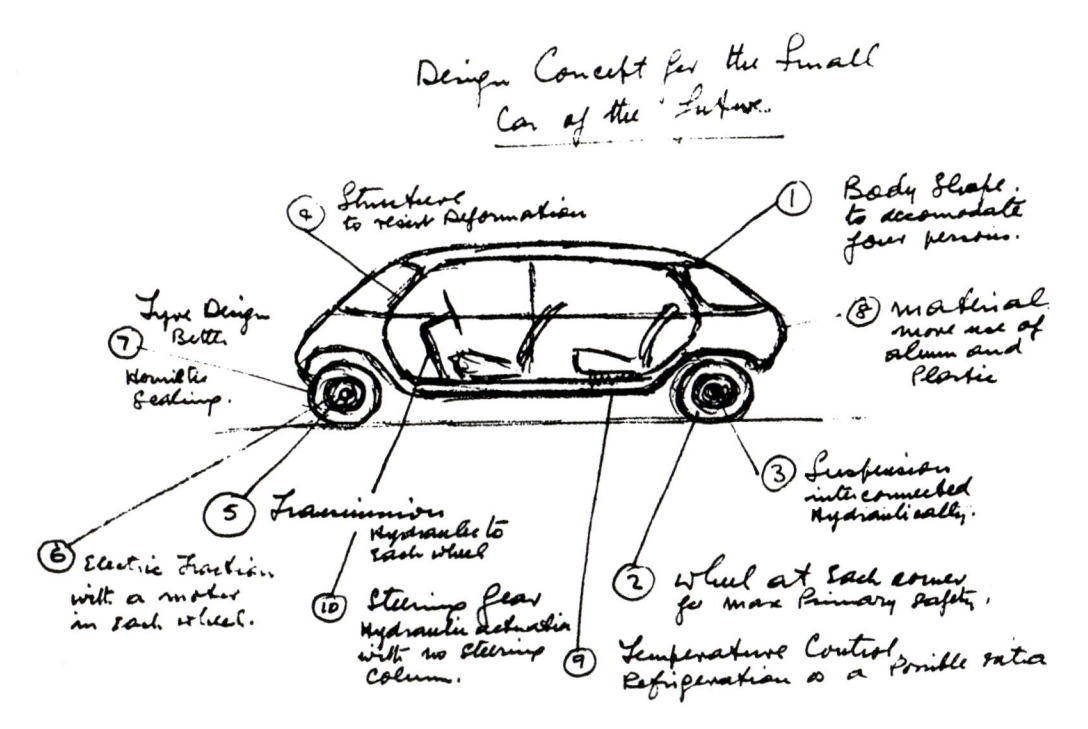

In the early 1960s Issigonis penned this vision of the future. It is of course, today's MPV type reality.

MG-EX – long tailed of Le Mans perhaps, but further proof of the talent that lurked inside BL. Another 'nearly' car. As preserved at the British Motor Museum.

Designed in 1969, on sale until the 1980s, Marina to Ital just about summed up the internal disorder that ruled BL. Not a 'bad' car, but neither a 'good' one. Merely trying to mimic the opposition: 'SLX' indeed.

BL Brilliance • 223

A good car – Montego estate, but tainted by the BL narrative. Much nicer than a Cortina or Sierra estate. Montego was packed with technology and very fuel efficient, if a little tame to look at.

MG Montego – badge-engineered but another good car from BL and ARG. The Turbo went well.

Above: A Honda Accord with a Rover body and seats. It was called a Rover 600. It looked nice but it crashed badly with EuroNCAP. At this stage Rover Group had few new cars of its own design. This was the unintended outcome of BL's earlier Honda liaison via the Triumph Acclaim.

Below: Sterling service. In fact this an 800-series fastback. It's Gordon Sked styling looked good, went well, and handled, despite short damping. Sadly, build quality issues yet again manifested, not least in the 'Sterling' variants for North America. Underneath lay its origins in the old, and then out-of-production Honda Legend.

800 was revamped and given a 'posh' grille and a revised interior that lacked the class of the original series. This one shows the later, single-colour moulding, lack of wood inlay and airbag modification to the fascia.

Rover turned out its own '200' series small car for the late 1990s – a car that should have been the Metro reborn say some. This BRM special edition is one of 1,100 and was very well engineered and is now a true collectors item of rising interest and value.

Rover's excellent 75 was a bit of retro-pastiche by BMW, but it was re-worked into something special – the later Rover and MG variants. And you could buy a V8 (Ford) engined version!

12

Austin to Roverisation

As Clear as Day

'We face a political, not a commercial problem and the politics of ownership appear to be outweighing the responsibilities of ownership to the detriment of the business and a large part of the United Kingdom motor industry. I have been assured that the recent appointment does not reflect upon my performance as a manager. I must therefore conclude there were other factors at work.'

Ray Horrocks to Trade and Industry Select Committee
House of Commons, 12 March 1986

Triumph was all but wiped out by the strikes it suffered in the mid-1970s. But you might have said that in the 1960s, when Triumph had to be 'rescued' by Leyland. Triumph's Lynx could have been a British world-beater said many, including *Car* magazine in April 1977 on its front cover. But all that would result for Triumph was the appalling Honda-Triumph Acclaim.

Bizarrely, having made a 'success' in sales terms of a Honda Ballade/Civic badged as a Triumph, BL then took the decision to launch its version of the subsequent-model Honda Civic *not* as the Acclaim MkII as logic and brand and marketing sense and costs-so-far would have suggested, but to dump the Triumph marque completely and rebrand Acclaim MkII as a Rover in the 213 series. Here was BL usurping the rules, again. Triumph meanwhile would be dead in British eyes, yet carry on as brand in India to 1989.

If only BL had done a deal to use the new, more modern, more aerodynamic, and much better, Honda Quint five-door hatchback instead of the base-model Ballade/Civic as the basis for the Acclaim. Then they might have got somewhere. Rumour has it that Honda simply did not show BL the Quint! A case of 'if you don't ask we won't tell'?

Rover had in its original and pure form, survived 1960s strikes too, but its new replacement for the amazing P6 in 1976, the SD1 – so wonderful to look at and sit in, almost destroyed Rover with its refusal to actually perform its intended task and drive reliably. And the workers wouldn't build enough of them. Customers went elsewhere rather than waiting a six months to a year for a new car. SD1 may have been badly built by annoyed workers, but the fact that the new paint shop did not work as its technology suggested it should, could hardly be blamed on them – could it?

Yet, in this era, one of the reasons Mrs Thatcher came to power, was that what went on in 1977 and 1978 at BL created her electoral chance. Strikes afflicted the country and BL workers still seemed to think that 'wild cat' strikes could solve smaller disputes. And did they also still assume that a Labour Government would automatically pour in taxpayers' money and never confront the issues of the workers' (their own voters) sometimes absurd behaviours?

With Labour in power, the unions were sure of a safe ride – weren't they? But Callaghan usurped his previous pro-union position and policies. And when Thatcher was replaced by the abnormality that was 'New' Labour, there would be no return to beer and sandwiches at Number 10. After all, New Labour was apparently 'intensely' relaxed about rich people and their practices.

Reality had slapped quite a few people across the face when in 1977 a 'true' Labour government told the unions that the time had come to buckle down and build cars, and build them well. Michael Edwardes was installed into BL on 1 November 1977. On that day, 1,500 Liverpudlian workers at Speke's TR7 production line walked out only a matter of hours after they had just returned to work from another disagreement. TR7's build quality at this time was truly appalling and there is no point in pretending otherwise. Even the Americans baulked at the panel gaps and clanging metal!

TR7 production would get moved south, and Lynx would soon be euthanised despite all the money spent on it to that date. A sole remaining example exists at the British Motor Museum at Gaydon.

BL was imposing new practices, but was it only 'imposing' them because no amount of union negotiation could bring an amicably agreed introduction to pass? And yes, the factories needed updating and working conditions and health and safety improved, *but* when faced with new factory investment from BL, the unions blocked its process when it came to installation and new working practices that resulted!

In yet another paradox, the survival of BL, and the improvement in the quality of the cars being built all became enmeshed in a government policy that was supposed to be on the workers' side, yet even the National Enterprise board (NEB) had threatened to stop funding for BL. But the truth was that BL's workers were pretty sure that no government would shut them down, whatever games they played, and especially not a Labour administration.

At this time, Alex Park and Derek Whittaker had left BL. And Edwardes had dug his heels in and started slicing, secure in the knowledge that he could simply walk away if any MP or Minister tried to stop him. The old Ryder Plan had gone out of the window. Even the most sympathetic, Left-leaning observer must by now have realised that the workers' chaos at Longbridge and across BL was a suicide pact for BL. But this disease was nothing new – remember, BMC had been crippled by strikes in 1959-1963 – as so often forgotten by Leyland bashers who only look as far back as the 1970s. Even BOAC, our national airline, had been similarly crippled by strikes in 1959. It all goes back that far – amid the great unresolved post-war sociological struggle and the turmoil within our class and political structures.

Labour's 1970s Industry Minister Eric Varley, had publicly stated that the Edwardes' management plan was here to stay. Government was not going to manage nor run BL. Incredibly, Varley actually publicly stated that he 'supported' Edwardes' approach. Was this some people's 'proof' that the workers and the unions really had gone too far? A Labour minister supporting a 'capitalist' CEO!

As we know, Callaghan was, eventually, compelled to point out that the tax payer had supported BL and now was the time for BL's workers to respond in kind. Things must have been pretty bad for a Labour prime minister to have had to publicly state that. In a curious way, Callaghan was acting as precursor to Thatcher's strategy. But it had been made clear to Callaghan that the very stability of the nation depended on sorting out BL and controlling its extremists. Is this why Callaghan changed his behaviour of a lifetime and switched from union support to union taming? No less a figure than Michael Foot suggested such rational answer.[1]

Underneath, there lay the secret goings-on, and the now alleged and sometimes evidenced drive of the far-Left to achieve their revolution in Great Britain.

Yet continued state support via taxpayers' money would be hard to justify; a nationalised industry that would not work, would become a millstone around any government's neck. In the background, lay Margaret Thatcher. She for sure, would scream and shout about tax payers' money being used to support an unwilling and uneconomic BL – even if she would distribute it with extravagant largesse to others more favoured.

But did the workers, supported by Tony Benn, still envisage a socialist or communist type 'five year' plan, full funding, no job losses and no new practices? Was Marxism and beyond, amid revolutionary politics still at work behind the scenes? If it was, its supporters were in for a shock. Labour would, in late 1978, invoke a 5 per cent pay policy. This opened the doors to the winter of discontent and the swift arrival of the shock of the new – in the form of Margaret Thatcher herself.

How bad were things in 1979? The answer was very bad indeed. The Callaghan government had to put the army on standby (40,000 troops) and deployed the Civil Contingencies Unit (CCU), a precursor body to COBRA – today's national emergency Cabinet committee. The Labour government's anti-inflationary cap on wage increases in the public sector, and resulting strikes that included fire-brigade strikes, and a range of industrial actions which included the closure by the workforce of a major port (Immingham), took the daily function of the nation close to the edge of collapse. The Army had to stand in for striking firemen.

In 1979 the BBC's rival, Independent Television (ITV), went on strike for more than three months – costing ITV over £100 million in lost revenue. Even the TV people – technicians and cameramen – were on strike and blank screens resulted. The settlement was long and drawn out but saw a significant pay rise conceded. Britain was strike-bound. The 'winter of discontent' was real, even if as some Left-of-centre observers say, the Right-leaning press made the most of it. Britain was on the edge, and so was BL.

Yet the incoming Thatcher was a woman so strictly brought up by an austerity-minded father, that it infected her thinking, her policies and decisions as the country's leader. She openly admitted that her father lived within his means and never, ever, made what she termed 'extravagant purchases' nor overt spending. Decades later, this psychology must have made it very hard indeed for her to agree to the hundreds of millions of pounds running into billions, that BL asked for. She would have seen it as 'extravagant spending' and reacted against it. This would surely have blinded her to the reality of life at BL, life in the Midlands, and the risks of it all collapsing – as it eventually did.

Thatcher's economic creed was to be in surplus at *any* price, or 'a price worth paying' to quote a politician of the day. Amid such thinking, BL had no chance, but by then it had shot itself in the foot anyway.

By the time Thatcher achieved her reign, BL was still endemically, chronically in debt, but the truth is, that that was not Thatcher's fault, she 'only' made it worse. Now, under Thatcher's privatisation mantra, the taxpayer was not compensated and in fact, the taxpayer had footed the BL bill, but the City had reaped the profits of the sale of a taxpayer-created entity. It seemed bizarre that new wealth could be created from old debt. BL would not prosper under such edicts, as BAE and then BMW would find out to the tune of over a billion pounds in the Rover experiment. But BMW would get four-wheel-drive technology and more from the deal. The

EU would latterly approve BMW's purchase of BL's Rover remains and BMW's sale of Land Rover to Ford. BMW needed to recoup some of its losses on Rover and Berlin was unlikely to veto that.

Thatcher's privatising of everything that moved and was not bolted down, created a short-term bubble yet one ironically of arrogant, self-indulgence that became Thatcherism's 1980s legend, despite her personal hatred of such extravagant and expensive behaviours. BL's cars, even fast Rovers advertised with Germanic themes, failed to appeal to such people. Germany's cars did. Hence the German car sales boom of the 1980s.

Thatcher, despite her scientific training and intellectual mind, similarly refused large spending on science and this led to a major crisis in university funding in the 1980s – not just operating costs, but in funding of actual scientific research. Thatcher unpatriotically denied UK academic science research its funding which led to a 'brain drain' to overseas, yet poured hundreds of millions of pounds into setting up De Lorean, Nissan, Toyota and Honda in the UK – effectively signalling that Britain was prepared to cull its own domestic car maker to gain inward investment and status on an international economic stage.

Amid such mindset, securing the willingness of Thatcher agreeing funding for BL's new cars must have been fraught with difficulty even for Michael Edwardes. But even Edwardes had trouble with Thatcher. As an example, the reader may care to know that in early 1981, just as Michael Edwardes was having one hell of a tough time securing more state money (£1 billion) for BL (which sold 372,000 cars in 1980) from Margaret Thatcher, she (via her Industry department) was 'throwing' money at a car company that was a direct BL competitor, and she was funding their building of a British, yes British car factory, which could wipe out BL.

Enter Nissan as Datsun to the British car building sector and sales market! How must Edwardes have felt – at the hands of a free-marketeer in the form of Thatcher? He had to plead, beg, convince and detail for BL's survival cash, only to see government (taxpayers') money running away to Japanese competitors inside Britain. Honda (BL's collaborative partner for whom BL was building early Honda Legends in BL factories) would soon be building cars in Britain, as would Toyota.

The new British Nissan plant and its 'Bluebirds' would also soon usurp the previous 'gentleman's agreement' that limited Japanese imports into the UK at around 10,000 cars per year which was in the early 1980s still in force. The factory, would, said the forecasts, build 200,000 cars a year and the productivity levels in this plant would be higher than BL's endemically strike-bound factories. Instantly BL faced a massive new Japanese competitor for its market share on home turf and one co-funded by the British tax payer and government direction in an act of what some might see as extravagance and totally contrary to Thatcher's inner psyche and patriotic claims. All from a government and a leader that would nonetheless wrap itself in the Union Jack. And had not John Zachary de Lorean 'charmed' £70 million out of Thatcher in those vital Unionist constituencies at the same time?

But, and here was the clever bit, building Japanese cars in Britain would also lower and thus improve, the adverse British balance of payment register by cutting imports (at the price of BL sales and jobs and more 'wasted' tax payer money). Such were the bizarre nuances of Thatcherite economic policy. Meanwhile, AR6, the greatest car design of the late BL-ARG era, a world class supermini that could have earned hundreds of millions, was culled, while money was liberally sprayed around by Thatcher's Government, often to direct competitors.

At the same time, ex-BL man George Turnbull was forced by reality into closing Talbot's Linwood, Scotland plant, and Thatcher gave no money to save it. BL would by 1984 need to close its Belgian plant at Seneffe. It is thought that over £200 million of the £1 billion went into funding that closure and many others around the myriad network of BL's British plants. Bathgate in Scotland would soon no longer produce BL products.

BL's ex-director Turnbull would help Hyundai get off the ground, and why not? British car building was dying and he knew it. He was asked to return to run the NEB (and maybe even BL) but turned the offer down. Sir George Turnbull had also suggested that letting Japanese car makers build cars, using British sourced components and built by British workers, would be a way to change the motor industry. His views were of course entirely prescient.

BL had already spent nearly £300 million modernising and 'robotising' Longbridge to produce cars that had limited appeal. Next up was Maestro and Montego, but sadly, the Honda-based Triumph Acclaim was also reality – in all its confusion and 'one-off' brand ethos.

General Motors had at this time put over £150 million of its own money into saving Vauxhall's Luton plant and then opened up Ellesmere Port factory to build German 'kits' of Astras.[2]

Thatcher of course was intent on securing her ethos of fiscal surplus, privatisation, cost-cutting and perhaps also a convenient electoral advantage from traditionally Labour-voting north-eastern constituencies where Nissan was to be located, and if BL had been the price, amid constituencies in Birmingham, so be it. In the end of course, Thatcher became impossible even for her own people to deal with, her own Cabinet revolted amid its chronic EEC/EU internal crisis.

Although the strikes at BL in the 1980s might have appeared different from those in the 1970s due to the Thatcher effect, the reality was that the unions, the Left-wing factions and the far-Left were still active inside the BL/ARG story.

Kenneth Warren MP was a Chair of the Trade and Industry Committee within the Thatcher Government. A committed Thatcherite, he was nevertheless ready to question policy and strategic decisions. A trained aviation engineer, Warren asked several difficult questions of the ministers who would oversee BL as ARG – Keith Joseph, Patrick Jenkin, and David Young.

Warren wanted detail when it came to their positions and statements on the car maker. Warren knew that Edwardes had made vital and difficult choices over which cars to build, which cars to cancel and which factories and brands to either support or close. Warren also pointed out something that many observers often omit, that by 1980, BL's European export market, notably in Germany was on its last legs. How could Edwardes' plan work if it had no viable export earnings? By 1989, BL's income from its American exports would also collapse at the altar of the end of MG, Triumph and the disaster that was the Rover 800 in America.

Warren also had views on what was going on at BL. It appears he knew just how much real cash a car company could consume just to get from day to day. But did Thatcher know that cost?

'Putting aside wild conspiracy theories, I was not alone in thinking that something else was indeed going on at or inside BL,' said Warren when I interviewed him:

> 'The unions were at war with each other and schisms in the Left and far-Left clearly revealed differing agendas and motives. I was not alone in suspecting that very hard-Left factions were intent on using BL to attack the government and to use BL for their own political purposes.
>
> 'There were those of us who thought that breaking BL up and saving the strong bits like Jaguar and Land Rover and Rover, was by now the only feasible way to stop the rot. BL was one of the things that caused us very real problems within government. The implications of a BL failure upon the Midlands were significant. There were so many factors to consider. The death of BL could have destroyed us. When advised that sell-off or closure were options for BL, Keith Joseph and Margaret Thatcher looked at the costs to the economy of that option – which was in the billions, and the electoral issues too.
>
> 'Michael Edwardes was a national figure of great profile – probably rivalling Margaret Thatcher herself for public recognition. She and her Cabinet were very reluctant to act, to close BL from under him because of the public relations and voter implications. Any verbal hint from Government

that BL really was being considered for closure would have actually been its mechanism. Keith Joseph and Margaret Thatcher were keen to be seen to be supporting Edwardes and BL. Internally there were huge disagreements as to the costs to the national exchequer. Some suggested three billion or five billion. The unions of course upped it to a more frightening ten billion. Geoffrey Howe went for a figure well below one billion and under half a billion as a direct cost, which made it sound more palatable. But Margaret Thatcher was not happy with the financial or electoral implications, so she carried on funding BL towards sell-off. Over a million direct, and supplier jobs would have been lost in one go if BL had been closed.

'Graham Day created great change for BL and his efforts to turn it into Rover Group did prepare the company for sell off to British Aerospace, whatever you might think of Roverisation. My only concerns about the deal Ken Clarke created for the sale to BAE were the issues of BAE's liabilities within Airbus financing. I asked for an assurance that no pay-off to that was involved in the Rover deal.'[3]

Sir Kenneth Warren's comments, irrespective of his own political position, provide the reader with a further reference point as to just how 'political' things had got inside BL.

Thatcher eventually lost the plot, but before that occurred, after a 'successful' Falklands war, with public support and an iron will (the miners' strike soon proved that to the workers) she careered ahead with her re-election. BL was now under the spotlight as perhaps never before. What was now officially entitled 'BL Ltd.' stood in many minds for 'billions lost'.

By 1984, it was clear that BL was going to need £1.5 billion. And in 1985, BL asked for that sum. This did not sit well with Margaret Thatcher. Michael Edwardes' contract was not extended and a new Chairman appeared from the ether. He was Sir Austin Bide, who had in fact been brought in as a 'city' adviser by Edwardes in his early years at BL. So although Bide new nothing of cars, he knew something of BL and he had proved his credentials running one of the world's biggest pharmaceutical companies. But Bide's new role at BL was a non-executive chairman on a part-time role. This all had shades of how government ran BOAC back in the 1950s!

Bide's orders from Thatcher were to prepare BL, or its best bits, for sell off.

General Motors had first looked at a BL buy-out in 1984 – to take over *all* of BL cars and commercials. But the 1986 shenanigans of conditions being imposed upon the deal by Government via MPs' pressure after the House of Commons debates on the matter, killed off the GM offer.

By 1986, Jaguar had been the only part of BL car manufacturing to be successfully offloaded and a privatisation 'carve up' of BL was what Thatcher ordered.

She had made a clear manifesto commitment in 1983 to privatise BL. Bide had years in financial and city experience and realised BL was not in a state to be sold off either as a whole or in bits. This may explain why his tenure at BL was so short – 1984-86 – as it conflicted with Thatcher's aims and promises. However, it was Bide who framed the potential sale of Land Rover to General Motors and ARG to Ford – both deals went a long way down the line before collapsing amid claim and counter claims of leaks to the media and the silent hand of political intrigue that saw Thatcher's sale of Britain's helicopter maker Westland to an American buyer being stalled by events.

Thatcher later stated in her memoirs that BL kept making repeated promises about profitability lying just around the corner, but in the meantime it always needed more money.[4]

Some believe that Thatcher's free-market economic ethos has taken Britain's automotive sector to where it is today in terms of efficiency and productivity, but that argument conveniently ignores the fact that no mass market truly British car maker exists!

Morris as a brand died in late 1984 when the Marina/Ital was finally put down. Triumph as a marque died as the last few Acclaims struggled from 1984 into 1985 via showrooms. But surely Triumph had died long before it was subjected to the Honda experiment?

On 5 February 1986, Labour's John Smith MP deplored the suggested selloff of Austin Rover and of Leyland's commercial arms and the resultant denudation of both manufacturing and design and development in the commercial vehicle field.

The final plan was to sell off Leyland Trucks and Land Rover to General Motors and to dispose of Leyland Bus to the Laird Group. Talks were latterly to take place with Ford on the future of the Austin Rover Group. But would GM have keep BL British if it had bought it in its entirety? Even if GM only purchased the truck division, would it retain its British-supplied content and workforce? For example, in 1980 David Brown (tractors) had been sold off to a new American owner and by 1986, 3,000 of the 4,000 British workforce had been dispensed with.

Some observers claimed that in 1985 the bus market had collapsed because of the Government's transport policy – which then impacted upon the viability of Leyland's bus building. Yet in terms of cars, their designs, and their sales, BL was now on the up!

Ray Horrocks had shown loyalty to BL even through its toughest days and was in line for the top job. Yet he was to become a victim of the even tougher world of politics. Horrocks (and the top team) had kept BL on the road even when it looked like a crash was imminent. Musgrove and Horrocks had worked together, visiting factories and getting involved in disputes on a face-to-face level with union men and workers. Yet in early 1986, rumours over BL's future viability made it into the press and claims of £240 million in lost sales for March-April 1986 as a result of the rumours were reported.

Austin Rover's managing director Mark Snowden made the claim – the possibility of sale to BL's rival Ford was now out in the open, as was its failure. Customers stopped entering showrooms and wanted to know what was what, reckoned Snowden.

Ray Horrocks reportedly 'slammed' the government's handling of the sale due to it creating highly damaging uncertainty. Horrocks had appeared before the Trade and Industry Select Committee on 12 March and criticised the government and its ministers for the manner in which it had pursued the potential sale BL and the criticisms made of him when he spoke against such moves.

Horrocks told the Select Committee:

'We face a political, not a commercial problem and the politics of ownership appear to be outweighing the responsibilities of ownership to the detriment of the business and a large part of the United Kingdom motor industry. I have been assured that the recent appointment does not reflect upon my performance as a manager. I must therefore conclude there were other factors at work.'[5]

In a matter of days, Horrocks said he had effectively been demoted – by not being made Chairman of BL has had previously been suggested to him by the government – after he led the opposition to earlier plans to sell of Austin Rover to Ford and Land Rover to General Motors.

Labour's Michael Foot kept a close eye on the BL story and spoke in Parliament on 17 February 1986 about the proposed sell-offs of BL (to GM) and pointed out that BL used British parts suppliers – whose existences could be threatened by new, 'foreign' ownership of BL's marques.

Foot asked in the House on 25 March about revised terms required by government over any possible GM bid to buy BL. GM wanted BL 'outright' but the government then revised its position with the Minister (Channon) looking for a compromise parting-out of BL with GM offered the trucks division. This led GM to withdraw. Foot asked very relevant questions as to how this affair took place, but no deeper explanation nor investigation ever took place.

At this time, Volvo and other major companies were interested in buying Leyland's bus and truck operations respectively. Land Rover's management

(Andrews and team) made its bid for the company in order to keep it British and stop GM getting their hands on it. Yet this bid was, it seems, consumed within the parliamentary and political process – to the anger of many interested parties.

Of great note, David Andrews, the BL commercial division director stated that an offer to buy Land Rover from a BL management consortium had been made in January and turned down by the government despite many MPs and top businessman supporting it.

This all had shades of the Westland affair – with government acting behind the scenes despite claims to the contrary.

Thatcher had not apparently replied to David Andrews' letter offering a management buy-out of Land Rover. Instead, the letter had gone to a minister at Trade and Industry (Paul Channon MP) whose department sat on the letter for eleven days during which time the rival General Motors bid for Land Rover was allegedly leaked from within government and the reality of it had to be confirmed by a statement to the House of Commons.

Thirty conservative MPs rebelled over the proposed sale of Land Rover to GM. They voted with the Labour opposition. Thatcher received her first really big internal shock.

Such was the politics of the affair that no less a figure than former prime minister Edward Heath protested in the House of Commons over the Thatcher government's apparently bungled handling of the BL-GM-Ford discussions of Spring 1986. Heath noted that the business world, and members of the Conservative party, were stunned by the revelation that the Thatcher Government were proposing to sell the remains of the motor industry to American firms. You could hardly call Heath anti-American, even if he was pro-EEC. But anyone who criticised government plans for BL to go to GM or Ford was attacked as being anti-American by a group of Conservative MPs.

There came about the utterly bizarre situation of Heath and Labour's John Smith destroying Thatcher's case for selling BL to GM via their respective statements in the House of Commons

Leaks, whispers, unhelpful statements and contradictions of argument all surrounded the Thatcher government's muddled and easy-to-attack conduct over BL in early 1986. So much for the Iron Lady or the firm hand of leadership. Minister Paul Channon in particular made some allegedly unwise statements in the House over BL and the Opposition's response. In response to stinging criticism of Government's handling of the affair by Andrew Faulds MP, Channon spoke to refute entirely the allegation that the Government behaved in any way 'deceptively'.

But Ray Horrocks stated of the Government:

'This inability to recognise the damage being done to a company's products and reputation – particularly in overseas markets – is to totally misunderstand the need of confidence within a highly competitive industry. That is why I call called it a cruel and shameful persecution in evidence to the Select Committee on Trade and Industry the other week.'[6]

Yet 18 March 1986 saw a company named Lancashire Enterprises cited as wanting to take over parts of BL and making an offer which was rebutted.[7] Who has ever heard of them!

Monday 23 March saw reports that talks with General Motors about its purchasing Land Rover had been broken off. By 23 April, reports of BL losing £39 million in 1985 had surfaced. Yet in 1986-87, Unipart and Leyland Bus and Trucks were both sold off, but not to GM! Little remembered is that the ancient company of Aveling Barford remained inside BL past BL and ARG's 1986 restructure as Rover Group, and was not sold off until 1988. In a bizarre act, an Indian Leyland offshoot, known as Ashok Leyland, now owns a company building buses in Great Britain that itself came about as result of being sold off from Leyland Bus in the 1980s and which produced the Optare bus until recently. As with Jaguar Land Rover, an Indian company stepped in to rescue the remains. Incredibly this company –Ashok Leyland has direct roots back to Leyland in India and still uses the same badge!

Leyland Trucks is today owned by the American company PACCAR Incorporated, founded over 100 years ago. So America did get its hands on Leyland Trucks – but it was not GM that managed it. DAF had originally purchased Leyland Trucks, then the entrails of that were sold into PACCAR of the USA.

Graham Day was soon brought in by Thatcher herself to enact the selloff of what remained of BL; the spring of 1986 unravelled for BL and its loyal team. Austin Rover would remain a brand but Day would quickly dump the legend of the Austin badge and create Rover Group which would be privatised, sold off to British Aerospace and reborn as Rover Group Holdings with inherent subsidiary including Land Rover.

Sir Michael Edwardes always gets the blame, but have you forgotten about Sir Judson Graham Day?

Day was an experienced Canadian businessman with time served in industry, notably at British Steel. He replaced Edwardes and was Margaret Thatcher's true instrument of privatisation for BL. The strategy was to add value and then sell off.

The strategy was not to preserve British mass market car building and heritage, but to clear up the mess, sort out some cash flow, add value if possible, increase the asset value and get rid. Day would attempt to enact his orders, and can we blame him for that?

Day started off on a controversial footing by criticising the highly experienced team of old hands in BL who had directed product and design policy – notably the new Rover 800 range. Given how much experience such men had, and how they had worked miracles in circumstances not of their own making, Day's criticism of the product and car design choices they had made seemed unfair to many. And what did he know about cars? This was the moment that several of BL's loyal top-tier survivors choose to leave.

According to Day, the old BL brands, even the old name of Austin, was contaminated and had little marketing strength at home, let alone abroad. So he enacted a policy of 'Roverisation'. Day thought that the old BL legacy brands were so hated by the car-buying public that a rebranding was the answer. The flaw in his logic was that he applied the Rover name to some of the very BL/ARG (old) cars that he cited as having ruined the branding and reputation in the first place! Couldn't he, didn't he, *see* his own contradiction?

'Fordisation' had not worked, but would 'Roverisation'?

How could it, given that it was predicated upon sticking Rover badges on the ancient Mini and the Metro, and then creating 'new' Rovers out of Hondas – some of them old Hondas? However, the temporary fix of a Rover badge and some very clever styling tweaks from the design department, created a brief halo, a brief window of opportunity for privatisation.

A quick revamp of MG was also considered – beyond 'special edition' MG branding of existing cars with added red seatbelts. The MG PR1/2/3 design concepts were developed at this time (1993) and it would spawn an outcome as the MGF mid-engined sports car; mid-engined was a significant decision and one that prompted great interest in this new MG. The long-established designer Stephen Harper made MGF reality. Peter Stevens touched the later MGF/TF series developments respectively. It was Gerry McGovern who had supplied the prequel via the mid-1980s MG F-16 concept series design that was not pursued, yet which would help rekindle the idea of a soft-top two seater MG once stronger finances were available in the early 1990s.

Rover Group's design concept team did amazing things with the Honda underpinnings and created really good looking cars – notably the R8 series of 214/216 series Honda Concerto-based hatchback and booted cars under Roy Axe's lead. Gordon Sked and colleagues worked wonders to create the

800 series stunning new suit out of Honda dimensions and tooling points. Rover's marketing, PR, and advertising all improved and these cars were well received, well designed, well built and sold strongly. Denis Chick sorted out Rover's PR function and got the motoring press on-side.

Rover was turning a corner – so it was time to sell it then!

The ageing Montego lost its branding but did not become a 'Rover'. Instead Montego wore a St George cross design badge set into a badge shaped like a Rover 'Viking' badge emblem, with its name set amid a red cross. This was branding bonkers! Metro went the same way and then became a Rover 100 for the 1990s, as a Mk3 iteration of a 1980 car design!

Rover was to become the dominant brand and badge. Montego customers were, under Day's plan, expected to transfer to a purchase of a soon to launch 1990s Rover 600. This was concerning enough, but when we consider that this Rover was in fact a badge-engineered Honda Accord, the idiocy of the brand coming before the car was once again exposed. As for winning 'conquest' sales to Rover 600 over a BMW 3 Series, a Mercedes 190? Forget it. Rover's 600, pretty though it was, offered nothing more than clever mirage and some nice wood and leather inside.

The new Honda Concerto-based, then Honda Civic-based, small to mid-range 200-400 series cars might well have carried on the Triumph branding idiom (upon which many millions had been spent) as successors to the Acclaim – which despite its banality had built up some goodwill – so why not use it?

But Day pushed for *all* new cars from the group to be badged as Rovers. This he thought would add value and prestige, yet somehow the obvious question was ignored. So all that work and money with the re-establishing of the Triumph brand (using a Honda base car) was dumped!

But if Rover was upmarket and 'posh', why and how could and would it sell mainstream family cars to people who would not normally consider something as posh, or as staid, as a Rover? And even if a bigger Rover could be made to appeal to younger people, was a 'Rover Metro' really sensible?

The logic of all this seems to have been bypassed upon Day's thinking. The questionable issue was turning the humble and basic Metro into a Rover Metro and thence into a Rover 100! Oh, and lets have a Roverised Mini while we are at it and why not make an automatic one called Mayfair with added stripes? Triumph? Kill it and make the next Honda-based derivative a Rover not an Acclaim Mk2.

Surely these tricks were a 'con' too far that would also damage the intended brand – Rover itself!

Suddenly, we had a rash of Roverised Maestro and Montego-replacement type cars notably as the Honda-Rover 214, 216 series and subsequent iterations; they were good cars yet were pitched and branded at a totally different prospective buyer – who may not even have existed. An extra challenge now existed – to 'convert' all BL and ARG's old customers into going 'posh' in a small Metro-based Rover or a bigger Honda-based Rover and sold in smart and expensively re-modelled 'Rover' dealerships, yet still to retain Rover's upmarket premium yield, big-car customers.

Here lay brand contamination and another vital rune on the road to Rover's downfall.

Inherent within this business strategy was the usurping of all known corporate, branding, and marketing rules as the forced-abandonment of the commercial product and marketing offer norms. As the 1980s closed, Day thought he had moved BL and ARG *upwards* to become Rover as a brand, a signposter. In reality, especially given the issues of the 800 series and Sterling, all he had done was move Rover backwards as a brand – down to a lower class sector. But temporarily at least, the cars were produced, the productivity up, the strikes mostly gone, and the company was fit to be sold or 'hived off' as soon as Thatcher could approve it.

Day's 'Roverisation' idea – of reinventing BL/ARG as 'Rover Group' and gentrifying old cars as posh Rovers – worked the Thatcherite edict over BL and its Austin Rover Group. As a result, the leaders of BL, the men who had seen it through to survival, however hobbled, were dispensed with and Graham Day went on to restructure and reframe the company and its brand from Mini upwards. A certain BAE waited in the wings. And that went well . . .

BAE bought the Government's majority shareholding (99.8 per cent) of Rover for £150 million in 1988.

But about half of Rovers' £1.6 billion-plus debts were effectively eliminated by being carried by the government, not BAE. Was government effectively 'giving' BAE money (£500 million+) in all but reality? The remaining loss could be claimed by BAE against future Rover profits and tax liabilities!

Some politicians and observers though the agreement made a mockery of the term 'privatisation'.

Honda retained a 20 per cent interest, which ensured the continued supply of car designs and parts.

Leyland Bus and Leyland truck were dispensed with. The famous Scammell brand name died. Oh, and Rover Group lost just over £800 million in losses and operational restructuring costs for 1986! Yet the figures were soon to improve and years before Day's selloff schedule demanded it, Rover was quickly sold off to BAE. There were no obvious 'synergies' as business speak would say, but at least Rover remained British. On the face of it, Thatcher had succeeded. Her successor, John Major, was unlikely to challenge the outcome and Anthony Blair performed likewise, ultimately to deny BL as Rover any further funding – which was an irony given that Thatcher *had* continued the funding. Observers may smile at the realisation that it was Thatcher who supported funding for BL and ARG/Rover Group, contrary to perceptions of her beliefs, and that it was New Labour that in the end refused funding for MG Rover.

So despite her many contradictions and internal conflicts, Margaret Thatcher believed in offering State-supported, scaled funding for BL, and then Blair and Brown once in power, did not. How ironical is that?

More proof that the 'narrative' of perceived wisdom can be so confusing.

Before all that happened, Rover tried to rebuild its American reputation with the 800-series and the related Sterling brand. 1986 dawned with the Conservatives still in power and Tony Blair's New Labour yet to spin its way to reality and then its inevitable fate.

With the Triumph Acclaim under its belt and a new relationship with Honda forging ahead, there had manifested the jointly developed Axe/Sked styled Rover XX – the car that became 800 in the 2.0-Litre and above executive car class. Here was a money making opportunity – as Graham Day quickly recognised. The 800s series could be a great way of redressing all the years of angst and setting the company's reputation on a better course. On the surface, it looked a tempting idea. But was due diligence missing?

Arguments over technical specifications – notably front suspension – had raged between Honda and Rover. In the end, Honda paid for the expensive double wishbone front suspension. Rover's version of the car – wearing a cloak of superb Rover styling – looked great and more modern than Honda's own Legend's rather tame styling.

Things looked better for BL post-1986. Rover's new 800 went down well in its home market and soon the rather breathless 2.5-Litre became a 2.7-Litre engined car with a Honda engine that had real ability. The Rover-engined 2.0-Litre 800s were very popular for a time. Quality problems and reliability had yet to manifest. The Rover 800 found its way to America, ultimately not least as the new sub-brand named 'Sterling' – apparently a derivation of the famous 'Sterling Silver' tag that was a global hallmark of British silver's quality.

Selling the Honda Rover 800 Sterling in America was going to cost a lot to set up, but the returns from re-establishing the brand in the USA could be significant.

Yet very quickly, there was a problem; Sterling was soon costing a fortune in warranty claims and damage to the brand's reputation in the UK and crucially in America. Had 800 been rushed through? And why were Honda's versions of the same car built by BL but fettled by Honda at Swindon, seemingly more reliable?

Austin Rover Cars North America (ARCONA) a part-private/part-Austin Rover owned body, even had to form a special 'Sterling Club' for owners. This was effectively a marketing device that could step in and deal with an ownership issue; there were many. The powerful American consumer lobby groups, headed up by *Consumer Reports* damned the Sterling range with faint praise and tales of woe about quality, fit and finish. The reliability issue was soon to manifest. *Consumer Reports* actually ran its own, individually purchased Sterling and the list of faults encountered just kept on coming.

Sterling as an ARCONA brand would have to be re-branded as Sterling Motor Cars yet would be dead in America by 1991. Another tale of BL build quality woe despite all the promises.

At this time, Graham Day had pushed the Sterling brand into America on the suggestion of over 20,000 cars per year sold in the USA. Production of the superb Rover 800 Sterling two-door coupé which had been especially created by the clever design engineering team was a good move in terms of Rover's branding.

The stumble at the start of 800 sales due to the Honda 2.5-Litre engine's breathlessness, and the late availability of the Rover 2.0-Litre was soon recovered. Somehow, Rover made the 2.7-Litre Honda V6 engine even more lively than its Japanese originator's own unit. It was much more sprightly and 'on the cam' – a real 'wailer'. This interpretation gave rise to the more modern 800 that was the 'Fastback', designed to appeal to younger buyers and younger executives on the company car ladder. A sports version was a must.

With lead input from product engineering director Rolando Bertodo and from marketing and sales director Kevin Morley, Rover came up with the 800 fastback as the 179 bhp, 2.7-Litre-powered 'Vitesse'. There must have been some technical or materials changes inside the Rover version of the Honda 2.7-Litre when fitted to the 827si and Vitesse – the thing reacted like a scalded cat when prodded and thundered away.

Morley put a lot of work into correctly pitching the 800 fastback specification and selling and Bertodo went to town on tuning the specification and handling.

With attention to the suspension via gas-filled dampers, revised spring rates and anti-roll bar thickness, Vitesse felt less under-damped than its brethren. Well specified, well-trimmed, and very sporty with excellent overtaking performance in the vital 30-60mph and 50-70 mph sectors, Vitesse was arguably the best interpretation of the 800-series. With a 140 mph top speed and 0-60 mph in 7.1 seconds, Vitesse could eat most BMWs for breakfast.

Apart from over-stuffed 'sport' seat bolsters, Vitesse was great to travel in, fast, economical (up to 33 mpg from nearly 200 bhp!), very stylish and a real winner.

Here again was proof that BL – or its descendants – really could produce great cars. Sales went up and rightly so. My own experiences with an 827 Vitesse confirm that it was a fantastic car, well made and superbly designed. Only the Honda under-structure remained of concern.

Curiously, the 800 Fastback was also sold as an O-series 2.0-Litre powered car without a 16 valve head and carburettor fed! It was slow but had great torque which could be wound up to great if rather raw effect. People liked them as town cars in basic 'family' trim.

The 800 Coupé was, like the 800, designed by Roy Axe's talented design team at Austin Rover. Coupé's design team saw Gordon Sked, Richard Hamblin, Stephen Harper, Richard Woolley, Adrian Griffiths, Wyn Thomas and David Saddington as key members/contributors. The 800 Coupé included (expensive) engineering improvements to the underlying Honda-originated structure. These were notably at the A-pillars, doors and sills and rear end. The Coupe's origins lay in the Canley design studios MG EX-E concept that was so good that Harold Musgrove wisely insisted was shown as a concept at the Frankfurt Motor Show. The Rover CCV design prototype would not be without later influence too. Ideas were commissioned from International Automotive Design (IAD) as consultants and, with internal Austin Rover input, the story seemed to amalgamate into the Coupé's design.[8]

Latterly re-engined from Honda unit to a Rover 2.5-Litre KV6, the coupé sold from 1992 and was popular with moneyed buyers in Europe (notably in Italy). In fact it had the air of a smaller Bentley or Rolls-Royce coupé and became very much admired, not least for its wonderful interior design and ambience.

Roy Axe's team added much identity to Rover at a difficult time – in a difficult brief amid the Honda inheritance – and the achievements of the design team should not go unappreciated.

The old brands, even the sporting and upmarket ones, had all been destroyed by the events of 1968-88. Only Jaguar and Land Rover escaped – proving that selling off the sustainable bits had been a viable strategy. The amicable and talented Axe was key to the high quality of the design unit's output. He must have felt a bit different from his days in America, but clearly enjoyed the challenge and the camaraderie at Austin Rover.

One of the toughest tasks inside BL, ARG, and Rover Group was that of PR and media relations. The PR/communications team went through many tough times managing externally framed issues. In the vital post-1985 era, Denis Chick led the function; Chick had joined Rover in 1965 as an apprentice and ended up in product planning and marketing then to head up Austin Rover's PR team after 1985.

This was no easy task at any time nor as ARG became the Rover Group. Denis and his team performed magic with what must have been a tough brief.

The one true golden star brand remaining was MG, yet instead of being nurtured, fed, and made to sustain Rover, or sold off, it was castrated. Sanctioning the building of a fifty-year-old MGB as a good but niche RV8, was never going to resurrect MG. The 1989 DR2/PR5 proposed MG styling sportster by Roy Axe could have been a winner, but only one was built (on TVR underpinnings) and instead we got red seat belts, and octagons on everything had been more wilful brand contamination. MGF and even a later MGTF? A good car and interestingly engineered but ultimately a sacrificial exercise. Roy Axe's team and men like Steve Harper had a good go at actual new cars (MGF) and the 'nearly' cars such as AR6. Gerry McGovern had joined Roy Axe's team at Austin Rover in 1982 and lead on MG project EX-E and worked on MGF. McGovern also worked on Freelander and led the Range Rover Mk3 development. But by the late-1990s, BL's design force was facing the consequences of political interference upon management decisions.

This period saw Thatcher get Day to prepare the company to sell to British Aerospace, sidestepping the existing Honda deal. But Honda had got what they wanted – BL's technical know-how, a foothold on British soil, and cultural and political acceptance of their brand. Leaving Rover Group behind and running away from any chance to own it was clearly sensible for Honda.

In the end, the decline of what was left of BL came very quickly and very simply. BMW bought Rover from BAE simply to grab Land Rover and to create extra production capacity. Honda declined the chance to buy Rover Group in its entirety despite last-minute pleading from top people inside Rover – in Tokyo.

BMW paid £800 million for Rover but in the end, after several years of conflict and losses, it sold it back to the British for £10 (with further inherent liabilities) and added in a very long term loan of £470 million and the limited rights to use Rover's name. However, at the same moment, BMW sold Land Rover for $1.8 billion to Ford!

BMW failed to reframe Rover, failed to use all the management expertise inside Rover and seemingly ignored the very good advice which experienced British experts offered. Is anyone really sure just what BMW planned for Rover – or if it had plan? BMW did not create a new mid-range car and poured hundreds of millions of pounds into its BMW-Mini and the Cowley plant. The excellent Rover 75 was too 'niche' to sell in massive numbers.

The EU then decided to investigate BMW's actions over funding, and a threat to remove Rover to eastern European production facilities. There was corporate blood all over the floor of the BMW Munich Boardroom and BMW created an albatross of Rover. BMW abandoned Rover, blaming the British EU relationship and currency issues between these parties. Ford ended up with Land Rover (and Jaguar) and bizarrely this was under the aegis of a Ford Europe director who used to run BMW Rover – a man by the name of Reitzle. If anything illustrates the internecine machinations of the car industry, we might suggest this ironic outcome does.

The dateline from the mid-1980s was clear.

1986: Land Rover management buyout refused by the Government and the potential saviour of General Motors walked away. Ford did not buy Austin Rover. Rover posts £890 million loss including over £500 million due to Leyland Trucks' sell off and liabilities. Actual ARG loss of £166 million for trading year.

1987: BL Corporate 'five year' plan given to Government. Rover produces nearly 470,000 cars. Leyland Bus sold to Volvo. Unipart sold to management buy-out.

1988: Lord Young pursues sell-off of ARG to be sold off to British Aerospace (BAE). No obvious reasons why BAE should want ARG but Thatcher happy with 'British' buyer. Graham Day retains CEO leadership of Rover and Kevin Morley becomes Managing Director of Rover Cars. 1989 ARG formerly becomes 'Rover Group'.

1994: BAE sold it all to BMW for an astounding £800 million. BMW produced a retro-pastiche of a Mini that relied on olde-worlde British image to triumph over actual design integrity and ability. The public succumbed to the magic and the rest is history. The Rover 75 was good, but a mirage that would have limited appeal – but at least it did not steal sales from the Five-series! Internal conflicts amid BMW's top management saw the likes of Bernd Pischetsreider, Wolfgang Reitzle, and Walter Hasselkus all battle for BMW's ownership of Rover. They, the BMW-owning Quandt family, and BMW's board, grabbed Land Rover technology, churned out the Freelander (an ex-Austin and Honda based project) and promised new cars. But in the end, the costs were too high. John Towers 'fronted' the British end of Rover for BMW.

Rover would soon launch a small car of all its own work – the nice little 200 that was everything a Metro replacement should have been except for its name and its price. Then came several more iterations of old Honda design that had worn Rover badges. This was more brand contamination and destroying of brand 'pillars' in marketing terms.

2000: BMW wanted out and New Labour failed to step in; calls for nationalisation of Rover were refuted. BMW began looking for possible partners or offers and entered into talks with Alchemy partners.

On sale to the Phoenix Group – BMW retained the rights to Mini but sold everything else out to Phoenix Venture Holdings, not to Alchemy and the unions had a hand in that. Egged on by Labour's Industry Secretary Stephen Byers MP, the Phoenix 'four' (ex-Rover man John Towers, Peter Beale, Nick Stephenson, John Edwards) relaunched the brands as MG Rover and began a process of facelifts of old cars and rather good but questionable (from a marketing standpoint) badge-re-engineering of the Rover 75 into MG Z-series cars. Considerably more questionable was the unwise investment in a sports car project – the Qvale Mangusta that became an MG V80 that became an X-Power Rover SV that only sold a handful of copies.

Kevin Howe, previously manufacturing director under BMW ownership (although not one of the 'Phoenix Four'), was the MG Rover chief executive who took a close interest in new model developments. In 2001, he reckoned that by 2004, all of MG Rover's old models would be replaced. This was optimistic to say the least.

However, new model programmes such as R30 and RDX60 were to be long delayed and allegedly much 'interfered' with by management amid various Chinese deals including the China Brilliance affair and a brief discussion with Malaysia's Proton.

2002: Losses of over £250 million incurred by MG Rover in nine months 2001-02. Investment deal with China Brilliance fails (but some interim funding received). Longbridge site sold for £45 million and leased back!

Negotiations with China's SAIC were supposed to see a £250 million joint venture production investment in Longbridge, but in the end, SAIC walked away with the rights to Rover's designs for just £67 million and no guarantees about making Longbridge work. Quite how this 'failure' occurred is a long story, but many suggest that Phoenix's negotiation team allegedly got out of their depth in China.

2005: Phoenix Venture Holding's MG Rover failed in April with loss of 6,500 jobs after a new prospective partner withdrew and the Blair government's bridging loan failed to be finalised and SAIC refused investment. MG Rover went into administration and the Chinese picked up the pieces in the confused deals between the main players of Shanghai Automotive Industry Corporation and Nanjing Automobile Corporation. Alleged MG Rover debts of £1.4 billion.

Ford exercised its contractual (via BMW) rights to the buy the Rover trademark. The Chinese Rovers become 'Roewe' branded (sadly interpreted as 'Rong Wei').

2007: Nanjing begin MG production – with MGTF, and saloons and hatchbacks. CKD build of MG's begins in Longbridge.

2019: MG China stops assembly of CKD of Chinese originated cars at Longbridge and begins the import of MG cars fully built in China.

In a move typical of politics, New Labour launched an enquiry that would take years to report, cost millions and actually not identify a solely responsible action or actor. No alleged illegality on the part of Phoenix Venture Holdings as Rover's 'saviours' was cited. But the 'Phoenix Four' had been well rewarded for their gambles via a reputed £42 million in salaries, bonuses etc. However, it must be said that respected accountants 'signed off' the accounts and that no illegality has been cited. Yet as a result of the then government's self-policed internal report, the four directors were latterly banned from acting as company directors. The four always denied any wrongdoing and blamed the Blair government for side-stepping responsibility for its own actions. Kevin Howe was not banned from being a director.

Of significant interest, Phoenix's accountants (Deloitte) appealed over being cited and fined in the MG Rover collapse and won that appeal. A prior £14 million fine was reduced to £3 million and a tribunal threw out eight of thirteen charges previously made against Deloitte's handling of the accounts in a case originally brought by the Financial Reporting Authority. A senior Deloitte partner had a prior imposed fine cut and a three-year ban reversed.

In 2018, over £50 million in recovered MG Rover assets was made available to its unsecured creditors. But this still only represented a recovery of 6.3p per £1 owed.

13

The Way to a Rusty Death

End of the Road – via diversions

'Ultimately the merger did not succeed in achieving its objectives.'
Tony Benn speaking post-Ryder on the 1968 BLMC merger.
In conversation with me in 2003 and stated at:
Hansard, HC/Deb 21.1975, vol 892cc1419-541,
House of Commons 21 March 1975

There were many reasons BL crashed; politics and power were some of them, but crucial to the failure were the strategic and structural issues of BL's own behaviour as a corporate entity.

BMC's earlier confused management policy and competing internal hierarchies and brands gave rise to the consequent contradictory product planning and confused and disrupted brand foundations of BL itself. Critically what is known as 'brand equity' was destroyed. In plain English, the value of the marques' histories and identities was not just diluted, it would be destroyed – Triumph, MG and others would be castrated, and the end would be framed ultimately by the 'Roverisation' of old Hondas and old BL cars.

A crucial key factor amid BL's errors and those of its mutated children that were BL, ARG, and Rover Group, was the forced abandonment of the norms and behaviours of the generic rules of the commercial (and specifically the automotive) product life cycle and marketing offer. Normal processes of management were also usurped by the BL 'process'.

All known mechanisms and proven theories were modified or even dumped, in an ad hoc, pay-as-you-go branding and product mix-up and mix-and-match lottery that was forced upon the management by circumstance and by governmental behaviour. Effectively, BMC and BLMC abandoned all accepted management practices and systems mechanisms.

The crucial abandonment of model cycles and brand structures was often as a result of several government policies and financial edicts upon BL and its leaders, but not always. Even when Stokes took over BMC in 1968, he had noted that the

BMC cars were old and the model cycles well beyond Ford's time-frame. The 'rot' went that far back.

BL disrupted the usual four-year model replacement cycle, keeping cars in production with or without facelifts for far longer (over a decade) than its competitors, who could entice customers into their dealers' showrooms with nice shiny new models every four or five years or so. Ford managed this spectacularly, despite the fact that some of its 'new' cars were the previous model underneath – but at least that fact was hidden from view, which was not something you could easy about Allegro version 3, Maxi part 4, or even Marina part 15 as Ital. As for 'big bumper' MGBs, and Triumph 1500/Toledo with front wheel drive or rear wheel drive (you could chose!), the less said the better.

Honda had a disciplined four to five year model cycle, with replacements coming down the line on time and without fail, as scheduled. BL and Rover did not, and in the end, Rover was selling Roverised versions of Hondas that were cars Honda had terminated up to a decade before! This was how 'brand equity' was killed.

Austin Morris ADO16 owners – the front-driven 1100-1300 range's loyal fans – had no choice other than to switch to the larger and very different rear-driven Marina or go elsewhere. Similarly, front-driven 18-22 Land Crab's buyers had also been offered the Marina. Mini buyers had been offered nothing for years. Metro buyers soon faced the same car badged as a Rover. Maxi and Maestro buyers faced nothing and then a small Rover that was on sale against an identical Honda version of itself. Patriotic Triumph owners had been offered a one-off, re-badged Japanese econo-box as the Acclaim – yet which the replacement thereof, was badged as a Rover not a Triumph. Top of the range Triumph and Rover prestige saloon buyers (ex-V8 men) were offered a 2.0-Litre (Rover engine) or at most 2.7-Litre (Honda engine) with Rover badges.

MG owners? Offered very little.

For BL there was very little product continuation. The brand 'pillars' had been thrown out with the bath water. All there was were stop-gap cars and mix and match hybridised brands of cars that conflicted with each other even more than Austin versus Morris had done in 1968. This was how BL's design, marketing and product strategy had gone awry. And there was, as fate has proven, no rescue.

But it was *not* for the want of design. New, brilliant BL and ARG cars existed in concept and running prototype form – Lynx, SD2, ECV3, AR6, MG, DR2/PR5. BL actually had the cars to save it, to hand – notably AR6. They existed! But they were binned by circumstances born well beyond the design centre.

Ultimately, Rover Group's product range was based on reinterpretations of Hondas and it left Rover with nothing new of its own in the design pipeline.

Whatever the facts, under Day, the brand (Rover) became the product definer, not the cars; again a reversal of known and successful automotive strategy. This was always going to lead to trouble in the long run once the 'bubble' had burst.

Of crucial importance, BMC had led the world in front-wheel drive design and marketing (under the Issigonis effect), yet then BL decided to go rear-wheel drive with the 'Fordised' Marina. BL continued to make and plan for medium and large class cars with rear-wheel drive. It also spent huge amounts of money designing a Triumph-Morris joint brand car that could have served both marques. Known as TM1, this car was worked on, just as the SD2 design prototype was also in preparation inside the BL tent. SD2 was rear-driven as well, although it looked more like a front-driven Citroën and was a huge loss to BL in its cancellation. Engineers who worked on it like Gordon Birtwhistle, still lament its loss today – as so poignantly told in *Classic Car Weekly* in 2019.

The so-called stop-car that was Marina *did* have an intended replacement (almost within model cycle guidelines!) known as ADO77. This looked like a quintessential 1970s car – reeking of a cross between a Ford and a Vauxhall, and it was rear-wheel drive too. It was cancelled. And Vauxhall were working on a family of front-drive cars even if Ford kept its foray into the expensive front-drive world to its Fiesta, only belatedly applying front wheel drive to Escort, but *not* to Sierra.

As all this BL rear-driven design was taking place at the former home of front-driven enthusiasm, the rest of the automotive manufacturers were finally embracing front-wheel drive! Effectively, BL created its own product-led chaos. So another factor in BL's collapse was that BL (and ARG) paradoxically created a product-led brand confusion and resulting product-led decline. Many observers and academics share this view.[1]

BL did this by rehashing old cars as new. Yet BL did this far less successfully than Ford had done in its 'new' 1970s cars – which were less 'new' than Ford's incredibly successful marketing machine had convinced they were. Austin Rover did it by changing names, changing badges on cars, and pitching the badges at the wrong market sector and then trying to flog Honda Rovers as something authentic when new, and something else when not. Austin Rover, despite the massive talent inside its design and engineering teams, stopped designing its own in-house, self-created and engineered cars.

Curiously, Rover would create the excellent Freelander, the last Rover 200 series as its own in-house car and the MGF, but they were to be anomalies in a sea of derivations.

Michael Edwardes had consolidated the vast tribes of internal BL offerings as cars, engines, badges and parts, into a leaner more cost-effective operation, but sadly he had to do this just as rival car manufactures were expanding their offerings. And then he had to invest money in the likes of the old Marina in order to make it an Ital – a pointless waste of about £10 million in order to bridge a product-cycle gap that should never have existed but which did for reasons not of his making.

Edwardes tried to put a normal, active, hierarchical management structure and process back into BL with his chosen men, but they all had a battle on their hands.

BL's top men and Edwardes envisaged the 'core' of three main model lines – all sharing cost-effective parts-bin components. Yet it foundered at the fate of events and the unintended consequences of the seemingly beneficial initial Honda-link up. This difficult collaboration was very well managed and enacted inside ARG, yet it was what an oldie might call 'Hobson's choice' in that it might not have been a choice at all.

What happened was that the 'pure' BL 'new' models were replaced by models stemming from the Honda-derived varietals. We might argue that 800/Legend was a new car, but it was more Honda than it was Rover – underneath it was a Honda in structure, suspension, dimensions and many hidden parts. The 800 and especially the next collaboration the 600, were Honda derived and certainly were not 'Rover' cars in the traditional pure sense that a Rover buyer would perceive, yet paradoxically they were pitched at *exactly* the traditional Rover buyer segment and marketing. Indeed, an effective and not unattractive 'posh' Rover grille and lashings of chrome and wood were added to the 800 facelift to make it even more 'traditional'.

The Rover 600 drove well – apart from its Honda-type ill-damped and short-sprung front suspension. Above all it was reliable, well finished, stylish and popular. Yet it was a Rover that would not appeal to thrusting young types who would prefer a BMW – *any* BMW. And neither at the other end of the scale would it sell to an ex-Montego man. Rover 600 also suffered its terrible EuroNCAP crash test outcome, but received less adverse publicity for it than the Rover 100 did when it suffered the same fate. But in that test result lay the truth about what lay underneath the Rover re-skin of an old Honda.

But as the 1990s evolved, for Austin Rover Group, all there was was the chance of updating and tweaking more cars from Honda, and that option soon went away. Which of course, is how we eventually ended up with the Peter Stevens cleverly re-styled Rover 75/MG Z-series 'disguises', and the post-Millennium Rovers as 25, 45, 200. These were decade-old Hondas by another badge and then they were added to by a few styling tweaks to create 'new' models out of old.

MGF/TF might have briefly shone, but it was one car. The 'CityRover' was another badge-engineered import best left described as a very expensive Rover 'trick' that fooled no one and which should never have been attempted. MG-Rover's top 'Phoenix' management must be allegedly to blame for trying to sell this car as Viking-badged Rover from 2003 – breaking every brand, marketing and product rule in the book in a perfect example of, how not to do it.

CityRover (in 2003 up to £9,300 to buy new!) was deemed to be one of the 'worst' cars of the modern era and was surely an insult to what had been 'The Rover Company of Solihull, Warwickshire, England'. Retired Colonels, and managing directors, revolved in their clubs, pubs, and graves. From Rover P5B to P6, to a Honda in drag, thence to an Indian econo-box with an ancient Peugeot engine Here lay the death (in the dreaded jargon) of the vital 'brand equity'.

However, the in-house Rover 200 Mk3 and its 'Streetwise' variants were curiously good – providing you kept an eye on the K-series engine's cooling and head gasket. Throw in 1,100 or so 'BRM' special editions of this Rover, fitted with limited slip differential gearbox/drive unit and designed to mark the two companies' previous liaison, and the story gets better – not least as these cars were seriously well specified and tuned (now collectors' items and rightly so). MG Rover added add a Ford V8 to an old Rover 75/MG ZT shell, and the last days of Rover and MG were intriguing to say the least.

The late 1990s-2000s 'Rover' import-derived, facelifted car range was a catastrophic model-policy outcome as an unintended consequence of 'saving' BL amid the tides of reality and politics. There could only be a crash ahead unless you separated the good bits off and made them a success – which could have happened to MG, but did not, because offers were refused or blocked – right up to John Moulton and Alchemy Partners. Moulton's plan had its correctness proven by hindsight, but that was little help to ex-MG Rover workers. They did not have Moulton's forensic appreciation of reality of his long term vision, they went with what they knew – or *thought* they knew.

One of the key elements in the story has to be the role of management and the changes in management style, structure and behaviour. Edwardes did very well indeed to change the BMC and BL management culture which had previously created the corporate entity's own personality construct abnormalities, its own culture and behaviours – which then fed into the disaster scenario. Edwardes finally put a stop to the tribes, the fiefdoms within BL's brands as their managements quite naturally competed to win the slices of the money-cake that developing their own specific brand's new cars demanded.

But of course, a *part* of the management style and behaviour was a consequence of and a reaction to the workers' behaviours; yet *part* of the workers' behaviours was a consequence of management's actions. 'Catch 22' achieved. And behind, or under it all, there lay the far-Left, the centre-Left, and the working class Tories, all of whom populated BL's workforce.

All this lay within the attempt to force a diverse range of corporate marques and their cultures together under one roof (or sell them off) and to manage these conflicting mechanisms. It began with BMC in 1953, then with BLMC in 1968 and was bound to encounter problems and resistance. The forced merging of so many proud and individual marques, engineers and employees, each ingrained in their own thinking, was a classic change-management disaster scenario – a crash that was inevitable in the opinion of many.

Keeping quiet, not standing up and speaking out, lying low and letting egos and bullying run riot, or being utterly powerless to do anything about such egos, *these* are the ingredients of how dominant personalities further their agendas and careers within hierarchical 'personnel' and 'authority gradient' structures. Is this in some way what happened inside BMC and to a degree inside BLMC in its management and functions?

The seeds of the BL strife, so often stated to lie solely with Stokes and the Leyland-BMC merger of 1968, or with Thatcher and her divisions after 1979, were cast down long beforehand.

Beyond this, there can now be appreciated the causes and their effects that lay beyond cars. There were proven and admitted 'revolutionaries' within BMC and BL, men whose aim was total political and sociological change for Britain. And their actions impacted on actual car building, then to impact upon strategic decisions about which new designs could be built because government dictated how much money would be available and BL had to make choices to satisfy a government.

So strikes *did* impact actual car design, and product planning, not just car building.

Sociological factors, so often ignored in the BL tale, can now be seen to be vital triggers that were way beyond the simpler subject of just cars. Yet go back even further and the post-war mentality of a mixed up, old world, new world Britain, was evident in the strikes and recession of 1959 and beyond.

For BL, there was a strand of elements that conspired to produce the outcome. On their own, each element might not have caused the crash, but it was the *combination* of these elements that created disaster – much like the elements and alignments of an air crash.

Conflicting management, and altered processes, notably within tribal product planning, dictated BMC's and then BL's strategy, their policies and the cars that were made. Many later industry observers concur with these suggested scenarios.[2]

But management were also being dictated to by direct route from Number 10 Downing Street across several governments of both political hues and political reaction to many factors, not least the court of public opinion and the egos in the House of Commons, many of whom had one agenda – their own careers. The trades unions and the workers also influenced the outcome of policy choices made by managers and politicians.

You can blame the 'red' workforce all you like, but you would be wrong to do so for everything, for in the main they were not all 'red', nor as portrayed by the media; many were proud motor industry men – true craftsmen from Midlands families with decades of experience and heritage behind them. Yes, the declining quality of their manual labour and the failing of their productivity did cause BL huge harm, but these workers did not become careless or slow-witted overnight. They did not all wake up one morning and decide to throw cars together and waste time, money, and life by dossing about and walking out on strike at the whim of a scent in the air. They were not *all* members of the Communist Party, International Marxist, or Workers Revolutionary bodies.

Some of the 'workers' became minded to become obstreperous, they became minded to work slowly and not care about the cars they were building, they were strike and dispute minded by circumstance, behaviour, manipulation (by Left and by Right) and other factors. They resisted change and new efficiencies stemming from the very investment they demanded. And it started long before Thatcher wielded her stick.

But were those who were the moderate, Longbridge and wider BL workforce, agitated and manipulated by hard-Left or centre-Left union activists within the BL workforce and union structures? Many people think that this is an accurate scenario. The tribal, 'them and us', Left and Right, and far-Left behaviours, were not invisible, but in fact they were underlying in post-war British society as the old class system and accepted norms were all challenged by a new world.

The long-established tradition of British Left-wing activism, be it on a factory floor or at a posh university, lay behind some of the events that befell BL.

Did not politicians force the managers to carry out orders and the workers to react? It appears so, and this all started this long before Thatcher's 'Eighties'. The course of our cars, who created them, who built them, and how they were finished, and sold, was on the same collision course as society and British politics. Everything, it seems, was wrapped up in its own crash test experiment from 1950 to 2000 and beyond.

Not everything Thatcher did was wrong, just as not everything BL did was wrong, but fashionable perceptions and media headlines – the narrative – might lead you to think otherwise at the time and ignore the truth of activism within BL or other corporate entities. However, the rational average man wanted a secure job and fair day's pay for a fair day's work. But Britain in the post-war decades was a polarised and divided society, escaping from that old pre-war world of doffed caps, class structures, and set rules. All of these ingredients were played out within the BL saga. And the far-Left truly were active and open about their aims for a changed society. Remember, they called BL the microcosm of the class struggle.

Those who ignore such sociological factors, fail to tell the full story of BMC and BL.

The workers (like the airline pilots dead at the scene of an air crash) were so easy to blame for everything. Yet were they also instruments of a higher will (of both Left and Right) and players within a culture of corporate and political power? To be clear, the BL workers are *not* blameless in the BL story, and they and specifically their unions seem to have created a 1950s-1980s culture that fed upon itself and became a self-perpetuating habit leading to industrial suicide. There seems to have been a choice to become victims, partially at their own hands and at the leadership of the Left. But there also remains the falsehood that the workers did not decide BL's strategy, nor its actual product strategies nor the resulting car designs.

But this view (as stated by Derek Robinson and others) that the cars' design and quality had little to do with the workers who made them was wrong, because strikes impacted BL's finances and that impacted its funding and negotiations with its funders – the governments of the 1970s and 1980s. Consequently, choices had to be made and if that meant dumping a nearly-production ready car design, or engine, upon which millions had already been spent, or its factory allocation, then that choice was made to satisfy government. So funding decisions and rules forced BL management to cancel and curtail vital new model streams and engineering developments, with consequent unviability of brands and entire BL edifice.

Union or worker power *did* influence management's strategic policy decisions on the grounds that BL management took decisions designed to secure funding and also to manoeuvre around, or avoid conflict with unions and workers factions, at certain plants.

What of the BL designers and engineers? They too did *not* decide BL's strategy and policy, they simply designed the cars they were told to design for production – by senior management whose hands in the end were tied by government and by events. And where did the origins of the strangest of car model policy decisions lie? The answer was amid BL's internally competing, conflicted tribal brands and their managers as BMC's legacies. Much responsibility lies in these areas – beyond design and engineering, way before 1979 or 1974.

Messrs Webster, Musgrove, Horrocks, Ball, Egan, Knight, and others, delivered talent and vision, but all these men who were at various times within the BL tent, left to pursue other more likely opportunities. Of the men of 'Fordisation' at BL, perhaps framed by John Barber's vision for BL, well, did he and they fail to see that they could not apply their success at Ford, to the entirely different beast that was BL, its internally conflicted brands, its 'hobbled' designs and the effects of its often politically and structurally insolvable problems? Barber, like others, was of course doing his best along with his colleagues, but this was a wider game, a bigger machination, one which was not Barber's fault.

Perhaps General Motors could have understood BL's tribes and its ethos better than ex-Ford men? But that is a historically unproven. And yet GM blew Saab to pieces with a failure to 'get' what Saab was about – which included selling Japanese Subarus with Saab badges. Bloody badge engineering again! Not even the visionary Bob Lutz could navigate around that particular pot hole. Although, like BL, not all Saab's later problems were the fault of its later custodians and managers – like BL, much of what was wrong at Saab had its origins in decisions made in decades past.

BL failed because of all the reasons discussed herein and that those causes had the effect of creating a range of cars that were underdeveloped and/or poor quality. Furthermore, a great confusion was created by the merger of 1968. As we know, Donald Stokes categorically knew that there were massive structural problems within the effects of the merger upon brands that were already in trouble or if not, likely to be at war with each other – he said so in January 1968 as the ink was still wet on the agreement! Some say he wanted to cancel the deal when he lifted the drain covers and discovered the 'truth'.

BMC and the BL became ill via decentralised brands and their strategies which were roped together under a tent that was muddled and which suffered from political interference and a forcing of an ethos where the ill-defined BL *brand* itself defined the cars. You only have to look to the late 1970s success of BMW, VW, Toyota, or Saab to understand how cars that defined the brand succeeded, as opposed to brands that defined their cars failed.

For BL, compromise and the dilution of design and marque branding became an accepted norm. So too did strikes, walkouts and utter intransigence of the workforce and unions.

But where did BL's apparent corporate personality construct disorder stem from?

Was it solely from the multiple brands, the history and the workers, or was it from management? In all parts, the answer was yes – but not entirely.

Other factors were at play. British society, Britain's class-system, and the post-war end-of-empire mindset and corporate construction, and British Communism, *these* were all ingredients in the social science of the BL story. The conflicts between pre-1939 'empire' Britain and the men who ran it, and the new age of post-war and the 1960s boom, all played a role in creating the circumstances that led to the crises of BMC, BL and beyond.

Politics, national politics and the machinations of men (and women) in power seem to have a far more direct influence on the BL story than some commentators of recent years have stated.

The real origins of decay and designed-in destruction lay in the forced mergers of the 1950s in the automotive industry (as in the aviation industry). Morris, Lord, and Austin, all cast the seeds for the BL tragedy decades before the wheels fell off.

We can blame what went on in the 1970s as the peak of the problems, but the originating cause lay many years beforehand when Morris, Lord, and Austin, all cast the destiny of the BL crash decades later. All this was amid a Left-to-Right, pro-Europe, anti-Europe, merry go-round of a truly British disaster that to this day, impacts the lives of people.

Engineers and designers had little chance to fight off the decisions of the leadership or the governments and the state, who were the main players in this frankly incredible story not just of cars, but of politics and human psychology and behaviour.

Remember, Britain lurched to the left under 1960s Labour – it had been of the old patrician Tory Right beforehand, before the Suez scandal and before other scandals, the Cold War, the threat of Communism, spies, and the rise of the sixties 'celeb' culture. Then came Harold Wilson, more 'white heat of technology', the early EEC/EU debacles, and then the Heath-led Conservative government in all its pro-Europe inconsistencies and expensive contradictions. Then came another lurch to Labour. Finally, there came the psychology of the Thatcher years and its effects upon society. Then came the paradox of New Labour and its continuation of Ken Clarke's Thatcherite economic policies from which it gained a boom that it turned into a bust.

But Thatcherism is where old Tory toffs, captains of industry, self-made millionaires, titled gentry, intellectuals, and ex-military men tried to tie up all their lose ends and govern under the rule of a leader who re-invented herself as a different personality construct to the one she was born and raised with. Her patriotism extended to the destruction of British industry whilst simultaneously championing the flag and British business in a hyper-inflationary recession and then in a socially explosive privatisation boom that New Labour would continue in economic policy terms, capitalise upon politically yet under which MG-Rover as BL's last incarnation, would finally die amid incompetent political management from Number 10 Downing Street and New Labour's refusal to support it with limited, State funding.

Amid these events, BL and its Rover entrails was reinvented, only to finally die.

Our fate may also be to realise that for BL, *something* had to be done. Further, to see that BL was something that actually defeated no less a figure than the 'Iron Lady' – Thatcher herself, in the reality of its outcome, despite all the headlines about her 'taming' of the unions and the 'revolutionaries' inside BL. After all, BL is dead. Thatcherism is dead. New Labour is dead. But the far-Left lives on. The far-Right is having a response.

Beyond the cars, this is the very politics of the stuff of the 'truth' about BL.

Intriguingly, and again often ignored, is the fact that two women and their actions, Barbara Castle of the Left in 1969, and Margaret Thatcher of the Right post-1979, were vitally important factors in the course of BLMC and BL and the fates of both. And at MG-Rover's end, a woman of New Labour, Patricia Hewitt, announced its death rites.

Labour, Conservative, New Labour, and others including the far-Left and have all had a hand in the giant national mess that became BL. Given the sums of money that BL swallowed, you might today suggest that it was a massive, slow-motion scandal that somehow slipped past the court of public opinion. It surely was one hell of a British scandal. Yet, did not BL, Austin-Rover, MG Rover, Rover Group etcetera, all die while Britain was a *full member* of the EU?

They did and Britain was.

Talbot at Coventry is long gone, so too is Chrysler, its cars, the Hillman Avenger and also Scotland's car industry and the Hillman Imp. Leyland once built and exported tractors and trucks at and from Bathgate. Leyland's tractors, notably its 1970s-80s small tractors, were highly respected and included a synchromesh gearbox fitted to a tractor range ('Synchro' 1987), and even included a 'Mini' range – a sort of modernised Ferguson small tractor. Sadly, even Leyland's tractor business fell foul of industrial relations and of politics. BL's tractor division was moved from Bathgate in 1982 and soon after its relocation, ceased trading as Leyland and was bought out and rebranded. Truck production at Bathgate finally stopped in 1985.

Tam Dalyell MP tried in 1985 to speak up for Bathgate in the House of Commons. But it got him precisely nowhere. Having been hobbled by a previous Labour Government, Bathgate was closed under a Conservative one.

Dalyell was categoric:

> What happened at British Leyland was one of the biggest scandals of the age. People do not realise that it nearly brought down Wilson, Callaghan and Thatcher. It astounds me that Bathgate was allowed to be closed. It contained the largest machine shop and tooling plant in Europe. It exported to the world. Closing it was madness. There must be a hidden story. If there is anything you can tell me, please do so.'[3]

All that we should remember is that Scotland no longer has a car, bus, truck or tractor factory nor the jobs that go with it. There was and is no sign of the Scottish National Party (SNP) resurrecting the Scottish car industry, but who knows, maybe the SNP's Scottish so-called 'independence' inside the EU will see the Chinese set up a factory there. But that is about as likely as finding an Allegro Vanden Plas that does not look like the northerly end of a south bound cow.

Some conspiracy theorists even suggest that BL was destroyed by politicians in order to remove it from competition in Europe in the EEC/EU, in order to give Germany and France a free hand in dominating European car making, with all the economic and employment benefits that would create. This may sound like a paranoid conspiracy to the reader, and whilst I may not concur with the theory, the *fact* is that today's reality *is* that the German and French car industries no longer face mass market competition from a large British car maker, because there is not one.

However, once again, the conspiracy theory is actual paradoxical reality. German car makers do not face the threat of British car makers – they just own the entrails of British car making, Mini, Bentley and Rolls-Royce. Yet above all this, above all the politics, one thing remains clear. Dear old BL has gone, sold off, sodded off, sold down the line, exterminated and defenestrated.

In Britain, it appears that will we never make our own mass market cars again. So, despite all the billions spent on BL (probably in excess of £12 billion) and all the pain to people, nothing has changed really, except that we no longer have a mass market car maker as that essential and true crucible of advanced design and employment in the heartlands of the British industrial core. Instead, we have a political and industrial madness, one that may well have even been started by the whole BMC and BL story.

Many blame Thatcher and her need for conflict for what happened at BL, but they are wrong. Thatcher and her effect were in part just the consequences of prior history.

To coin a phrase, 'the truth' about BL lay in an earlier age, not in the merger of January 1968, nor 1972, not 1981, nor 1989 or beyond, but back on 31 March 1953 as a prophetic decision taken by well-meaning but perhaps blinkered men of a certain British attitude, to create a merged BMC 'monster' that was always going to be at war with itself. And this in the 1950s, is where management and government must be held to the account of responsibility. Leonard Lord wanted his 'revenge' and big British business and powerful men wanted to increase share price and assets values. Wilson and Benn had yet to come along with their plan that would facilitate such factors – via other motives.

Look back to Nuffield, Lord, Austin, to see where the foundations of the BL failure were laid, in 1953. Of 1968's Donald Stokes – well that was afterwards and not before and frankly it is unfair to blame the man for the outcome. Like Edwardes after him, Stokes played the hand he had been given. The strategy he deployed was not of his choosing, it was forced by circumstance and realpolitik. You might argue the same of Graham Day, although some might refuse your view and suggest he was more involved in the context.

Of the MG Rover Phoenix Venture Holdings Four the men who 'earned' a reputed £42 million from the venture, we might ask, if they knew so much about cars, how the hell did they get it so apparently wrong? Who was it that 'cost' so much in the new model development programme and its changes, delays, engineering, design and styling arguments and overruled design and engineering decisions as alleged by some?

Was a management 'consultant' really paid up to £1,000 a day on top of a consulting fee of over £1 million?

The last true BL legacy cars such as SD1, Maestro, Montego, Rover 20 (R8), Discovery, MGTF, *were* good cars, and eventually achieved build quality. But it was too late. Sticking snobby grilles, and lashings of chrome and wood veneer on BMC, BL, and finally Honda-Rover cars, would not a class-leading best-seller create. Had we not learned this when we added grilles to the tarted up Austin Morris 1100-1300 in the 1960s, and then tried it again with the Allegro Vanden Plas? They even tried such a VDP grille on a Princess; thankfully it was still-born.

Even at the last minute, Birmingham had a saviour on its hands, for inside the Rover Group under BMW, and then MG Rover (MGR), there lay the brilliant design team and a shedload of ideas for new cars. Of significance were plans for a new five door hatchback in the prestige class, a saloon to replace the Rover 75, and a series of models using existing bases over which new bodies could be draped. These would quickly and cost effectively serve up a new MG Rover model range.

Under BMW ownership, Rover's design team had created a new mid-sized five-door model under the R30 code. Intended to be an MG-badged car in its initial guise, it had potential but was subject to too many external factors to reach reality. Was its design re-born as the BMW 1-series? Many think so.

Of significance, under the new MGR/Phoenix Group the Rover RDX60 project used Rover 75 basis for a large new hatchback body. A derivative-of-derivative plan would then see a 'new' large Rover as an outcome. But RDX 60 foundered on the failure of MGR's talks with China Brilliance (who seemingly forfeited the 'deposit' they had paid in and which in-part funded RDX60 development).

Tom Walkinshaw Racing as TWR had been the design and engineering consultants on RDX60's long drawn out and much modified basis, but TWR as a business failed in 2003, which threw the whole affair into chaos. RDX60 would be much 'fiddled' with – less by engineers and designers and more by managers and marketeers. It would also see expensive derivations of its floorpan created to see potential Chinese investors happy, in that they could have their own domestic-market version of the car. In other words, MGR's leaders reverted to BMC and BLMC badge engineering and delays, costs, internal arguments and the usurping of engineers and designers opinions and works!

It was all happening again as 2003 merged into 2004!

RDX60 could have been a big new Rover and a range of MG derivatives. Like the old Lynx, the AR6 and other earlier BL design projects, it was ready to go – some suppliers and some tooling had even been engaged and realised. But no, allegedly duff decisions by men at the top, fate, and events, saw it die in a long drawn out saga that was depressingly familiar. MG would end up seeing its badge attached to a revised MGF as MGTF then to family hatchbacks and booted derivatives such as the MG 3 and the MG Six.

The communists have had the last laugh because the worthy Rover 75 has been re-born as Chinese 'Roewe'. The Roewe as a Rover 75-based car remained in production until as recently as 2017 – nearly twenty years on from its original launch. BMW had sold Rover to the Phoenix Group and they had raised much needed cash by tarting it up into some rather nice MG variants, and then selling the model rights to the Chinese at Shanghai Automotive Industry Corporation (SAIC). SAIC then bought into Phoenix and the Rover brand. But SAIC walked away from the deal which precipitated a crisis. National Automobile Corporation of China (NAC) then scooped up the rights to the Rover 75 but not the Rover name and in its restyled form put it into production as a Roewe 750 and as an MG7. SAIC then bought NAC! Over 100 former MG Rover engineers are reputed to have worked in China on productionising the cars via the Ricardo Company acting as a consultant.

The Roewe 750 benefited from an extended wheelbase, new rear styling, and an updated interior and revised engines, what a shame it was never sold in Great Britain say many.

We can only look back in shame at the behaviours of leaders and their civil servants, and of workers too, yet with pride at the great cars that still, somehow, emerged from the cauldron of British Leyland and all its brews. Those cars gave us great enjoyment and the genius of BL prototypes, such as the ECV3, AR6, as they were pointers to a future now framed – but by others who have reaped BL Technology's rewards. But BL is not here to take the credit nor earn the money. Right up to the late-1990s, BL's legacy was producing advanced, future-proof, low-emissions, high-efficiency engines and car designs people wanted. Yet still, all this talent was, for want of a better word, wasted.

All we have left is memories and the rust of time as nostalgia lane becomes a digital highway as badge-engineering gone berserk, fades into the mists of memory. British mass-car making is dead.

We no longer design and build mass market cars, motorcycles, airliners, trains, or ships. The reader must ask him or herself why, and how, and what it means. Were such men, such engineers, designers and industrialists, 'little-Englanders'? Of course not, it is just that what they did and the things they built, have been destroyed, as was British Leyland. And you can always purchase a Chinese MG but with the profits sent offshore to a republic of a communist state. Isn't that an irony, especially if you are a Communist, Marxist, or a Trotskyist who once worked at BL.

The reasons for BL's collapse are clear as outlined herein, but there is now an obvious ingredient – that being that Britain was being undermined from within by a political process that may have taken it to the edge of an undisclosed socio-political explosion at the end of the 1960s or in the 1970s. A takeover by the far-Left, or a coup by the forces of the Right, came much closer to being real than the powers that be have ever dared admit. British Leyland was part of the process and its actual car design had little to do with that, other than to be its victim.

The truth about BL is that it and its cars may have been used in the most stunning, audacious, and almost-successful attempt by the far-Left to launch its political revolution in Great Britain. Few have ever dared suggest it or evidence it. Anyone who does is framed as a 'nutter' or conspiracy theorist. But the facts speak for themselves.

Unless of course you just want to just blame the cars and suggest that they achieved it all upon their own?

If so, how?

It was not *all* the fault of the far-Left or Left, or the unions; some management and politicians are heavily implicated, but we must realise the politics of BL cars and their production, the mechanism of government, the implications of revolutionary sympathies, to know what really happened.

It is surely fair and rational to all but the most rabid Lefty, to suggest that union power *did* get out of hand in its refusal to embrace new technologies and new efficiencies.

The key question has to be, how did this BL tragedy happen? The answer is far more complex than some have stated. It really is a multi-layered story of product, politics, management, power, personality, disorder and delusion amid a failure of *both* the Left and the Right. A plague may have to fall upon both their houses. And Labour's Patricia Hewitt wept tears as British mass car making died at Labour's hands. Who would have thought it when Edwardes was the 'enemy' under Thatcher's command?

Of interesting significance is the social science of the BL story. We ought perhaps to recall that in the mid-1970s, British society achieved something it had never reached before (nor since) – this being a narrowing to the rate of inequality between rich and poor; in fact it was smaller than ever before. At the time of BL's worst strike years, the gap between rich and poor in terms of wages and access to a better quality of life, was at its lowest recorded variance in British society.

At that time, only Sweden was ahead of Britain amongst European countries in terms of equality of life between the haves and the have nots.

Nearly four decades on, and long after the death of the great British BL marques, here we all are, still arguing about what happened. Oh, what characters those BL era cars had. Annoying they may have been, but anodyne they were not. And they were British – in an age when patriotism and nationalism were acceptable and politically 'correct'.

We British, the so-called 'little Englanders' built the amazing machines of genius and which brought change upon the world. And now we do not – in a sort of reverse-engineered paradox where, if you cite the rest of the world, the one beyond a Europe-centric narrative and cause, you are called a 'little Englander'. BL's Donald Stokes would have had none of that rubbish; he sold to the world – you know, that place that lies *beyond* fortress Europe and its inwards focused 'Little Europeaners'.

British engineering and design genius still exists, but we are it seems, 'group think' coalition thinkers constrained by a created narrative and a myopia from which few dare escape. Don't you dare think beyond the fashionable narrative. So our past is decried and only its demons cited. Our future is hobbled by a prescribed mind-set.

Imagine if Issigonis had thought that way!

It used to be acceptable for Donald Stokes to sell Leyland products to the world, didn't it? Or was that him being a little-Englander? In fact Stokes was pro-EEC in terms of business – which was clearly sensible back in 1972 and remains so.

We can blame Margaret Thatcher only for a *part* of the BL disaster. And some people credit her with saving BL from the Left and the revolutionaries, but she reaped the benefit of others' works. Thatcher wrapped herself in the Union Jack, screamed of patriotism and then, in a great paradox of hypocrisy, sold off our national assets, significantly our engineering base to foreigners who could and *would* walk away.

Thatcher seemed to have no idea of the vast seas of money needed to run a car company, she divorced herself from the real lives of the real people that built BL's cars, and the suffering they would endure if they did not build the cars. But who gave Honda, Toyota, and Nissan, massive, truly massive amounts of tax payers' money, inducements, tax advantages and planning consents, to come and build cars in Britain? Thatcher.

Meanwhile, our Midlands car making foundry was left gelded of its soul and its seed, thus billions of pounds were wasted and people withered, as the end of car making manifested upon the Midlands, that vital, essential crucible of England. Come to think of it, why not import bargain basement Polish and Russian cars that were as 'unsafe' as their 1960s underpinnings suggested? Let the lumpen proletariat drive crap cars, or buy British, buy BL – whilst they still could.

And guess what, Blair and Brown got rid of MG Rover in such a haste, it all went wrong. Due diligence seemed to be missing. The unions stopped the sale of Rover to Alchemy and supported the sale to the 'Phoenix Four' group. That went well; then the unions lambasted the group that it had previously lobbied in favour of, over the sale. As I say, it went well . . .

The end of BL might have been much of its own fault and marked the end of the Britain that built it. Less than 20 per cent of our current economy is engineering manufacturing-related, and a smaller percentage is car building-related. And the cars are not British, of note despite Vauxhall's claptrap of an advertising slogan stating 'British brand since 1903'.

Maybe the whole role of the EU in the BL story was all part of some great plan that its defenders would deny and attack as a conspiracy theory if such was stated, yet which is a current truth of factual reality. The conspiracy was real. Time has proven that whether you view it from the Left, or from the Right – true British car making is dead!

We can only look backwards in the mirror of our motoring as it rests upon the hard shoulder, awaiting our remembrance. It is time to fold-down the seats on the beige Maxi 2 HLS, brew a cup of tea, tuck into a Marmite sandwich or a Tunnocks' teacake, and watch an Audi, BMW or Hyundai storm past in spume of success, and to wonder why on earth this journey ended in such a tragedy.

The answer lies with the people, the politicians, the nation, and mess that was and remains post-war British history – the end of England on a road upon which BL lost and cost many billions.

The deeper tragedy of BL is the waste of world-class engineering and design genius; the waste of RDX60, ECV3, AR6, Lynx, SD2, Puma, Nomad, Apache, MG EX, Rover P9, and even as far back as the Road-Rover. It was all there, and it looks like it was all sabotaged either by accident or maybe even by design. The only thing left is what kept it going – the cars and the men that created them and manufactured them. Perhaps it is time we took a kinder view of the men that designed them and those that enjoyed driving them.

BL and its final Rover Group iteration did not lack talent, knowledge nor capability. There were *no* 'missing' engineering or design ingredients in comparison to other car makers – quite the opposite in fact as the BL and Rover teams were world class. They kept fighting to the end.

Other factors were to blame.

BLMC to BL to ARG, Rover, and MG Rover had more heroes than villains. The national tragedy and the inaccurate national narrative have treated such heroes and their cars very unfairly. At its worst BL was dire, at its best, BL was brilliant and of global design intellect. Sadly, the wheels came off.

Now you know how and why.

Notes

Introduction
1. *Building a Corporate Identity* June 1973. British Motor Museum Archive/BMIHT.

Chapter 1
1. Insurance Institute of Highways Safety, O'Neill, B., (Chairman IIHS) media statement, 1999.

Chapter 2
1. Bardsley, G., *Issigonis: The Official Biography,* Icon Books Ltd. 2005.
2. Setright, L.J.K. Sir Alec Issigonis: The Ideas Go On, *Car*, April 1978.
3. Mackay, M. Professor, media statements and author communications.

Chapter 3
1. Daniels, J., *British Leyland the Truth about the Cars,* Osprey Publishing, 1980.

Chapter 5
1. Benn to L.F. Cole, interview, Wyvern Theatre, Swindon, 2003.
2. Benn, Tony, *Out of the Wilderness*, Diaries 1963-1967; Hutchinson, London 1987.
3. Benn, *ibid*.
4. Annual Sales figures BMC records BMIHT.
5. Deeley, P., The *Observer* 21 January 1968, citing Stokes, D.
6. Benn to L.F. Cole, interview, Wyvern Theatre, Swindon, 2003. Also refers to Benn in House of Commons 21 May 1975: Hansard HC. Deb 21. 1975, vol 1892, cc1419-1541.

Chapter 6
1. Winsbury, R., 'The Labours of British Leyland', *Management Today*, October 1969.

Chapter 7

1. 'In Place of Strife: A Policy for Industrial Relations', Cabinet Papers 1969 The National Archives, London.
2. Rochester, Lord, In Place of Strife debate, House of Lords, 18 March 1969, Hansard Vol 300cc719-871.
3. As evidenced by advice to News International by Farrer & Co, London. January 1986. Externally referenced as published by Costello, M., *Morning Star* 4 February 1986.

Chapter 8

1. Daniels, J., *British Leyland the Truth About the Cars*, Osprey Publishing, London. 1980.
2. ADAC & UK Consumers Association archives.
3. Society of Motor Manufacturers SMMT official figures.
4. Turner, G., *The Leyland Papers*; Eyre & Spottiswoode, London. 1971.

Chapter 9

1. Sir M. Edwardes personal communication to author as Jaguar Lyons Scholar, London. 1984.
2. Edwardes, Sir M., *Back from the Brink: An Apocalyptic Experience*, Collins, London. 1983.
3. M. Snowden to R. Hutton, *Autocar* w/e 11 October 1980.
4. Whyte, A., Jaguar: *The History of a Great British Car*, PSL/Jaguar 1980. Also from author at Jaguar as 1983 Lyons Scholar.
5. Carver et al, *British Leyland Motor Corporation 1968-2005*, The History Press, Stroud, 2015.
6. Edwardes, Sir M., *Back from the Brink: An Apocalyptic Experience*, Collins, London 1983.

Chapter 10

1. Tony Benn to author at Wyvern Theatre Swindon, 2003.
2. *Car Industry Crisis: A Policy for BL Workers*, 17 September 1980; Workers Socialist League/ Folrose Ltd.
3. Thatcher, M.H., *The Downing Street Years*, Harper, London. 2003.
4. M. Foot as communicated to the author in person, Piccadilly Rare Books, with Paul Minet, Sackville Street, London 1980.
5. Frolik, J., *The Frolik Defection: The Memoirs of a Czech Intelligence Agent*. Leo Cooper Ltd. 1975.

6. Eden, D., We came close to losing our democracy in 1979, *The Spectator* 3 June 2009.
7. Thornett, A., *Militant Years: Car workers' Struggles in Britain in the 60s and 70s*; IMG
8. *Car Industry Crisis: A Policy for BL Workers*. 17 September 1980.Workers Socialist League/ Folrose Ltd.

Chapter 11
1. Mann, H., to author at Gaydon July 2019.
2. Mann, H., 26th March 1976: BL Press Release.
3. Sharratt, B., *Men and Motors of the Austin*. Haynes Ltd. 2000.
4. Axe. R., personal communications to author, 1989.
5. Weakley, S., *Practical Classics* 26 June 1988.

Chapter 12
1. Foot, M., Personal communications to the author, Sackville Street, Piccadilly Rare Books with Paul Minet, 1981.
2. Warren, Sir K., FRAeS, interviews and personal communications to the author at the Garrick Club 2013 and via telephone interviews to Cranbrook.
3. *Car*, April 1981. FF Publishing, London.
4. Thatcher, M.H., *The Downing Street Years*, Harper, London 2003.
5. Horrocks, R., to Trade and Industry Select Committee, House of Commons, 12 March 1986.
6. Horrocks, R., public statement Leeds 9th April 1986; also reported by M. White, The *Guardian* 10 April 1986; Also cited to author 1989.
7. Reuters, 18 March 1986.
8. International Automotive Design, author's communications Shute.J., 1984-89.

Chapter 13
1. Walker, J., *Determinants of the Decline of British Leyland: The Roles of Product Quality, Advertising and Voluntary Export Restraints* (1971-2002), London School of Economics, University of London, Department of Economic History, London.
2. Oliver, N., Carver, M., & Hollweg, M., 'A Systems perspective on the death of a car company'. 2008. *International Journal of Operations and Production Management*, vol 128, no 6. pp562-583.
3. Dalyell. T., MP to author, personal communications March 1997.

Bibliography and sources

BOOKS

Bardsley, Gillian, *Issigonis: The Official Biography*, Icon Books Ltd. 2005.
Benn, Tony, *Out of the Wilderness, Diaries 1963-1967*, Hutchinson, London 1987.
Carver, Mike, Seale, Nick, Youngson, Ann, *British Leyland Motor Corporation 1968-2005*.The History Press, 2015.
Edwardes, Sir Michael, *Back from the Brink: An Apocalyptic Experience*, Collins, 1983.
Daniels, Jeffrey, *British Leyland the Truth about the Cars*, Osprey Publishing, 1980.
Frolik, Joseph, *The Frolik Defection: The Memoirs of a Czech Intelligence Agent*, Leo Cooper Ltd, London. 1975.
Knowles, David, *MGB, MGC & MGB GT V8: A Celebration of Britain's Best Loved Sports Car,* Haynes Publishing, Yeovil. 2004.
Pullen, Steven, *British Leyland: From Steam Wagons to Seventies' Strife.* Mortons Media Group, 2015.
Robson, Graham, *The Cars of BMC*, Motor Racing Publications 1987.
Ruppert, James, *The British Car Industry: Our Part in Its Downfall*, Foresight publications, 2008.
Thatcher, M.H., *The Downing Street Years*, Harper, London 2003.
The National Archives, London.
Thornett, Allan, *Inside Cowley: Trade Union Struggle in the 1970s – Who Really Opened the Door to the Tory Onslaught*, IMG Press.
Thornett, Allan, *Militant Years: Car Workers Struggles in Britain in the 60s and 70s,* IMG Press.
Turner, Graham, *The Leyland Papers*, Eyre and Spottiswoode, London 1972.
Whisler, Timothy, *The British Motor Industry 1945-1994. A Case Study in Industrial Decline,* OUP Oxford, 1999
Whyte, Andrew, *Jaguar: The History of a Great British Car*, PSL/Jaguar 1980.

PUBLICATIONS, PAPERS & ARCHIVES

Autocar 1977-1989.

Business History, Volume 59, 2016 - Issue 1: 'The stagflation crisis and the European automotive industry, 1973-1985', Jordi Catalan Vidal/ Department of Economic History, University of Barcelona, 2016.

Business History, Volume 59 (1), 75-100. 2016 'Industrial Policy and the British Automotive Industry under Margaret Thatcher', Tommaso Pardi/ ENS-CHCAN, France.

BLMC publications and brochures.

BMC publications and brochures.

British Leyland Annual General Meeting, Report, May 1981.

'British Leyland: The Next Decade'. National Enterprise Board, UK Government.1977.

British Motor Museum, Gaydon, Archive.

British Motor Industry Heritage Trust, Archive.

Car 1972-1983, FF Publishing/as Bauer Media Ltd 2019.

'Car Industry Crisis: A Policy for BL Workers' Workers' Socialist League/ Folrose Ltd, 17 September 1980.

Engineering and Physical Science Research Council.

Hansard, Vol 300cc719-871. Vol 91 cc310-54310

International Journal of Operations and Production Management, vol 28, no 6. pp 562-583. 'A Systems perspective on the death of a car company'. Oliver, N, Carver, & Hollweg, M. 2008.

Management Today, archives -1968-1975.

Hart, Anthony, I., Left Library and Archive.

'In Place of Strife: A Policy for Industrial Relations', Cabinet Papers 1969. The National Archives, London.

Jaguar Cars Ltd. Archive / Author at Jaguar 1984 as Lyons Scholar.

Morning Star, People's Press Printing Society Ltd, Bow, London.

Practical Classics, Bauer Media Ltd.

'Report on the British Leyland Corporate Plan, 1981 and Business Plan 1978', UK Government/Society of Motor Manufacturers and Traders, publications. London. 1978.

SMMT-Society of Motor Manufacturers, London.

Telegraph Media Group Ltd. The *Daily Telegraph* Archive.

'The Ryder Report. British Leyland the Next Decade', Ryder, D., Clark, R.A. Gillen, S.J., McWhirter, F.S., Urwin, C.H., UK Government, DoI, C (75) 53, 23rd April 1975. HMSO.

Trade and Industry Select Committee, House of Commons, BL/AR Hearing 12th March 1986.

Warwick University. Archives and Library (BLMC collection).

'Who Killed Saab Automobile: Obituary of an Automotive Icon', Oliver N, & Hollweg, M., Edinburgh. University of Edinburgh 2011.

On-line resources

Etheses lse.ac.uk, 'Determinants of the Decline of British Leyland: The Roles of Product Quality, Advertising and Voluntary Export Restraints (1971-2002)'. J. Walker, London School of Economics, University of London, Department of Economic History, London 2009.

www.ADAC, (Allgemeiner Deutscher Automobil Club /ADAC).

www.ARonline.org, (Adams, K.).

www.auto-motor-und-sport.de.

www.TRL.com, (Transport Research Laboratory, Crowthorne, UK. Cited as TRRL/TRL).

Personal communications
(Titles and awards, uncited)
Axe. R
Atkins, D.
Ball, T.
Barker, R.
Benn, A.
Boole, D.
Chick, D.
Conway, D.
Dalyell, T.
Daniels, J.
Dewis, N.
Edwardes, M.
Foot, M.
Gunn, R.
Hollweg, M.
Horrocks, R.

Hughes-Jones, M.
Hutton, R.
Lyons W.
Mann, H.
McKechnie, S.
Rankin, A.
Read, M.
Scarlett, M.
Shute, J.
Walshe, J.
Warren, K.

Index

Abingdon, 17, 36, 82, 89, 108, 110, 126, 172
Adams, J., 192
Allard, S.H., 59
Alchemy Partners, 253
Alvis, 65, 120-121, 214
Amalgamated Union of Engineering Workers, 123, 191, 192
Andrews, D., 185, 237
Ashok Leyland, 238
Austin, 9, 10, 16, 62-71
Austin, H., Sir, Baron, 59, 67
Austin-Morris, 8, 71, 73
Austin Rover Group (ARG), 8, 13, 16, 17, 21-29, 36, 84, 121, 147, 151, 172-189, 210-244. 259
Austin Rover Cars North America, 243
Austin cars (Key Models):
  Allegro, 8, 12, 16, 25, 34, 83, 96, 124, 150, 155, 172, 208-210. Ambassador, 37, 188, Apache, 25, 80-83, Atlantic, 70. Cambridge, 60, 73. Devon, 70. Dorset, 70. Land Crab (1800-2200), 37, 55, 56, 61-64, 73, 75, 77, 81, 121, 208, 250. Maxi, 9, 34, 61, 62, 75, 93, 95, 124, 133, 186, 266. Metro, 15, 17, 24, 170-182, 190, 200, 210, 240, 250. Mini, 9, 24, 25, 37, 54, 60-63, 72, 93, 159, 172, 209. Maestro, 7, 22, 29, 156, 157, 178-183, 205, 211-13. Montego, 13, 23, 137, 156, 177-181, 190, 212. Princess (1800-2200), 9, 19, 32, 34, 100, 131, 146, 153, 157, 188, 207-211, 271. Seven, 66. A35, 66. A40, 23, 66, 70, 72. A60, 70. A90, 70. 3.0-Litre, 73, 75-78. 1100-1300, 10, 14, 23, 25, 61-64, 81-83, 113, 134, 183
Authi, 83
Autocar, 15, 27, 102, 134
Axe, R., 13, 27, 36, 206, 220, 242-246

Bache, D.E., 9, 21, 36, 67, 91, 101, 165, 211, 214
Bahnsen, U., 129
Bagshaw, J., 190
Ball, A., 36, 185-187
Barber, N.J.R., 118, 123, 132, 146-147, 158, 194, 257
Bashford, G., 59, 211
Bathgate, 259
Beale, P., 247
Beech, I., 211
Benn, A.W. 27, 32, 111, 112-125, 140, 159, 161, 198, 229, 249, 261
Bertodo, R., 13, 243
Bide, A., Sir, 36
Birtwhistle, G., 36, 251
Black, J., Sir, 59
Blair. A. 25, 32, 241, 247, 265
BMW, 13, 33, 40, 41, 59, 60, 72, 113, 179, 194, 230 240, 245-248, 252-266

Index • 275

British Aerospace (BAE), 33, 39, 230, 234, 241, 245
British Leyland Motor Corporation (BLMC/BL), 10, 17, 18, 20, 21, 22, 30, 40, 42, 53, 63-71, 72-84, 93, 101, 106-110, 111-127, 128-132, 140-149, 150-162, 185-197, 200-222, 249-265
British Leyland Australia PTY, 79-8. (Key Models): Kimberley, 79. Lancer, 79. Nomad, 150, 266. P76, 80-82
British Leyland Technology Ltd., 16, 102, 212, 218, 219, 263. AR6, 206-210. ECV3, 202-226
British Motor Corporation (BMC), 10, 17, 20, 25, 40, 53, 68-71, 72-84, 111-127, 128-136, 140-149, 150-162, 185, 200249, 262
British Motor Holdings, (BMH), 68, 74, 118-122, 130
British Motor Museum Gaydon, 228
Brown, G., 27, 242, 265
Buffum, J., 172
Burzi, R., 46, 66
Byers, S., MP, 247

Callaghan, J., Sir, 32, 136143, 160, 186, 197, 228, 230, 260
Canley, 124, 204, 244
Car magazine, 12, 22
Carver, M., 179
Castle, B., Baroness, 32, 139-144, 161, 259
Castle Bromwich, 119
Channon, P., MP, 236-237
Cherry, W. 211, 236
Chick, D., 240, 244

Chrysler (UK), 31, 59, 70, 112, 123, 152, 162, 171
China Brilliance, 247
Clark, M., 192
Clark, R., 58
Clarke, K., 258
Consumers Association, 183
Coultas, F., 36, 173
Craig, P., 176
Crayford, 28
Creese, I., 85
Cropley, S., 12
Communist Party of Great Britain, 15, 37, 19, 198-200
Confederation of Engineering and Shipbuilding Unions, 199
Costello, K., 36, 59
Cowley, 15, 48, 113, 126, 133, 140, 157, 181, 192, 198-200, 245
Culcheth, B., 172
Curtis, A., 109

DAF, 238
Daimler, 49
Dalyell, T., 259-260
Daniels, J., 21, 38, 76, 134, 146
Day, J.G., Sir, 13, 36, 131, 186, 207, 234, 238, 241, 246, 261
Deloitte, 248
De Lorean, J.Z., 232
Dewis, N,. 59
Dick, A., 59
Dobson, R., 151, 159

Easter, P., 59
Edwards, J., 247
Edwardes, M., Sir, 12, 21, 27, 33-36, 108, 126, 131-133, 141, 145-153,

158, 161, 176-190, 192-200, 228, 229, 230-238, 252, 264
Egan, J., Sir 36, 175, 185
England, F.R.W., 59
Etheridge, R., 191
European Economic Community/EEC/EU, 16, 38-41, 78, 112, 142, 178, 183, 199, 211, 260, 265

Faulds, A., MP, 237
Fogg, A., 123
Ford (Motor Company), 18, 20, 32, 61, 112, 118-127, 128-138, 179, 195, 210, 245
Ford Cortina, 126-138
Foot, M. M., MP, 198, 236

Gaydon Advanced Technology Centre, 206
General Motors, 8, 24, 32, 60, 68, 115, 183, 190, 232-238, 246, 257
Griffiths, A., 244

Hamblin, R., 244
Hancock, A., 65
Harriman, G., Sir, 59, 74, 116-123, 140
Harris, P., 173
Harper, S., 239, 243-244
Hassan, W., 59
Hasselkus, W., 246
Haynes, R., 36, 75, 132, 134
Hayter, D., 59
Healey, Donald, 59, 67
Healey, Denis, 160, 162
Heath, E., Sir, 111, 141-143, 162, 237, 258
Hedges, A., 59

Helfet, K., 102
Hewitt, P., 159, 264
Heynes, W., 102
Hill, G., 58
Hindustan Motors, 84
Hodgkinson, M., 175
Honda, (Motor Company,) 13, 22, 23, 30-33, 40, 83, 108, 158, 159, 175, 183-201, 202-224, 227-248, 251-265
Hopkirk, P., 59
Horrocks, R., 21, 36, 176, 185-188, 227, 235, 238, 257, 267
Horsman, F. 113
House of Commons Industry Committee, 184
Howe, G., Sir, 188
Howe, K. 246-248
Hutton, R., 15, 21
Hyundai, 232

Ireland, I.M., 59
Innocenti (Motors), 10, 63, 78-79, 155, 131, 209
International Automotive Design, 189, 244
Issigonis, A. Sir, 59, 60-66, 70, 74-76, 120, 124, 128-134, 174, 206-208, 251, 265
Insurance Institute for Highway Loss Data, 31

Jaguar, 16, 29, 39, 51, 72, 74, 101, 106, 113, 120, 146, 151, 157, 175-178, 187, 244
(Key models): E-Type, 51, 88. XJ6, 24, 29, 67, 72, 90, 101, 111.

Jones, J., 141, 173, 192
Joseph, K. Sir, 201

Kimber, C. 69
King, C.S., 18, 59, 202-206, 211, 219

Lancashire Enterprises, 238
Lanchester, F., Sir, 63
Lanchester, G., 120
Lanchester, 66
Leyland Albion East Africa, 83
Leyland Bus, 11, 235, 258, 241, 246
Leyland Trucks, 235, 238, 246
Leyland Vehicles, 175
Loewy, R., 66
Longbridge, 8, 14, 35, 39, 66, 73, 119, 157, 172, 181, 190, 191-200, 232, 247
Lord, L., (Baron), 59, 61, 66, 71, 114, 258, 261
Lyons, W., Sir, 39, 59, 57, 67, 103, 120, 123

Mackay, M., Prof, 24-25, 175-176
Major, J., Sir, 241
Mann, H., 9, 18, 19, 25, 27, 36, 50, 74, 90, 132-136, 147, 180, 202-211, 221
McGovern, G., 231, 245
McKechnie, S. Dame, 183
MG, 15, 10, 25, 52, 69, 72, 82, 90, 108-110, 122, 140, 159, 163, 220, 239, 242, 245
MG Rover, 209, 213, 242, 245-248, 251-263
MG Magna, 202
MGB, 25, 36, 52, 58, 59, 101, 108-110, 163, 202

Michelotti, G., 11, 49, 50, 79, 82, 85, 107, 218
Morley, K., 13, 243
Morris, W., 59, 68, 69
Morris Cars (key models): Ital, 130, 135, 174, 190, 222, 235, 252. Marina, 10, 17, 65, 95, 128-138, 154, 158, 208, 231. Minor, 10, 23, 47, 61-62, 72. Oxford, 60, 73
Moss, P, 59
Moss, S., Sir, 58
Moulton, A., Sir, 209, 253
Mundy, H., 59
Musgrove, H. 21, 36, 154, 174, 180-185, 206, 201-211, 236, 244, 257

Nanjing Automobile Corporation, 247
National Enterprise Board (NEB), 33, 111, 147, 158-161
Neale, E., 66
Nicholls, M., 12
Nissan, 231
Nuffield, 61, 67-79, 208, 261
Nuffield Australia PTY, 79

Palmer, G.M., 48, 60
Paradise, F., 154
Park, A., 229
Peugeot, 11, 15, 31, 39, 152, 178, 184
Phoenix Venture Holdings, 206, 246-248, 261
Pininfarina, 66, 109, 135, 166, 176, 221
Pinin farina, B., 66
Pressed Steel Fisher, 29, 71
Pressed Steel, 109, 119

Pischetsreider, B., 246
Pond, A., 172

Quandt, 246

Randle, J., 36, 102
Reitzle, W. 246
Renault, 12, 27, 40, 41, 72, 152, 153, 177, 188
Ricardo (Compamy), 262
Riley, 17, 25, 68, 70, 121
Riley brothers, 69
Riley cars (Key models): Pathfinder, 73. RM-Series, 47. Sprite, 43. 1.5, 80
Robinson, D., 15, 113, 126, 161, 172, 186, 191-200, 256
Robinson, G., Sir, 176
Rochester, Lord, 141
Roewe, 262-263
Rootes, 70-77, 116-122, 170
Rover, 8, 13, 33, 65, 79, 101-110, 172-201, 225-248, 251-266
Rover cars (Key models): P5B, 65, 67, 89, 103. P6, 9, 10, 23, 65, 76, 90 101-106. SD1, 9, 19, 21, 24, 30, 84, 159, 160, 163, 210. Land Rover, 11, 58, 103, 152, 177, 180, 185, 189, 231, 233, 235-238
   Sterling, 29, 224, 242-243. Rover 100, 24, 173, 174, 209. Rover 600, 240. Rover 800/827, 13, 23, 31, 169, 179, 181, 185, 224, 240-244
Rover Group, 225-266
Ryder, Lord, (Report), 82, 132, 146-151, 176, 196, 229, 249

Shanghai Automotive Industry Corporation, 16, 262
Saddington, D., 244
Sartotelli, S., 10
Sayer, M. G. 59, 67
Scanlon, H., 123, 141, 192
Sherpa (van), 130-131, 189
Shute, J., 189
Sked, G., 13, 169, 180, 239-244
Smith, J., MP, 235
Snowden, M., 172, 236
Socialist Labour League, 199
Speke, 107, 160, 170, 200, 228
Standard Triumph, 102, 114
Stephenson, N., 247
Stevens, P., 239
Stokes. D. G., Sir, 33, 35-36, 42, 78, 103-109, 111-126, 130-134, 145-148, 159, 186, 191, 201, 254, 257, 261-263

Talbot, 12, 15, 16, 39, 152, 155, 170, 184, 232, 259
Tata, 84
Taylor, T., 187
Thatcher, M. H., 8, 11, 17, 27, 32-36, 11-112, 126, 140-143, 154, 158, 160-162, 170-178, 180, 184, 192, 200-2006, 228-238, 241, 242, 256, 260-266
Thomas, M. Sir, 70
Thomas, W. 244
Thompson, W.P. 176
Thornett, A. 37, 38, 198-199
Tjaarda, T, 10
Towers, J, 246-247
Trades Union Congress, 141

Transport & General Workers Union, 35, 123, 160, 147, 188, 198
Triumph, 107-110, 227
Triumph cars (Key models): Acclaim, 83, 108, 227, 232, 235, 242. Herald, 23, 49, 59, 60, 73, 79, 81, 107. Lynx, 9, 202, 216, 227. Stag, 107, 157, 162, 176, 202. 2000/2500, 82, 98, 107. SD2, 108, 176, 182, 202, 215, 251.
Toyota, 39, 153, 178, 213, 231, 265
Trotsky, L., 193
Trotskyism, 193-199, 263
Tucker, R., 212
Turnbull, G. M. Sir, 40, 109, 123, 131, 145, 154, 232
Turner, G, 21, 38, 122, 159-160

UNITE, 191
Unipart, 178, 238, 246

Varley, E., 94
Vauxhall, 34, 39, 65, 68, 1895-195, 203, 211, 232
Volkswagen, 8, 12, 147, 148, 153, 178
Young, D., Lord, 246

Warren, K., Sir, 233-234
Webster, H., 59, 134
Whittaker, D. 151
Wilks, (brothers), 59, 65, 101, 102
Wilks, M., 67
Wilson. J H., Sir, Baron, 110-138, 139-143, 162, 197
Wolseley, 17, 48, 60, 66, 69, 70, 80, 146
Woodcock, J., 74
Woolley, R., 244
Workers Revolutionary Party, 199
Workers Socialist League, 191